Praise for *Goodbye Homeboy*

"Steve Mariotti's moving memoir is a call to action for anyone who dares to dream, and dream big! Steve's entrepreneurial spirit led him from calming his contentious classroom and nurturing his students' 'street smarts' to becoming the founder of a booming nonprofit. *Goodbye Homeboy* powerfully illustrates how Steve went from reaching one student to reaching millions with the Network for Teaching Entrepreneurship (NFTE)."
—**ERIN GRUWELL, teacher and author of** *The Freedom Writers Diary*

"*Goodbye Homeboy* truly captures Steve Mariotti's amazing journey as a teacher and an innovator. It's engaging, heartbreaking, hopeful, and ultimately triumphant. This is the story behind the entrepreneurship-education revolution!"
—**JIMMY "MAC" MCNEAL, founder of Bulldog Bikes Worldwide**

"Steve Mariotti is one of the great teachers of our time. In this deeply personal memoir, he describes how a bunch of high-school dropouts in the South Bronx helped him discover the power of entrepreneurship education. *Goodbye Homeboy* is a page turner—once you open this book, you won't be able to put it down."
—**VERNE HARNISH, author of** *Scaling Up* **and founder of Entrepreneurs' Organization**

"I'm so inspired to finally read the inspiring, intense, and hilarious story behind the organization that helped me so much as a high schooler. NFTE taught me entrepreneurship skills that I still use to this day, as the CEO of a company that employs thousands and is transforming the real-estate industry."
—**ROBERT REFFKIN, founder and CEO of Compass**

"So many personal stories today are described as 'inspiring,' but *Goodbye Homeboy* is the rare true story that genuinely transcends the word. Steve Mariotti's memoir conveys the heart, soul, and determination that have catalyzed the lives of so many young people."
—**RAY CHAMBERS, World Health Organization Ambassador for Global Strategy**

GOODBYE HOMEBOY

GOODBYE HOMEBOY

How My Students Drove Me Crazy
and Inspired a Movement

STEVE MARIOTTI

Founder of the Network for Teaching Entrepreneurship (NFTE)

with DEBRA DEVI

Foreword by WES MOORE

BenBella Books, Inc.
Dallas, TX

This book is a memoir. The stories within reflect Steve Mariotti's present recollections of experiences over time. Some names and characteristics have been changed, some events have been compressed, and some dialogue has been recreated.

Copyright © 2019 by Steve Mariotti

All rights reserved. No part of this book may be used or reproduced in any manner whatsoever without written permission except in the case of brief quotations embodied in critical articles or reviews.

BenBella Books, Inc.
10440 N. Central Expressway, Suite 800
Dallas, TX 75231
www.benbellabooks.com
Send feedback to feedback@benbellabooks.com

Printed in the United States of America
10 9 8 7 6 5 4 3 2 1

Library of Congress Cataloging-in-Publication Data is available upon request.
9781948836005 (trade paper)
9781948836302 (electronic)

Copyediting by Scott Calamar
Proofreading by James Fraleigh and Lisa Story
Text design and composition by Katie Hollister
Photos on pages 4, 255, 262, 273, 274 by NFTE
Cover design by Pete Garceau
Printed by Lake Book Manufacturing

Distributed to the trade by Two Rivers Distribution, an Ingram brand
www.tworiversdistribution.com

Special discounts for bulk sales (minimum of 25 copies) are available.
Please contact bulkorders@benbellabooks.com.

To my mother, Nancy Mason Mariotti, a beloved special education teacher, who taught me that "a great teacher affects eternity"; to all my students, who have inspired me and given meaning to my life; and to my friend Diana Davis Spencer.

"My dream is not to die in poverty but to have poverty die in me."
—Michelle Araujo, NFTE graduate

CONTENTS

FOREWORD

I first spoke on the phone with Steve Mariotti when I was studying at the University of Oxford on a Rhodes Scholarship in 2001. That sounds like I was born with a silver spoon in my mouth, but actually I grew up much like the struggling low-income students Steve comes to know and love as their teacher in *Goodbye Homeboy: How My Students Drove Me Crazy and Inspired a Movement*.

My sisters and I were raised by my widowed mother in poor neighborhoods in Baltimore and the Bronx infiltrated by drug-dealing gangs. Like Steve's students, I didn't always see a connection between my schoolwork and finding my way to a better life.

Goodbye Homeboy is Steve's deeply moving—and often very funny!—memoir of his career as a special ed teacher in New York City's most dangerous public high schools from the Lower East Side to the South Bronx during the early 1980s. It's a great read, and it also offers a real answer to this question: How do we engage our low-income youth in education that will equip them to rise up out of poverty?

In *Goodbye Homeboy*, Steve discovers that teaching his rowdy students about entrepreneurship awakens a passion for learning in them, and an eagerness to start their own small businesses and take charge of their lives. He realizes that they are brave, street-smart, and resourceful, just like all great entrepreneurs.

Steve shared this with me during our first conversation. I still remember Steve exclaiming, "Street smarts equal business smarts! We have to help our at-risk youth understand that they have a gift they can use to get out of poverty, and teach them about entrepreneurship so they can!" He told me he had founded the Network for Teaching Entrepreneurship (NFTE) to fulfill that mission.

Steve said he believed that many teens in America's inner cities were being misevaluated and their enormous potential overlooked. Our public schools fail to teach low-income children how to enter our economy and succeed, Steve argued. As a result, students drop out. Many enter the illegal drug trade. Sadly, they often pay a terrible price for choosing this path.

As Steve describes so vividly in *Goodbye Homeboy*, he was inspired by his students to found NFTE in 1987 to bring entrepreneurship education to as many low-income youth as possible. By the time Steve and I spoke in 2001, NFTE was a global leader in entrepreneurship education, and had both the anecdotes and research to prove that NFTE programs were helping low-income teens stay in school and change their lives for the better.

I felt very inspired by our initial phone call; so inspired that when I returned to the United States in 2006 after completing my service with the Army's 82nd Airborne Division in Afghanistan, I reached out to Steve again. We picked up easily right where we had left off, and our lively conversations continued.

I eventually returned home to New York City, and I began volunteering for NFTE. My wife, Dawn, was also inspired by NFTE's mission and became NFTE's Director of Business Development, Corporate, and Foundation Philanthropy. In 2017, I became CEO of the Robin Hood Foundation, one of the largest poverty-fighting organizations in the country. Dawn and I both consider Steve a valuable mentor and friend, and always will.

To have this opportunity now to read Steve's unflinchingly honest memoir of his trials and triumphs as a teacher, and how NFTE came to be, is a real treat. We thoroughly enjoyed getting to know Steve's wonderful students and reading about his adventures with them in *Goodbye Homeboy*, and were inspired anew by his story. We know you will be, too.

—WES MOORE
BALTIMORE

PREFACE

I t takes roughly twenty-six minutes to travel the eight miles from Boys and Girls High School in Bedford-Stuyvesant to the Waldorf Astoria on Park Avenue, depending on traffic.

It took me thirty-one years, one month, and seventeen days.

I felt awestruck as I entered the Waldorf's glittering ballroom for a gala celebrating the silver anniversary of the Network for Teaching Entrepreneurship (NFTE). The nonprofit I founded in 1987 to bring entrepreneurship education to low-income youth had survived twenty-five bumpy yet exhilarating years. As NFTE's founder, I was the guest of honor at this milestone event. I could hardly believe it.

During that quarter century, NFTE grew from a dream I had when I was a teacher in New York City's roughest high schools into a multimillion-dollar nonprofit. Today, NFTE is a global leader in providing entrepreneurship education to low-income youth from Chicago to China. Studies of NFTE programs by researchers from Brandeis University, Harvard University, and RAND Corporation prove that entrepreneurship education reduces dropout rates and disrupts the school-to-prison pipeline in low-income communities. NFTE graduates are more likely to finish high school, go to college, find employment, and start businesses.

I never intended to become a teacher, let alone found a non-profit. In 1977, I graduated with an MBA from the University of Michigan and went to work for Ford Motor Company as a financial analyst. A few years later, I moved to New York City and started a small import-export company. I was happy. Life was good. But everything changed one sunny September afternoon in 1981, when I was jumped by six knife-wielding teenagers as I jogged along the East River.

Plagued by debilitating nightmares and flashbacks after this attack, I took my therapist's advice to face my fear perhaps a bit too literally. I closed my business and became a high school teacher, choosing to work in the city's poorest neighborhoods. From 1982 to 1988, I taught primarily special ed in Bedford-Stuyvesant, Brooklyn; on the Lower East Side of Manhattan; and in the decaying, gang-ridden section of the South Bronx that police had nicknamed "Fort Apache."

When I began teaching, I was rapidly driven to despair by my rowdy students. My classes devolved into pure chaos. I discovered, though, that whenever I talked about how to make money with a small business, my students were riveted.

I had stumbled onto the truth. My students acted out in school because they were struggling with soul-crushing poverty and mortal danger around every corner. They saw zero connection between paying attention in school and improving their lives.

I consistently witnessed angry, disillusioned teenagers light up whenever I explained that entrepreneurship is a viable way for anyone to earn money and create a pathway out of poverty. They were eager to learn more. I almost couldn't believe the positive changes I saw in my students as they discovered entrepreneurship. When they got excited about starting their own small businesses, they *wanted* to learn to read, write, and do math. They were motivated to behave better, and to treat other people with respect once they viewed them as potential sales prospects.

I discovered that my low-income students had a natural aptitude for entrepreneurship, born of their stressful lives. They were comfortable with risk and ambiguity. They were brave and unselfconscious. They were gutsy and resilient, and they were natural salespeople.

Entrepreneurship education empowered these highly at-risk children, who had not previously envisioned surviving into adulthood, to imagine good and prosperous futures for themselves. Most of my students had been raised on welfare, but when they got hands-on experience with entrepreneurship and learned how business works, they became excited about participating in our economy. They also became valuable employees because they were financially literate.

I mean, who would you rather hire? A young person who can read a balance sheet? Or one who has never heard of a balance sheet?

I came to believe so strongly in the transformative power of entrepreneurship education that in 1987 I founded NFTE on my meager teacher's salary. My dream was to bring entrepreneurship education to low-income youth all over the world who felt as frustrated and left out of the economy as the teens I had come to love as a teacher.

As I made my way through the Waldorf Astoria's ballroom, hugging and shaking hands with NFTE teachers, students, and donors, I was nearly overcome with tears of gratitude. Goldman Sachs, Mastercard, Southwest Airlines, Ernst & Young, E*Trade, Microsoft, and hip-hop mogul Sean "Diddy" Combs were among the gala's sponsors, yet I still remembered, as if it were yesterday, how NFTE had almost failed during our first year because we couldn't pay our bills.

I eagerly visited the displays manned by NFTE's Global Young Entrepreneurs of the Year winners, who had been invited to the gala to accept their awards. Tyler Hansen had opened a paintball arcade in his Central Valley, California, hometown. Lakeisha Henderson told me her pet-grooming business, Besties for Life, in East Cleveland, had inspired her to major in business in college, which she would be attending in the fall. Niall Foody from Letterkenny, Ireland, who has Asperger's and dyspraxia, showed off his ingenious line of luminous stickers that make keyholes, light switches, and doorbells easy to find in the dark. Abdulaziz Al-Dakhel from Jeddah, Saudi Arabia, displayed innovative products he had created from camel's milk and wool.

At the NFTE 25th Anniversary Gala at the Waldorf-Astoria with with (L-R) Erika Pittman, Jamila Payne, and Jasmine Lawrence. Photo by NFTE.

Many of these young winners were from impoverished communities plagued with gangs and crime. They proudly delivered their well-practiced pitches to gala guests, making eye contact, shaking hands firmly, and making sure everyone who stopped by their displays left with business cards and brochures.

Such amazing young people illustrate what I have seen happen many times. Teaching low-income youth about entrepreneurship transforms their lives—whether they become lifelong entrepreneurs or not.

There are countless incredible NFTE success stories. We have experienced terrible losses, too. Fourteen NFTE students have been murdered. I have attended too many funerals. Each tragedy has only strengthened my commitment to entrepreneurship education as a pathway out of poverty.

My first office was a wooden table at West 4th Street Saloon in the West Village. Today NFTE occupies 18,000 square feet of offices at 120 Wall Street with spectacular views of New York Harbor. As I write this, NFTE is operating programs in twenty-three locations in eleven countries, with more locations slated to open in the near future. NFTE students have been invited to the White House and profiled in the media around the world. The idea that entrepreneurship education can fight poverty, crime, unemployment, and violence, while spreading free-market and democratic ideals, is steadily gaining momentum.

To date, nearly one million young people have graduated from NFTE programs. To me, all of them are my kids.

CHAPTER 1

GIVE US YOUR MONEY

"If the Martians ever find out how human beings think, they'll kill themselves laughing."
—ALBERT ELLIS, *Reason and Emotion in Psychotherapy* (1962)

can't say I wasn't scared. It was September 1982, and I was headed to my first day as a teacher at Boys and Girls High School in Bedford-Stuyvesant, Brooklyn.

Boys and Girls High generated newspaper headlines like:

TEACHER'S HAIR SET ON FIRE
AT TROUBLED BOYS AND GIRLS HIGH

TEACHER BEATEN AND DRAGGED DOWN STAIRS
AT BOYS AND GIRLS HIGH

The headlines were only the tip of the iceberg. The school had been in serious trouble for years. In just one semester in 1977, forty-eight teachers and staff members were physically assaulted. Once, a teacher had a heart attack on the school grounds. As he lay dying, his watch and wallet were stolen. Students were regularly robbed and assaulted on school grounds.

I was amazed that Boys and Girls High was still open, let alone functioning as a learning institution. It was considered the most dangerous high school in New York City, if not the nation.

As I walked from my Greenwich Village studio to the West 4th Street subway station wearing my favorite Brooks Brothers suit, I felt intense fear. Nothing in my background had prepared me for this challenge.

What had I gotten myself into?

In 1977, while teachers were being beaten up at Boys and Girls High, I graduated with an MBA from the University of Michigan. Upon graduation, I was awarded a scholarship to study economics over the summer at the Institute for Humane Studies in Menlo Park, California, thanks to my paper "A Statistical Test of the Austrian Theory of the Trade Cycle."

I was overjoyed to be one of twenty young economists selected nationwide. Our reward was three months of theory, discussion, and research with F. A. Hayek, the 1974 Nobel Prize winner in economics. I was in geek heaven.

At the end of that magical summer, I began my career on the tenth floor of Ford Motor Company's sleek world headquarters in

Dearborn, Michigan. I had the best job a young MBA could dream of landing. I was an analyst for the legendary Ford Finance Staff developed by the "Whiz Kids," ten young army officers, including Robert McNamara, hired by Henry Ford II in 1946 to revitalize his company after World War II.

Ford Motor Company would hire twenty young men per year to work at world headquarters and only expect to keep one. This extremely competitive environment had produced more *Fortune* 500 CEOs than any other organization except Harvard Business School.

I was a financial analyst for two Ford divisions: South Africa and aerospace. I survived by also leading a team that devised strategies lowering Ford's interest payments on its corporate debt by several million dollars annually. My youthful enthusiasm and knack for international finance earned me the nickname "Stevie Wonder."

At twenty-four, I was leapfrogging over career hurdles and getting an inside look at how one of America's largest corporations operated. It was thrilling!

I soon learned, however, that speaking one's mind on controversial subjects went over like a lead balloon in the corporate world.

I had become a fan of civil rights leader Reverend Leon Sullivan. In 1971, Sullivan joined the General Motors board of directors, becoming the first African American to serve on a major corporation's board. Sullivan helped expand GM's employment of African Americans and creation of more African American–owned dealerships.

During a trip he took with GM board members to tour the automaker's facilities in South Africa, only Sullivan was detained and strip-searched at the airport by South African authorities. This humiliating experience galvanized Sullivan into fighting apartheid. In 1977, he published the Sullivan Principles. These were guidelines for American companies operating in South Africa under the white minority government's apartheid regime, which was severely oppressing the country's black majority.

Sullivan argued that American companies had a moral obligation to treat their workers in South Africa as they would be treated in the United States. American companies should, therefore, desegregate factory floors and company cafeterias in their South African factories and provide equal pay for equal work, regardless of race. Sullivan also lobbied GM and other large corporations to disinvest while apartheid was still in effect.

I began corresponding with Sullivan in my capacity as an analyst for Ford's South Africa division. I disagreed with him about divestment, because I thought closing plants would only take jobs from South Africans who needed them, but I wrote Sullivan that I supported his other initiatives and would seek to promote them at Ford.

I began openly questioning in meetings and memos whether Ford should continue selling surveillance equipment to a racist government. The National Party was cracking down on any opposition with brutal force, including the death by torture while in police custody of anti-apartheid activist Stephen Biko on September 12, 1977.

When you were hired at Ford, you signed an agreement stating that if you witnessed any employee make a political statement in writing, you would report it immediately to your higher-up. I still remember my poor supervisor running down the hall to the assistant treasurer's office, waving one of my many memos about South Africa and shouting "Code 728!"

I made enough of a stink that it reached the board of directors, and Henry Ford II created a thirty-person committee to study Ford's dealings with the apartheid regime. Ford Motor Company did eventually reduce its business with the South African government. As international outcry against apartheid grew, Ford divested from South Africa entirely in 1988.

I had been on the fast track at Ford, but now I heard my colleagues whispering to each other when I walked by them in the hallways. When I entered the cafeteria for lunch, a thousand people would turn and stare at me.

One day, my supervisor told me I was simply too controversial. After twenty-five months at Ford, I was sacked, with eighteen months' severance in recognition of my financial achievements at the company.

I had grown up in Flint, Michigan. My dad was a professor at General Motors Institute, and I had always dreamed of a career in the auto industry. When I was fired, I cried in front of my supervisor. I was twenty-six and convinced my life was over.

I was allowed to finish that awful workday in order to avoid further humiliation. As I walked through the parking lot for the very last time, I looked up toward my old office on the tenth floor. Around thirty of my colleagues were standing at the windows, solemnly waving goodbye.

In 2000, a year before he died, Reverend Sullivan came to visit me in New York City. He brought fifty letters I had written to him during my tenure at Ford. He told me that he had always wanted to meet me. I was deeply honored to meet him.

Burned out on corporate life, and with zero prospects in Flint, I decided to move to New York City. I needed a fresh start far from home where no one would know how badly I had flamed out.

I thought maybe I would open a small business. I had always loved entrepreneurship. I started a golf ball resale business when

I was eleven. I mowed lawns, did home repairs, and even ran a laundry service. All told, I had seven businesses from age eleven to twenty-one.

New York City was the perfect place to lick my wounds. I loved walking the streets and meeting wonderful people from so many different cultures. I made a Jamaican friend who told me he was having a tough time finding someone to represent him and other Jamaican artisans who wanted to sell their products in the United States.

"Gee, there's an opportunity!" I thought.

I traveled to Jamaica with a few contacts he had given me. I was searching for simple artisanal products like wood carvings, python-skin belts, handmade jewelry, textiles, and pottery that might sell well in the States.

I named my new business Mason Import-Export, after my maternal grandfather, Lowell B. Mason. He was a libertarian lawyer and Illinois state senator appointed to the Federal Trade Commission by President Harry S. Truman, serving from 1945 to 1956. Soon, I was meeting fascinating people from all over the world looking for someone to represent their products to American stores.

I brought these entrepreneurs to New York City one at a time. Each would stay with me for a month and help pay my rent. In return, I would take him around town and introduce him to contacts I had developed at wholesalers and stores, earning 7 percent commission on whatever we sold. Every month someone new and exciting would come stay with me. I was having a blast!

Becoming an entrepreneur had an immediate beneficial effect on my self-esteem and outlook. At Ford, I was near the bottom of the corporate hierarchy. In New York, I was making less money, but I was the boss. I didn't have tons of capital or thousands of employees, yet I felt on top of the world.

I also felt really good about assisting my fellow entrepreneurs from Jamaica, Kenya, Bangladesh, and other distant places. I was helping them make money and improve their lives, too. I loved being self-employed, and started thinking about expanding into other ventures.

But then I learned another life lesson—about the dangers of living in a large city.

One sunny September afternoon in 1981, I set out for a jog. I had been a high school state wrestling champ back in Michigan and still liked to keep in shape.

I cruised down East 11th Street until I hit my favorite stretch, the wide paved walkway that runs along the East River and offers glorious views of the Brooklyn Bridge, Williamsburg Bridge, and Manhattan Bridge. Lots of people were out enjoying the cloudless bright blue sky and warm weather.

I passed some Latino and African American boys around fourteen years old, lounging against the railing that ran along the riverfront. They were looking at me rather intently, so I nodded and grunted, "The water's down a bit," as I trotted past them.

"Get him," one of them said.

Next thing I knew, someone had grabbed me from behind and wrenched my right arm behind my back. Stunned and in agony, it took me a moment to realize I was surrounded.

"Give us your money," a stocky boy with curly hair shorn into a high fade demanded.

I was shocked by their brazen attack. There were people everywhere. I was in so much pain, though, that I feared if I screamed for help the kid twisting my arm would break it. Six teens were surrounding me, and since I'm five foot six, they were effectively blocking me from view. I craned my neck, desperately trying to look past them to see if I could signal for help somehow. All I could glimpse was a nearby soccer field where a game was in full swing.

Somebody punched me hard in the chest. Someone else shoved me. Metal glinted in the afternoon sun. They had knives. Large knives.

Panicked, I fought with all my might, broke free and ran. They chased me and cornered me again.

"You better give us your money, you sonofabitch, or we're gonna slice your dick off," one of them snarled.

I had a ten-dollar bill in the pocket of my running shorts. I handed it over with trembling hands and tears streaming down my face. I couldn't believe this was happening in broad daylight. Rage poured off these kids. They waved their knives in my face, punched me, shoved me around, and taunted me. They backed me up against the railing. Two of them picked me up and lifted me over it, laughing and threatening to throw me into the river. I kicked and struggled, feeling utterly powerless and humiliated. Luckily, one kid signaled for the others to put me down.

After knocking me to the ground, the teens sauntered off. The attack was over as suddenly as it had begun. Dazed, I got to my feet, blinking in the bright afternoon sun. No one seemed to have noticed a thing.

As I stumbled out of East River Park, I nearly fell headfirst into three policemen.

"I've been mugged!" I gasped, pointing in the direction of my attackers. I put my hands on my knees and tried to catch my breath. I did my best to provide a useful description of the boys, and two officers bolted into the park. The third took me to the station to file a report.

Afterward, the entrepreneur in me wondered why these boys

would mug someone in broad daylight and risk prison for ten dollars. If they had been able to sell me something, or ask me to invest in a business, they could have gotten a lot more money and it would have been a win/win situation for everyone.

Becoming an urban statistic was traumatic. I was plagued by flashbacks and nightmares that became more stressful than the experience itself. I was afraid of any tough-looking teenage male—and that described a lot of kids in New York City. I also felt a deep shame that I had been unable to defend myself against attackers half my age.

My sleep patterns were a wreck. I was struggling to keep my import-export business going because it was hard for me to wake up for the appointments my clients and I had with store buyers.

I knew I had a serious problem, so I dug out one of my favorite books: psychologist Albert Ellis's cognitive behavior classic *A Guide to Rational Living*.

I had read this book many times because it really helped me. My mother gave it to me when I couldn't stop moping after I failed to qualify for the varsity baseball team my junior year of high school. In two years, I had gone from being one of Flint's best shortstops to not making the team at my own school. Not a week would go by without some friend shouting at me in the school corridors, "Steve, what happened! You used to be so good at baseball!"

I knew why I hadn't made the team: While my former teammates had grown like weeds over the summer, I had barely grown at all. It seems silly to me now that I was so upset, but at the time I was inconsolable. Then, I read *A Guide to Rational Living*.

Ellis argued in his book that one's feelings could be changed by consciously changing one's thoughts. I couldn't feel any worse, so I decided to give his method a try.

The first step, I learned, was to identify and write down the thoughts disturbing me. That was easy: "You tiny little shrimp, you let your lack of height and strength get the better of you and you lost your seat on the team. If you're not good at baseball, what are you ever going to be good at?"

These caustic words were constantly running through my mind, making me miserable. Following Ellis's next instructions, I wrote down new, positive sentences designed to change my thoughts, and, hopefully, my gloomy teenage feelings: "I am a great wrestler, and in wrestling size does not matter, skill matters. I was AAU Michigan State Champ in 1969. Leaving baseball gives me more time to focus on wrestling!"

I felt better immediately! I wrote those sentences down over and over, said them out loud, and repeated them in my mind, as Ellis recommended, until I truly felt free of the pain of not making the team.

Over the years, I used Ellis's self-help method many times. It saved me during the breakup of my first romance, whenever I got poor grades in college, and when I lost my job at Ford.

Maybe it could help me now, I mused. Then, I had an exciting realization: Albert Ellis practiced psychotherapy in New York City! I wondered if I could possibly obtain an appointment with this legendary therapist. I just knew he would fix me right up.

I phoned the Albert Ellis Institute, located at 45 East 65th Street, and was told the doctor was not taking any new patients. Luckily, I had an ace in the hole. I knew Ayn Rand. Rand and Ellis were not exactly friends—they were more like intellectual sparring partners. But they ran in the same circles.

I actually had a meeting coming up with Ayn Rand, arranged by my grandfather Lowell Mason. He had been Rand's lawyer and friend for decades. Maybe she would help me connect with Albert Ellis.

I was not hugely hopeful, because I had already discovered on my previous meeting with Ayn Rand, also arranged by my grandfather, that she was rude and imperious. She was also extremely charming and charismatic. Ayn Rand scared the crap out of me, frankly, yet I also had a massive crush on her, even though at seventy-five she was nearly fifty years older than me.

When I was fourteen, my grandfather sent me *Atlas Shrugged*. It took me two months to read all 1,069 pages of Rand's famous novel. *Atlas Shrugged* was the first work of fiction I ever read that talked positively about entrepreneurs and the wealth they created. Today, I disagree with many aspects of Rand's philosophy, but back then, as a mini-entrepreneur, I loved *Atlas Shrugged*!

My first appointment with Ayn Rand was at 11 AM on Memorial Day, 1980. I was overdressed for the weather, and sweat streamed down my face as I paced around the block at 34th Street and Lexington Avenue several times, too freaked out to enter her apartment building. I could barely breathe. I was both exhilarated and terribly nervous. She was a great hero of mine. I had memorized many passages from *Atlas Shrugged* and *The Fountainhead*.

I finally entered the Tudor-style building at 128 East 34th Street and rang the bell for apartment 6D. The name on the directory was O'Connor, for Frank O'Connor, Rand's husband, who had just passed away.

"I never agree to meet with anyone," Rand declared in her dramatic Russian accent, when her maid opened the door, "but you're right on time. That tells me something about you. Your grandfather has been my close friend since I started writing *The Fountainhead*. He gave me good advice on some legal issues.

"His *Language of Dissent* was brilliant," she continued, waving me in and pointing to a copy of my grandfather's book on a shelf. "Otherwise, I would never have agreed to see you. I am old and do not have the energy."

Rand wore a simple black dress with three-quarter-length sleeves. Her short auburn hair was combed into a sleek bob that accentuated her strong jawline. She positioned herself directly beneath a painting of a stunning topless woman who could have been Rand in her younger years and examined me intently, wearing the same sly smile as the woman in the portrait. Rand's seductive gaze seemed to say: "And I am still this sexy?"

She was. With her high cheekbones, full bosom, and bright green eyes, she looked like an earthly goddess who had stepped out of one of her novels. I called her "Dominique" and then "Dagny," both female heroines from her books, and she smiled and touched my arm. I told her how beautiful I thought she was, and she laughed a loud Russian laugh.

I was twenty-six and in love.

She escorted me around the apartment—everywhere but the bedroom; she said it was too untidy for me to see. She showed me the massive drafting table on which she had written every page of *Atlas Shrugged* by hand. I shyly handed her three economics papers that I had written, which she accepted and promised to read.

As we headed out for lunch, her housekeeper, a soft-spoken African American woman, said, "Ms. Rand, please do not be long, and absolutely no smoking." I didn't know at the time, but Rand had been diagnosed with lung cancer.

As we walked down Lexington Avenue, I quoted my favorite passages from her novels at length until Rand finally interrupted my chattering with: "Can you be quiet?"

Chastened, I walked alongside her silently.

We found a diner on 33rd Street and settled into a booth.

Rand ordered cereal and I got a hamburger. She lit a cigarette and didn't stop smoking and blowing smoke in my face for the next four hours, during which she held forth on philosophy, economics, her career, and the love of her life, Frank O'Connor. She did not eat at all. When I pointed out that she wasn't supposed to be smoking, she shrugged and said, "I can't do this in front of my housekeeper because it's bad for my health. Do not be such a complainer."

Rand spoke in short, perfectly formed sentences. She was extremely judgmental, and the few remarks I was able to insert into her monologue were dissected thoroughly. Throughout the conversation she laughed often—loudly and joyously. Time flew by as I hung on her every word. She was a powerful intellectual force, and I was enthralled.

As our visit came to an end, Rand declared, "You listen and talk well but too much sometimes. You would make a good teacher. I've been taking math lessons in arithmetic. Can you show me how to do this problem?"

It was a simple problem that involved dividing fractions. I showed her how to solve it, feeling the pleasure of for once knowing something she did not.

After I paid the check, we walked back to her apartment building and said goodbye at the front door.

"You are a great teacher, Ms. Rand," I said. She smiled tightly and walked into her building.

A few days later, I sent her a book about Hollywood she was mentioned in, with a handwritten thank-you note. She didn't reply, so a few weeks later I sent another gift—some Russian candy—with another note.

She mailed my gifts back, accompanied by a letter from her

secretary explaining that Rand had only seen me out of courtesy to my grandfather.

I was devastated. She had seemed to enjoy my company during those smoke-filled hours, which made the letter from her secretary even more distressing. I believed then what I had often heard about Ayn Rand: my idol was nothing more than an egotistical, self-absorbed recluse.

Fifteen months later, a few weeks after I was mugged, we both got another chance. My grandfather had intervened, calling Rand and apologizing on my behalf. To me, he said: "You were too intellectually aggressive, Steve." I was shocked but held my tongue, not mentioning my virtual silence for those four hours in the diner.

"Because she hurt your feelings," my grandfather continued, "she will see you one last time—for fifteen minutes. Don't mess it up this time. She is a genius and you can learn a great deal from her. Do not talk or take issue with anything at all."

I met her in the lobby of her building. I had been so shaken by her return of my gifts, not to mention my recent mugging, that I must have looked like a chagrined child.

"Don't be so weak," Rand said, with a hint of a twinkle in her eye. "Weakness sickens me. Do not make me feel pity."

She was quoting from *The Fountainhead,* so I quoted the preceding and following sentences back to her.

Rand laughed. "Okay, you're forgiven!"

She peered at me intently, though. "What is the matter with you?"

"W-well," I stammered. I really didn't know how to tell this attractive woman who had just admonished me not to be weak that I was suffering from nightmares and flashbacks due to a mugging.

"Come upstairs!" she snapped.

In the elevator, I told her that I had been mugged at knifepoint and was having trouble sleeping. I added that I was a big believer in Albert Ellis's therapeutic approach and had tried but failed to get an appointment with him.

The moment we entered her apartment, Rand headed for her phone and dialed the Albert Ellis Institute. I heard, "This is Ayn Rand!" followed by, "Put him on the phone. Now!"

Ellis took her call, because next I heard Rand inform him that her lawyer's grandson needed to see him immediately. Over the doctor's apparent protests, Rand barked, "You *will* see him, Albert! Immediately! Yes, yes, you will!"

I was mortified by her rudeness. But it worked. Rand hung up and turned to me. "You have an appointment with Dr. Ellis at four PM tomorrow. Do not be late!"

We went to a restaurant on 33rd and Lexington, where I gave her a simple gold bracelet. She slid it on over the green blouse she was wearing underneath a ratty blue cardigan with an elegant gold brooch pinned to it.

We sat at her favorite table by the door. She knew all the waiters, who were very respectful to her. I excused myself and went to the bathroom. On the way, I asked one of the waiters, "Do you know who that is?"

"Of course," he replied. "She's a writer, right?"

This time, Rand and I talked for at least five hours. I mentioned some local activism for gay rights in which I had taken part, thinking she would be pleased. She scowled and I dropped the subject.

She was still grieving over the death of her husband. She smoked continuously and confided, "No one knows how sad I am. This pain from Frank is killing me."

She blew a cloud of smoke in my face and added, "You should

come to my funeral." I smiled when she added: "And I mean it"—
four words that had guided her life.

Rand told me that she met Frank O'Connor in 1926 on the
film set of Cecil B. DeMille's *The King of Kings*. O'Connor had a
small part and Rand was an extra. After meeting O'Connor briefly
on the extras bus, Rand came across him by chance again at the
studio library, where he was reading about art history.

With a breaking voice, she told me she had kidded him about
his sagging pants, and he had laughed at her accent. Upon discovering that they both liked the poem "If" by Rudyard Kipling, she had
recited it to him from memory.

"For me," she murmured dreamily, "it was love at first sight."

Rand showed me notes O'Connor had written her after his
stroke. They were in large letters that looked like a third-grader's
printing.

Then she started to cry. I felt so bad for her—and startled,
because she was legendary for never crying.

Trying to console her, I said, "You will see Frank again in a spir-
itual sense. There are billions of calculations a second for the body
to function. That is so incredible, someone had to create that. And
if that is so, then anything is possible."

Even though Rand was a staunch atheist, she nodded, her face
heavy with tears.

"I hope so," she sobbed. "I would do anything to see him one
more time." After a long pause, she added: "I will find out soon
enough."

"Let me know!" I said. That made her laugh.

"You should let the public know that you have doubts about
atheism," I added. "So many people follow you."

Rand waved her hand dismissively. "So what. Let them find

their own way; I cannot help them. You should be a teacher. I think you'd have a knack for it," she said, repeating her comment of fifteen months prior.

After our long chat, I walked her back to her building. We arrived just as the housekeeper was coming out. "Ms. Rand, I was just coming to find you!" she cried.

Rand turned to me and whispered, "You made me feel better."

I smiled. "I thought people were not supposed to feel."

She gave me a quick one-finger handshake and said, "Do not count on me for any more visits."

"Okay," I replied, "but you did say we could have coffee again sometime, and I love being with a beautiful woman. Can I get a picture with you, please?"

I handed my camera to the housekeeper.

"No, absolutely not, I'm too old! If I'm alive next year, perhaps," Rand laughed. "If not, come to my funeral."

This time I sent no notes or gifts and waited a month to call. When I got Rand on the phone, she said, "I can see you for a cup of coffee, perhaps, but only for twenty minutes. You wear me out."

I was pleased and promised not to talk at all. We went to the same restaurant, but she was irritable and tired. We left after twenty minutes, having exchanged very few words and no laughs.

On November 21, 1981, Rand delivered her lecture "The Sanction of the Victims" at a conference in New Orleans sponsored by the National Committee for Monetary Reform. In it, she declared: "It is a moral crime to give money to support ideas with which you disagree. It is a moral crime to give money to support your own destroyers."

Shortly thereafter, I received a letter from her, out of the blue:

I had seen you out of respect for your grandfather. You turned out to be a terrible disappointment. The fact that you support the immoral acts of homosexuals shows me you are a second-hander who likes his heroes with clay feet. Do not call me again or contact me in any way. Here is the bracelet—I do not want it. I am burning your papers.

I felt like someone had taken a hot knife to my stomach. That was the last time I ever heard from her, and "The Sanction of the Victims" was her last public speech. Ayn Rand passed away on March 6, 1982.

CHAPTER 2

MR. MANICOTTI GOES TO BROOKLYN

"A good teacher, like a good entertainer, first must hold his audience's attention, then he can teach his lesson."
—JOHN HENRIK CLARKE, "A Search for Identity" (1970)

When I walked into Albert Ellis's brownstone for the first time, I was amazed by how powerful his energy was. Dr. Ellis was tall and lean, with a shock of white hair and an impressively large Roman nose. He flashed a toothy grin as he sized me up with penetrating brown eyes swathed in crinkles behind his horn-rimmed glasses. His face almost knocked me over with its intensity.

"You don't look so bad!" he exclaimed, after we walked

downstairs to his office. He nodded toward the copy of his book in my hand. "So, what are you saying to yourself?"

"I . . . well, I got mugged and beat up by some teenage boys. I was unable to defend myself and cried in front of them. Now I'm jumpy. I'm afraid of any teenage boy I see. I'm having nightmares. I feel like a loser because this is affecting me so much."

Dr. Ellis looked so bored that I thought he might cry.

"That's it?" he said.

"Um, yes," I replied, cringing inside. What was I thinking bothering this great man with a garden-variety mugging?

"Well, you know what to do, right?" He gestured at the blackboard in his office. "Write!" he cried, clearly amused by his play on words.

I wrote "I am a loser because I let some teenage kids mug and humiliate me" on the blackboard in my large, awkward print.

"Change the sentence," Dr. Ellis said calmly. I noticed that two of his staff had followed us into his office and were sitting behind him, watching.

I turned to the board and started to write a more positive sentence underneath the one I had already written down.

"No!" Dr. Ellis barked. "Erase the first one before you write a new one! Erase it from the board and from your mind! Now, get the *accurate* one right. My two assistants will help you. I will come down and see you when you have the new sentence."

Dr. Ellis got up abruptly and left the office, his long feet flopping noisily as he galloped up the stairs.

With the encouragement of his kind and friendly staff, I erased and wrote many sentences until we all agreed I had gotten one right: "By heroically withstanding an attack by six armed thugs, I was able to prevent injury to myself and anyone else."

The two staff members had me stand on a chair and recite this sentence over and over. After about an hour, I heard Dr. Ellis's feet flopping down the stairs. Upon entering the office, he examined my new sentence intently.

After a solid minute of intense contemplation, he said, "Better."

"What are you thinking about, Steve?" he demanded next. "Right now!"

I was startled and didn't know what to say. Then I realized something amazing. I was no longer obsessing over what a loser I was for being mugged by a bunch of kids.

"I think I'm cured!" I exclaimed. "Thank you so much!"

Dr. Ellis and his staff members cracked up.

"Steve!" Dr. Ellis said, when he caught his breath. "You have post-traumatic stress disorder. It's not cured in one session, but today you have taken the first step. Pay upstairs and call me tomorrow morning. I want to figure out tonight what your next step should be, so this never plagues you again."

That night, I slept well for the first time since the attack.

When I called the next day, Dr. Ellis coldly ordered me to come to his office immediately. I jumped in a cab and worried during the entire ride about what I must have done wrong. Did I forget to pay? Did I say something inappropriate?

To my relief, Dr. Ellis met me at the door with a warm greeting and his firm handshake. "I was up half the night thinking about your treatment!" he exclaimed eagerly, as we trundled down the stairs to his office. "It hit a nerve with me. I got mugged years ago and also felt ashamed and humiliated. Hearing your story brought back a lot of memories that I had forgotten."

He gestured for me to sit down. "All to your benefit, as I came up with the perfect treatment for you, which will prevent your obsessive negative thoughts about the incident—and your nightmares and flashbacks—from ever coming back."

I nodded, feeling both flattered and intensely curious.

"You are going to become a teacher of difficult students in a difficult school!" Dr. Ellis announced.

"I-I . . . what?" I stuttered. "You mean, like 'flooding'?"

From reading his books, I knew Dr. Ellis believed in treating anxiety with exposure therapy. Flooding, specifically, treated phobias by exposing the patient to the feared stimulus until the patient's fear response was so overwhelmed that it collapsed. Flooding used what psychologists call "in vivo" exposure—real-life exposure to the feared stimulus. You're afraid of spiders? Come sit in this room full of spiders!

Today, psychologists take a more cautious and gradual approach to treating PTSD and phobias, as flooding can overwhelm a patient with so much anxiety that the patient may dissociate. But at the time, Albert Ellis was the foremost proponent of the anxiety-busting properties of flooding.

"Yes, Steve!" Dr. Ellis practically shouted. "We will flood your fear out of existence forever!"

Oh dear God, I thought, horrified.

"Um, I'm not a teacher," I protested weakly. "I'm an entrepreneur. I run a small import-export business."

"Doesn't matter!" Dr. Ellis declared. "You need to do this! You *must* do this!"

Compelled by the sheer force of his personality, I found myself actually considering this loony idea. After all, my mother had been a beloved special education teacher in some of Flint's most disadvantaged schools. She loved teaching and her students. And Ayn Rand kept telling me I should be a teacher.

I knew one thing for sure—I couldn't go on living in New York City scared of my own shadow and every teenage boy I saw.

I tested the waters by volunteering at the Boys & Girls Club on the Lower East Side for a few hours each week. I was working with children who were younger than the teens who had attacked me, but it was a start. I found that I enjoyed being with these spunky kids, and I noticed that my nightmares were diminishing in frequency. Maybe I was ready to try teenagers.

I figured I could still run my import-export business part-time on weekends and during the summer. But I had no idea how to become a high school teacher.

One sticky summer morning, I was delivering shoes to an importer's warehouse on 23rd Street and the West Side Highway. As I was pulling the boxes from my rental truck, I chatted with the burly guy helping me unload. It turned out Mike had recently quit his job as a high school teacher.

"Why'd you quit?" I asked.

"The discipline problems were overwhelming," Mike said. "I burned out."

"I'm actually interested in teaching," I told him. "How would I find out about any openings?"

Mike laughed. "Depends on what kind of school you want to teach in! There's a glut of applications for top schools like Bronx Science or Stuyvesant. But if you're willing to teach in more challenging schools, you can have your pick! All they ask is that you have a college degree. There are literally hundreds of positions open." He peered at me intently. "Are you serious about this?"

I nodded enthusiastically.

"All right, then go to the Department of Ed on Court Street in Brooklyn and see the personnel director, Rufus Thomas, on the seventh floor. The man's a legend. He taught math in the city's worst schools for twenty-five years and now he hires every teacher in New York City. We call him 'the black Napoleon.'"

"Wow, thanks!" I exclaimed, hardly believing my luck.

"Ha, don't thank me 'til you've done some time!" Mike chortled. "But if you can handle it in the rougher schools with those kids who are barely hanging on, Thomas will freakin' canonize you!"

As soon as I left the warehouse, I went straight to 65 Court Street.

The Department of Education building was the most depressing place I had ever seen. It was dark and dingy, and everyone trudging through it looked miserable. I got into an ancient elevator that climbed so slowly that several times I was convinced it was stuck. After a minute or so, it would jerk suddenly and begin its agonizing crawl upward again.

By the time I made it to the seventh floor, I was ready to turn around and go home—taking the stairs. But then Rufus Thomas changed my life.

Thomas was a perfectly dressed man in his forties with close-cropped hair who radiated confidence and intelligence. His suit was crisply pressed and his shoes gleamed. He wore a red tie and a very nice watch.

I was sweating in a worn blue suit going thin at the elbows and a wrinkled navy shirt. My shoes were scuffed and cracking. Despite my disheveled appearance, Thomas greeted me like I was the greatest thing since sliced bread. He joyfully ushered me into his plain office, furnished with a long table made of cheap particleboard, metal shelves, and fluorescent overhead lighting. I quickly understood why he was nicknamed "the black Napoleon." Despite the decrepit surroundings, Thomas positively sparkled with energy. He looked like Denzel Washington and exuded more pure charisma than most world leaders. He was the kind of guy you would gladly follow into a war zone.

With far more bravado than common sense, I told him I wanted to teach in the most troubled schools and work with the most difficult children.

Thomas asked me dozens of questions, ferreting out that I was specifically interested in teaching low-income youth with learning issues. Finally, he asked me earnestly, "Steve, why do you want to teach?"

Something my mother often said popped into my mind, so I repeated it: "A great teacher affects eternity."

Thomas beamed at me so warmly that I felt kind of guilty. After all, my real dream was still to become a great entrepreneur and make millions. I was only going after a teaching job in hopes of vanquishing my PTSD. Somehow, though, Thomas was starting to make me believe something else my mother often said: teachers were heroes. I wanted to be a hero, too.

Together, we went over his list of high schools having an especially difficult time keeping teachers. "When discipline breaks down in a school," Thomas mused, "it's like watching a ship slowly sink. Everyone is trying to get out." He shook his head. "It's terrible." In that moment, I sensed how deeply he cared and how many schools he had seen fail up close.

"Let's start you off at Boys and Girls High in Bed-Stuy," Thomas said. "We've got a special ed teacher there dying of that awful new immune disorder, and three of his students are facing felony charges for chasing another young man into the street where he was killed by a car."

I gulped. Thomas had taken my request to teach in New York's most troubled schools seriously. As I would soon learn, Boys and Girls High had a frightening reputation, even though it had only been open since 1976 and had cost $30 mlllion to construct. The school was teeming with four thousand under-supervised students. Seventy-two teachers simply refused to report for duty at Boys and Girls. They preferred to be unemployed. The dropout rate among students was an astounding 70 percent. In 1978, the New York State Board of Regents took the unprecedented step of putting the entire school on probation.

Bed-Stuy was comprised of 650 blocks in the center of Brooklyn and was home to approximately 350,000 people in the early eighties. If Bed-Stuy were its own city, it would have been one of the thirty largest in the United States. The population was 85 percent African American and 12 percent Hispanic. In 1983, the median income in Bed-Stuy was $8,500—40 percent below the average income in the rest of New York City. Bed-Stuy's incidence of violent crime, in contrast, soared above the city's average.

"Can you start in September?" Thomas asked.

I nodded nervously.

Thomas looked pleased. "If you can teach at Boys and Girls, you can teach anywhere," he said, "because those students will make you into a good teacher. If you do well there, Steve, come back and see me and we'll find you an even better challenge!"

He stood up and we shook hands, after I wiped my sweaty palm off on my pants leg.

"Steve," Thomas declared with a broad smile, clapping me on the back, "I think you will be a good teacher. Maybe even a great one."

His faith in me would give me strength during the painful months ahead.

On my first day as a high school teacher, it took me forty minutes to travel from the West 4th Street subway stop in Manhattan to Utica Avenue Station in Brooklyn. As my train rattled from station to increasingly grimy station, my anxiety grew.

By Nostrand Avenue, I was the only white person in a packed subway car. Three black teenagers sitting to my right were giving me the stink eye. They reminded me of the kids who had mugged me. I tried to avoid eye contact with them.

Finally, the train screeched into Utica Station. I got out and walked up the concrete ramp to Schenectady Avenue. As I approached the imposing brick facade of Boys and Girls High, I saw fifteen to twenty teenagers sitting on the steps outside the front doors under the indifferent gaze of a plump security officer. The smell of marijuana was overwhelming. I nodded as I walked by them into the school, and they nodded in return.

Dr. Ellis's "flooding" strategy appeared to be working, though. Within an hour of arriving at the school, I began to view the students with less animosity and fear. They were smiling, laughing, and goofing around like teenagers anywhere. I had a good feeling that I would like teaching. I was hopeful that I had found a new vocation.

Reality set in quickly, however. There were fifty-nine students in my remedial math class—a number far too high, in the best of circumstances, to teach effectively. Remedial programs are for students identified as having deficiencies in core subjects like reading, writing, and math.

I looked around my classroom. There were only forty-two seats and thirty-nine books. If two-thirds of the class showed up, I would be in trouble.

"Are you the new teacher?" a six-foot-two young man asked in a baritone voice as he entered the classroom. At first, I thought he was a security guard. He turned out to be nineteen-year-old Robert, whose math was at the seventh-grade level, according to his file.

"Yes, I am. My name is Mr. Mariotti."

"Okay, Mr. Manicotti," Robert smirked.

"Hey Robert, where'd ya get the midget?" yelled the next student coming through the door.

"Sit down, please," I said, trying to pitch my soft nasally voice as low as possible. More students trickled in and the noise level rose dramatically.

"Who says?"

"I do. I'm the teacher," I intoned, in my best Humphrey Bogart imitation.

"You're a shorty—what's it like being a midget?"

"Please sit down, now."

"Hey, he thinks he's a bad motherfucker."

"Chill out, teach, ain't nobody hurting you."

"Please sit down."

"Bust a move, teach."

"Nice suit, Manicotti. Too bad you didn't get it in the right size."

There were now forty-six students in the room, which meant that four had to stand and seven didn't have books. The students were actually quiet as I introduced myself and wrote my class rules on the board. I closed with a plea for them to learn basic math because without it they would find it difficult not only to get jobs but also to function effectively in their personal lives.

I passed out the books I had and a basic diagnostic test. Twenty percent of the class had no pencils or paper, so I had to go in search of supplies.

The tests came back with disheartening results. Only a third of these high school seniors could solve 1/3 + 1/16, for example. Clearly, we needed a lesson on fractions, so I launched into one.

I soon realized that everyone was talking—to everyone else.

Two girls in the back of the room were showing each other new dance steps. The boys in the back rows were talking more loudly than I was.

"Please be quiet," I said calmly.

No effect.

"Please be quiet!" I yelled.

Still no effect.

I sat down, hoping to shame them into silence. Instead, their conversations accelerated in volume and raucousness. After a few minutes, I continued the lesson for the five or six students who were paying attention, hollering to make myself heard above the din.

I lost control of my classes on a daily basis. If a student was acting disruptive and I asked for his name, the response would be "Muhammad Ali" or "John Wayne." One wag declared himself to be George Wallace. In each of my three special ed classes, there was a group of six or seven teens whose behavior was so unruly that I had to stop the class every five minutes to get them to quiet down.

I decided to make a seating chart and memorize the name of every student in all my classes. I noticed an improvement in classroom demeanor as soon as they realized that I knew their names. But it was not enough to prevent major ongoing disruptions. One student set fire to the back of another student's coat. The kid set on fire was as astonished as I was and flew out of his chair, flailing wildly. After blasting him with a decrepit fire extinguisher that, thank God, still worked, I furiously ordered the arsonist out of the class. He was expelled the same day. At least I had gotten his name right.

On another occasion, I was locked out of my eighth-period class when I left the room on one of my many hunts for supplies. The students would not open the door for what seemed like an eternity. Finally, one of the girls took pity on me and opened it just as I was about to admit total defeat and go look for a security guard to let me back into my own classroom.

In my third-period class, I threw out all the boys for two days and sent them to detention. They were so wild that it was the only way I could get control of the class. It was these young men, though, who provided me with a valuable insight. I invited all fifteen to join me in the gym for pizza after school one day. Seven showed up.

I passed around the greasy pizza box and a handful of paper napkins. After we had all grabbed a slice, I said, "Look, I asked you to meet me here today because I want to know why you act up so much in my class. What exactly is the problem?"

"Man, your class is *boring*!" Lamar declared with a mouthful of cheese.

The other young men nodded in assent.

"You talk too much, yo. I couldn't figure out what you was try-ing to say half the time," Darnell muttered as he picked pepperoni discs off his slice and stashed them in his napkin.

More nods.

It dawned on me, for the first time, that it didn't matter what a math whiz I was if I couldn't reach and teach the students entrusted to my care.

"Did *anything* I said in class interest you?" I asked, dreading the answer.

Trevon, a senior who read at the fourth-grade level, piped up. "I dug it when you talked about your business! That was mad cool how you got people from other countries to come here to sell they shit."

"Yeah," some other students murmured. "Yeah, that was all right."

"Like that dude you brought over from Haiti," Trevon

continued. "You said it cost him two dollar to make his wall hang-ings, but you got him that deal selling six dozen a month for four hundred thirty-two to some big store."

"Pier One," I said.

"Yeah," Trevon said, "so it was costing him, like, one forty-four to make them, but he was getting four thirty-two, so he was mak-ing, like, two hundred eighty-eight dollars every month. That's sweet money, yo!"

"Yeah, it is!" Lamar shouted, giving Trevon a high-five.

I was dazzled that Trevon, a student labeled "borderline retarded" in his file, had just calculated cost of goods sold, revenue, and gross profit in his head. This kid was not stupid. In fact, he had an aptitude for business.

I shoveled pizza into my mouth and chewed furiously, thinking hard. This was my first inkling that something was wrong not only with my teaching, but also with the standard remedial curriculum.

I was on to something. I just wasn't sure what it was.

CHAPTER 3

NO MORE MR. NICE GUY

"The learning process is something you can incite, literally incite, like a riot."
—AUDRE LORDE, "An Interview with Audre Lorde," *Signs: Journal of Women in Culture and Society* 6, no. 4 (1981)

In my eighth-period class, I was too afraid of the boys to throw them out.

The most disruptive young men were Andre, Brayton, and Jamal. Andre, the trio's leader, was charismatic, with a biting wit. Brayton was a wiry, hyperactive kid who literally bounced off the walls. Jamal was a stocky, pissed-off pit bull of a boy.

They really seemed to hate me, and I didn't like them much, either. They would disrupt the class by howling like hyenas, cursing me viciously ("Suck my sweaty balls, Manicotti!" was very popular), and treating their fellow classmates with great hostility. I tried threatening them with failure. I also tried not to lose a joking manner, which, it turned out, they saw as a sign of weakness.

One Friday, I knew I was off to a particularly bad start when I sat in my seat and felt something stick to the back of my suit coat. I got up and found an enormous wad of gum stuck to my jacket. The class roared with laughter. Then, seeing the hurt and disgust on my face, they fell silent.

A student named Therese came up to me and said, "You all right, Mr. Mariotti? You have gum on your back. Let me help you." She tried to pull off as much of it as possible.

I tried cracking a joke: "Judging from the amount of gum, I'd say it came from someone with a big mouth."

No one laughed.

Therese sat down and I resumed my decimals lesson. As I passed out a page of math problems, rap music blasted from a radio in the back of the room.

I took a deep breath. "Please turn off the radio."

"It ain't the radio," a skinny kid named Ramon shouted, "it's the PA." The class busted out laughing, and Ramon bounced out of his seat in the last row to take several dramatic bows. I glimpsed a boom box under his chair.

Andre and Brayton hopped out of their seats and started dancing. The rest of the class began to clap in unison. I ran to the back of the room and threatened Ramon: "Turn it off or I'm going to fail you!"

Ramon ignored me. He was dancing, too, spinning on the balls of his sneakers. His unzipped blue tracksuit jacket, with three white stripes running down each arm, flew around him, exposing the thin white tank top clinging to his bony chest. Andre ran to the front of the room and leapt on top of my desk, where he began performing karate moves to the music.

Furious, I turned back to Ramon. "Turn off the goddamn radio, you twerp!"

Someone, imitating my Midwestern twang quite well, shouted primly, "No swearing, Mr. Mariotti!"

I ducked under Ramon's chair, grabbed the boom box, turned it off, and marched with it to the front of the room. To my relief, Andre slid off my desk and strutted back toward his seat, muttering "fucking motherfucker" when he passed me. As I shoved Ramon's radio under my desk, I could feel my face twitching.

"Look, Manicotti's having a nervous breakdown!" Jamal squealed.

"You can't control this class, Manicotti," Brayton sneered, "'cause you ain't got juice."

"Shut up and sit down!" I snapped. "Work on your math problems!"

For a few moments, the class grew quiet. I was still shaking when a student named Aiesha came up to my desk and gently asked, "Can you show me how to do this problem, Mr. Mariotti?"

As I picked up a pencil to work through the math with her, I was hit in the eye with a large spitball.

"WHO THREW THAT?" I thundered, a wave of rage ripping through me.

The class erupted again in total chaos. Andre ran to the front of the room, grabbed the American flag off the wall, and brandished it like a spear, pretending to poke me with it. He raised it up as if to throw it at me.

"Put the flag DOWN!" I screamed, trying not to look as freaked out as I felt. I could picture the *New York Post* headline:

TEACHER SPEARED BY FLAG
AT BOYS AND GIRLS HIGH

Abbott, a sturdy Bermudian boy, snuck up behind Andre and grabbed him around the chest, pinning his arms. As he held Andre tightly, I wrested the flag out of Andre's hands and placed it into its holder.

That used up my last shred of composure. Without saying another word, I walked toward the classroom door. As I passed a kid named Darius, he proclaimed loudly, "We need a new teacher. This asshole can't teach."

As I exited, I was hit in the back with another massive spitball.

I stood in the hallway outside my classroom, trembling with fury and frustration, fighting back tears. I desperately wanted to walk out of that school and go home to the peaceful leafy streets of Greenwich Village.

I paced the hallway for several minutes, trying to calm down. If I didn't go back in there, I would lose my job, plain and simple. I had already failed at Ford. I wasn't going to let that happen again. I prayed for strength and thought about my pizza dinner with the young men from my third-period class. They had said I was boring—except when I talked about business, about money.

I reached down and untied my shoes. I took them off and threw them down on the floor with a satisfying clatter. I loosened my tie and removed my watch. My inner high school wrestler took over and, ludicrous as it surely looked to those passing by in the hallway, I clenched every muscle in my body and drew my fists together in front of my torso in the bodybuilding pose known as "the crab."

I snorted like a bull. I was ready.

I threw open the classroom door, letting it bang hard against the wall. I slid back into the classroom on my socks like Tom Cruise in *Risky Business*, holding my watch aloft in one hand and pointing at the class with the other.

"How much would you pay for this watch?" I shouted. "C'mon, lemme hear it!"

It gave me great satisfaction to note that, for once, my rowdy students were struck dumb. They looked stunned.

"Make me an offer! What's it going to take to get you into this fine timepiece today?"

"Five dollars!" Ramon yelled from the back of the room.

"Do we get to keep it if we say the highest price?" Shawan shouted.

"OF COURSE NOT!" I bellowed as if I were on a Broadway stage. "You have to get nearest to the price I paid. Then it's yours!"

Shawan bopped over to me. "Yo, Mr. Mariotti, can I inspect the merchandise?"

"Absolutely!" I cried.

Shawan took the watch from me and examined it closely.

"Naw," he grumbled, "I don't want it. It ain't got no style."

The class roared with laughter.

"*Au contraire, mon ami*!" I countered. "This watch is the ultimate in style because it is a *classic*. This is not a trendy piece of crap. It'll never go out of style!"

"Aight," Shawan nodded. "Five fifty."

"I've got a bid for five fifty! Can I get five seventy-five?"

"Five seventy-five!" somebody said.

"Can I get five eighty?"

"Five eighty!"

"Five ninety-five!"

"I'll give you six fifty for it, Mariotti!" Shawan declared.

"No way, that is much too low!" I objected.

"But that's the highest price so far!" Shawan said, looking confused.

"Do I hear seven dollars?" I called. "This watch is reliable, waterproof, and keeps time perfectly!"

I noticed Andre, Jamal, and Brayton glowering at me as they leaned against a side wall and observed the negotiations silently. I would deal with them later.

"Seven dollars!"

I shook my head. "That is the wholesale price. I would never sell something for wholesale that I bought retail!"

At the puzzled looks on my students' faces, I asked, "Who can tell me what 'wholesale' means?"

No one raised a hand.

"'Retail'?"

No hands.

Apparently, my students thought the retail price was the only price for a product. That meant they had never been shown how wealth is created. I went to the chalkboard and wrote:

MANUFACTURER
↓
WHOLESALER
↓
RETAILER
↓
CUSTOMER

"This is the product distribution channel," I explained. "At each step along this chain, wealth is created in the form of profit."

I wrote dollar amounts next to each word in the chain:

MANUFACTURER - $3.50
↓
WHOLESALER - $7
↓
RETAILER - $10
↓
CUSTOMER - $15

"Manufacturers make products, like this watch, in their factories," I continued, "and wholesalers buy those products in large amounts from manufacturers. The wholesaler then sells the products in smaller amounts—by the dozen, for example—to retailers. A retailer is any store open to the public—like Jimmy Jazz or the corner bodega—that sells to customers like you or me. Each link in this chain raises the price of the product in order to make money. That money is the business's gross profit.

I pointed at Shawan. "If it costs the manufacturer three fifty to make this watch, and he sells it to a wholesaler for seven dollars, what is his gross profit?"

"Um, three fifty?" Shawan ventured.

"That is correct! Very good, Shawan! Now, when the wholesaler sells the watch to a retail store like Chess King for ten dollars, how much gross profit does the wholesaler make?"

Several hands shot up. I called on Therese, who said, "Three dollars!"

"That's right, Therese. Let's say I buy this watch for fifteen dollars at Chess King. How much gross profit does Chess King make off the sale?"

"Five dollars!" Therese declared proudly.

"Right!" I exclaimed.

By the end of class, my now-attentive pupils could recite the product distribution chain. They understood that markups along the chain created profit. They understood the business concept "buy low/sell high." I even managed to lead the class through a lesson on calculating return on investment that involved fractions and percentages. These were math concepts I had been unable to teach the class previously.

This incident, born of sheer desperation, was my first breakthrough as a teacher.

On the subway ride home, I wrote extensively in my teaching diary about what had happened. Although I was happy and excited, as I wrote I also began to feel very angry. It was clear that the agony of poverty was being perpetuated by our public schools, which were failing to teach our poorest young people fundamental insights into how our economy works.

That night I called my mother for advice on how to deal with Andre, Brayton, and Jamal. She had taught special ed for years in some of Michigan's toughest public schools, such as Flint Northern High School.

"Don't smile, Steve," she told me. "You can't smile. Don't show any emotion, except anger. Show them when you are angry. That tells them you mean business."

I would have to get tough, she said. No more Mr. Nice Guy. No more friendly banter. No more jokes.

I spent the weekend writing lesson plans with lots of simple math exercises based on the distribution chain. I also visualized different challenging situations that might arise in the classroom and how I would respond. Samuel Johnson's famous observation that nothing focuses a man's mind so much as when he's about to be hanged kept running through my mind.

I was filled with the adrenaline-fueled courage of a man with his back to the wall. I would not let these teenagers cost me my job. Nor would I let them down as their teacher. Unless I could bring my classes under control, I was of little value to the students who were there to learn—and many actually were.

I understood now that I had to come to class ready to be instantly angry. I worked on altering my facial expression in front of my bathroom mirror. I furrowed my brow and tried to look stern. My face still looked friendly and good-natured—rather like Winston Churchill in his later years, with senility approaching.

I tried again, using the Incredible Hulk as my role model.

Better.

<hr>

When I returned to the classroom Monday, my students noticed the difference right away.

Marco: "What's wrong with you today?"

Tanya: "Why you busting our chops, Mr. Steve?"

Tawana: "Why you no smile, homeboy?"

The noise level in my classes declined from the roar of Niagara Falls to the murmur of a fashionable café.

Finally, eighth period arrived. I got to the classroom early, cleaned up the debris from Friday's debacle, and straightened the chairs.

I stood at the door, awaiting my students' arrival. As they filed in, they immediately sensed that something was different. Some said a quiet "Hi" as they walked past me.

On the blackboard I wrote:

DO NOW: SIT DOWN
TAKE OUT A PIECE OF PAPER
PREPARE FOR QUIZ

The late bell rang. I locked the door and passed out the quiz. About five minutes later, I heard a telltale stream of profanity echoing in the hall. The trio that had humiliated me Friday had arrived. The students who were already in their chairs looked at me. I could sense their apprehension.

Andre, Brayton, and Jamal kicked at the closed door.

I felt a sudden burst of adrenaline. It was them or me.

I opened the door a crack. Andre tried to squeeze into the room, but I put my hand on his shoulder and pushed him back. Had I assaulted him? At that moment, I did not care.

"Hey man, what you doing pushing me?"

I said nothing and kept my face impassive as granite.

"What's wrong with you?" Brayton asked with genuine curiosity.

"I want a written apology for your unacceptable behavior on Friday," I said calmly.

"We didn't mean nothing. We was just foolin' around," Jamal muttered as he bounced up and down impatiently.

"We didn't do nothing to you!" Brayton shouted as he tried unsuccessfully to muscle past me into the room.

Andre watched me intently. I knew I was going to win.

"I want an apology and it must be in writing," I repeated coldly.

Brayton's protest, "Nobody hurt you!" was followed by an outpouring of profanity.

"You swear at me again and you'll be thrown out of this school so fast you won't even know it," I said, showing zero emotion.

"What's wrong, Mariotti?" Andre muttered. "No one touched you."

"You jerk-offs ruined the class Friday," I said forcefully, deliberately showing them how angry I was. "You keep everyone else from learning anything. What kind of morons are you?"

"Mariotti, chill, man," Jamal said nervously.

"Shut up!" I snapped over their noises of astonishment. "Understand this: I'm here to help you learn. If you aren't interested, don't come to class. I'm here to teach math. Don't get in my way."

"Mr. Mariotti, are you all right?" Therese called.

I ignored her.

"If you don't know basic mathematics, you'll never be able to get a job or . . ." I caught myself. I couldn't dilute my anger with concern. I forced myself to look and sound as stern as possible, remembering the Incredible Hulk's famous line from my old Marvel comic books: "The *madder* I get, the *stronger* I get!"

"If you ever disrupt my class again," I said, "you will never set foot in this room again, and you will never set foot in this school again, either. Do you understand me?"

The trio glared at me silently.

I glared back.

"All right," Andre finally said. He tried to push open the door. I blocked him again.

"No. I want a written apology from each of you. Here are some pencils and paper. Write your apologies and when you're finished, slide them under the door."

I closed the door, locked it, and walked back to my desk. The class had obviously overheard everything. They were awaiting the outcome, just as I was.

"Please get back to work," I ordered.

One by one, three pieces of paper were slipped under the door. I waited a minute and then went over to pick them up. I could hardly believe it. I felt the sweet elation of victory as I read the apologies, but by now I had learned to show no emotion, except for anger when I needed it.

I went to the door, opened it, and calmly said, "Please take your seats."

The behavior of all my classes improved markedly after this episode. I made Andre, Brayton, and Jamal sit in the front of the class with me in eighth period every day while I solved problems on the blackboard.

At first, they were embarrassed by this special treatment. Brayton even asked me to keep my voice down as I was explaining to him what "percentage" meant. As I had suspected, these young men knew very little math. Embarrassment had prompted much of their wild behavior, and embarrassment was something I understood. By encouraging them and discreetly giving them extra help, I was slowly able to gain their trust that I was out to teach them, not humiliate them.

Whenever I could tie a lesson to entrepreneurship, I had my students' rapt attention. One day, I brought in a glass jar filled with change and announced, "We're going to play the shop game."

I divided the class into two teams: shopkeepers and customers.

"Jamal, come up here, please. You're going to sit at this desk and play the owner of the shop."

I placed five objects on the desk that I had brought from home—a coffee cup, a vinyl record, a videotape, a lighter, and a baseball cap with price tags taped to them —along with a pencil, some paper, and a receipt book.

I motioned to Brayton to come up to the front of the room. He ran up like Rocky, pumping his fists in the air. The class cracked up, and I handed him some dollar bills.

"Brayton, you are the shop's first customer," I said. "You can use your money to pretend to buy any product in the store, and Jamal has to give you the correct change. Count your change carefully because if you catch him making a mistake, he loses his turn as the shopkeeper."

I had given the "products" prices like $2.99 or $3.48, so that both students would have to do some math and count their change carefully.

The shop game treated math as a practical reality rather than an abstraction. It also gave the student playing the shopkeeper the opportunity to experience how it might feel to own and operate a small business.

I had learned that in neighborhoods like Bed-Stuy, shopkeepers often took advantage of teenagers by handing them back incorrect change for their purchases, accurately assuming that their customers didn't know how to count their change. I hoped the shop game would teach my students to count their change carefully in the real world, too.

"Okay, Brayton," I said, brandishing my stopwatch, "You get five minutes to buy as many products as you can. Jamal, your job is to give him the correct change—or you can try to trick him by giving him the wrong change! If he accepts the wrong change, his team loses.

"You both also have to complete the sales receipt before five minutes are up, like I showed you how to do yesterday," I added.

I could feel anticipation rising in the room.

"Ready, set, go!"

"I want to buy this here lighter for one dollar and forty-eight cents," Brayton announced. "Here's two dollars. I want fifty-two cents back as my change."

"'I want fifty-two cents back as my change, please,'" I interjected.

"I want fifty-two cents back as my change, *please*," Brayton repeated, rolling his eyes.

"Why certainly, Mr. Bray," Jamal smirked. "Here is your purchase and your change."

Brayton counted his change with immense concentration. "Motherfucker, this ain't fifty-two cents! You ripped me off four cents!"

"'Motherfucker' is not an appropriate way to address someone while conducting business," I said. "But congratulations, Brayton, you win!"

The shop game was so popular with my classes that I wound up carting that heavy jar of change around with me every day.

One Monday, I brought in a dozen copies of the *Wall Street Journal* that I had picked up at my West Village newsstand. I told each class that the CEOs of America's largest companies were reading, that morning, the very same newspaper that they were.

We used the stock listings in the *Wall Street Journal* to set up a new exercise I called the stock market game. Each kid got to pick a stock and track it. I offered prizes for the biggest gain at the end of the month.

One class was so interested in the *Wall Street Journal* that I ended up supplying each student with a daily copy at my own expense. I had to pinch myself sometimes to make sure I was really awake and discussing the *Wall Street Journal* with students in the most infamous high school in New York City.

I began to notice that many of my students had a natural aptitude for business. Fifty percent of success in sales is being willing to risk rejection, and these kids were comfortable with risk and ambiguity. Their challenging lives encouraged independence of spirit, toughness, and unselfconsciousness. These same qualities—along with difficulty thriving in structured environments—have characterized history's greatest entrepreneurs, from Henry Ford and Conrad Hilton to Richard Branson.

I began to encourage the students to come up with ideas for their own small businesses. "You have unique knowledge of your market that no one else has," I told them over and over. "Use that to develop a business. What problem can you solve in your community? What much-needed service or product can you provide? What is your competitive advantage?"

We spent time in class designing flyers and business cards. I couldn't help but grin when I handed students their business cards. They looked so incredibly excited to see the words "president" or "CEO" after their names.

Some students, however, were reluctant to get on board the entrepreneurship train.

Tawana rarely looked up or made eye contact. She shuffled slowly down school hallways, hiding under a bulky hoodie and dirty, baggy jeans. Her family had been on welfare for three generations. I was desperate to get her to come up with a business idea.

One day, she finally mumbled, in response to my relentless prodding, "I guess I could do manicures."

"Great!" I exclaimed. "Let's get you set up!"

Tawana decided to offer manicures after school in her home for seven dollars. She was a little halfhearted about it at first, but as she began giving out her flyers and business cards and booked a few appointments, Tawana realized that she had a real business.

As her clientele increased, Tawana's behavior began to change in unexpected ways. Previously, she had rarely changed her clothes and smelled pretty strong. Now, she showed a marked improvement in personal hygiene. This, in turn, improved her ability to make friends and attract clients. Her school attendance rose from an average of one and a half days per week to five days per week.

School was where her potential clients were, so Tawana wanted to be there, but she also became a better student. I required all the students to submit a simple weekly income statement for their businesses. Tawana struggled with the math involved, but because she wanted to show me how much money she was making each week, she worked at it. Her income statements improved and so did her math skills.

For Tawana, entrepreneurship was an avenue out of herself, a link to other human beings. She discovered that she really did have unique knowledge of her target market. She knew which girls would be likely customers and which trendy nail polish colors they would love.

Tawana's business became her lifeline to interacting with other people in a bond of mutual self-interest. I loved watching Tawana blossom from a social outcast into a girl with lots of friends and a strong, healthy ego. As her real personality emerged, I heard her boisterous laughter more and more. It was a very sweet sound to me.

My student Sonya was definitely *not* a social outcast. She was relentlessly flirtatious. Her self-esteem seemed to be tied to having sexually charged relationships with lots of different students. When Sonya developed a little business braiding her classmates' hair, it enabled her to interact with other boys and girls in a nonsexual way. Sonya discovered that she had something to offer besides sex. Her business permitted her to have friendships and share some safe touch without necessarily becoming sexually involved.

The primary act of business is providing a product or service for a higher price than it costs you. This act takes place over time, with money as the reward. I noticed that running their own small businesses helped my students make better decisions in their personal lives because it taught them the value of delayed gratification. Many times, I saw a student's sense of the future expand right before my eyes.

–––

Even though I had survived my baptism by fire at Boys and Girls High, I lost my position there when a tenured teacher who had not been coming to work was given the choice to either take over my position or lose his tenure. Although I would miss my students, I wasn't too upset, as I was eager to test my entrepreneurial approach to teaching in a new environment.

My eighth-period class and I had been through hell together— an experience I would never forget. Yet when I announced I would be leaving, my students had no noticeable reaction. I was hoping that they didn't feel abandoned by me. I wrote my phone number on the blackboard and assured them that they could reach out to me anytime, even though I would be teaching at another school.

My last day at Boys and Girls affected me more than I would have ever thought possible when I began teaching there. My first-period class gave me a card saying I was the best teacher they had ever had. Another class applauded and made so much noise that my supervisor ran in, thinking there was a fight. Three students came up to me in the hallway and warmly told me that I was the best teacher they had ever known.

I was deeply touched by this outpouring of emotion.

When I walked into eighth period on my last day, a basket of fried chicken was waiting for me in the front of the room. On my desk were two carefully wrapped gifts: a bottle of cologne and a vinyl record, *The Best of the Temptations*. Covering the entire blackboard in huge chalk letters was the message:

GOODBYE HOMEBOY
FROM THE ENTREPRENEURS OF BOYS AND GIRLS
HIGH SCHOOL

Underneath were my students' signatures. I teared up and just about lost it.

I felt particularly gratified when Brayton told me: "Mr. Mariotti, I've decided to start my own business." I kept in touch with Brayton until about 1990. He became a sales representative for a computer company and moved to the Midwest.

Tawana was still operating her manicure business when I checked in with her in 1989. Two of her cousins had joined her enterprise. All three were sharing an apartment and successfully supporting themselves with their manicure business and part-time jobs.

Andre and I stayed in contact, too. He successfully graduated from high school and credited this to his interest in entrepreneurship. He became very good at math and could do spreadsheets better than I could. After graduation, Andre landed a job as an assistant manager at a Brooklyn flea market, got married, and began raising a family.

In 1991, I ran into Therese on the Lower East Side, standing behind a sidewalk table laden with Afrocentric clothing and jewelry. She was twenty-four and looked positively regal in a beautiful dashiki dress adorned with an ornate beaded collar.

Therese told me that she had obtained a city vendor's license. Just as she had learned in class, she was purchasing her inventory wholesale and selling it for a very good profit.

"I have a child at home," Therese told me with a happy smile, explaining that she sold every afternoon while a sitter watched her toddler. "I'm working on saving up enough money to rent a storefront and open up my own clothing boutique," she added shyly. "I've even gotten my mom involved. She is so proud to be in business with me!"

Therese added that she was attending community college at night and still used handouts from my classes to help her run her business.

"Thanks to you, Mr. Mariotti," Therese said, "I have always been able to take care of myself and make a living."

I have never received a higher compliment.

CHAPTER 4

FORT APACHE, THE BRONX

"It's not a police station, it's a fort in hostile territory, you understand?"
—OFFICER APPLEBAUM, *Fort Apache, the Bronx* (1981)

For the next year or so, I rotated through the worst schools in the poorest neighborhoods in New York City, from Alphabet City to the Bronx. I worked as a floater for the school system's special education department, covering for teachers who were ill or on leave.

I was searching for a school that would let me test what I had discovered at Boys and Girls High: Tying lessons to entrepreneurship got even the most resistant students excited about learning.

Starting a little business not only motivated them to pay attention in class, it also prompted them to behave better, make smarter decisions, and take care of themselves.

At each new school, I introduced myself as eager to teach business skills. The principal would invariably respond by stashing me in the typing department, where I would be assigned to teach special ed classes in typing and shorthand.

During my travels through the school system, I learned that special ed was where administrators warehoused kids for whom nothing was working. Although many special ed students were genuinely disabled, others were not disabled at all. They were just trouble: rude, threatening, and mean to other students and their teachers. Often, both students and teachers were afraid of them.

Principals tried to avoid expelling even the most disruptive special ed students, however, because homeroom count determined a school's budget. Some principals simply let the special ed kids leave school after homeroom.

I turned all my special ed classes into entrepreneurship classes, because it was the only thing I knew I could teach that would keep my students from rioting. I lugged my heavy jar of change to every classroom because whenever I snuck business lessons and games into my classes, my students would perk up and become very interested.

Word inevitably got out, though, and soon I would find a note in my inbox to see the principal.

I would be reprimanded.

Discussing money in a public high school "wasn't appropriate."

Perhaps this school was not a good fit for me.

I might want to move along.

Things came to a head at a high school on the Lower East Side where I was teaching four special ed classes and one regular class. As usual, I hauled my change jar to every class so we could play the shop game, or the sales call game, which involved letting students pitch each other products and negotiate prices. All five of my classes were going smoothly. I was eager to get to school in the morning and often stayed late in the teachers' lounge, working on my lesson plans.

One day, in my fourth-period special ed typing class, I passed around the change jar and instructed the students to each take out a handful. Their assignment was to count their change, categorize it by denomination, and type a one-page memo with a chart listing their findings.

Suddenly, Miss Perkins, the head of the typing department, threw open my classroom door and stormed in shouting, "Put the money DOWN!" My students and I dropped our change and instinctively threw up our hands as if we were being robbed at gunpoint. Nickels, dimes, quarters, and pennies fell clattering to our desks and rolled onto the floor.

Miss Perkins was shaking with rage as she shoved me out of her way and grabbed my change jar. "This is a blatantly illegal act," she yelled, brandishing the jar, "I am going to make *sure* you are fired!"

Miss Perkins made us pick up all the change and put it back into the jar before she stalked out with it, taking the equivalent of two days of my meager teacher's salary with her.

I got really angry. Here was a government employee, paid by our taxes, preventing children who lived in poverty from learning about money. Screaming at them like it was wrong for them to even touch money.

I'm afraid I shouted "Fuck you!" after Miss Perkins as the door closed on her.

Two school employees had witnessed this blowout from the

hallway—the principal and a security guard. When they walked toward me, I thought I was about to be forcibly escorted off campus. Instead, they came into my classroom, told me that they were both part-time entrepreneurs, and asked if they could speak with my students.

As we all sat in a circle, the principal told us that he ran a very successful summer basketball camp. He fascinated my students with stories about his business. The security guard revealed that he was working toward his dream of starting a security company. Then, he and the principal encouraged my students to share their dreams for the future. Even though I knew I was in serious trouble, I was deeply moved by the kindness of these two men. That afternoon remains a magic moment in my memory book.

I found a letter in my inbox the next morning, requiring me to appear for a disciplinary hearing at the Department of Education building in Brooklyn where I had met with Rufus Thomas.

I was escorted to the hearing by a young woman the United Federation of Teachers had sent to protect my rights. We sat in a small room under flickering fluorescent bulbs, waiting for the official who was probably going to end my career.

After fifteen nerve-wracking minutes, an older gentleman with thick white hair entered the room toting an overstuffed folder with "Steve Mariotti" printed on it. I had no idea I had been generating that much paperwork. Now I was really worried.

"So," Mr. Bolden said after he introduced himself, "you're the guy who's been creating all the fuss by teaching our students about money."

"Um, yes, sir," I stammered nervously.

"Well, keep it up! You're doing the right thing!" he said cheerfully.

I was stunned.

"We have so much poverty in this city," Mr. Bolden continued, "yet all the children of the poor learn in school is that they're not good enough for college. The girls are told that *maybe* they can become secretaries. The boys learn nothing useful and wind up in prison. Good for you for teaching them some information that might help them avoid that fate. In my book, you're a hero!"

I was numb with joy and astonishment. Before I could thank him, though, my union rep launched into a spirited defense of me, vigorously defending my right to "create unique lesson plans" and so on.

Mr. Bolden and I stared at her, bemused, as she argued passionately for another minute or so, clearly relishing the fight until she finally realized there was no fight to be had. At that, all three of us burst into laughter.

"I am writing you up for cursing at your superior, Mr. Mariotti," Mr. Bolden said sternly, but with a merry twinkle in his eye. "I want you to sign this letter affirming that from this point forward you will follow the lesson plans assigned to you or risk termination."

I signed. Although my job had been spared, I felt so frustrated. I had experienced firsthand that teaching low-income teenagers about entrepreneurship lit a fire for learning in them, yet within the school system I was fighting a one-man culture war.

I felt very glad that a few teachers and administrators were confiding in me that they also thought teaching poor teenagers about small business could be valuable. Collectively, however, the school system treated any mention of money in the classroom as an outrage and provided no business training to low-income children beyond secretarial skills.

Our society constantly conveyed to low-income teens that they were not worthy people because they did not have money. Yet our public schools were failing to teach them how our free-enterprise system works and how they might participate in it.

These children were at such a disadvantage that it hurt my heart. President Ronald Reagan's Omnibus Budget Reconciliation Act of 1981 lowered asset limits for welfare recipients to just $1,000, penalizing recipients who attempted to save up any capital. This made business ownership virtually impossible. Most of my students and their families had no experience in owning or acquiring assets they could use to earn money to start a small business and get off welfare. There were very few jobs available in their communities because there was so little business formation.

I understood now why so many low-income teenagers joined drug-dealing gangs. The gangs taught them how to buy low, sell high, and market a product. If working your way up the drug-dealing ladder was the only option you knew for making real money, it might look pretty attractive to you, too.

My next assignment landed me at Jane Addams Vocational High School, located at 900 Tinton Avenue, on the edge of the notorious section of the South Bronx known as Fort Apache.

During the 1970s, police officers nicknamed the 41st Precinct's dilapidated station house at 1086 Simpson Street "Fort Apache." It was their only safe haven in a neighborhood dominated by violent gangs and scarred with burned-out buildings and empty lots filled with weeds and trash. By the early 1980s, Fort Apache came to refer to the neighborhood itself, a ravaged symbol of urban decay with the lowest per capita income—and the highest unemployment and homicide rates—in New York City.

Founded in 1937 before the neighborhood had deteriorated so badly, Jane Addams High had a long history of preparing working-class South Bronx students for careers as manicurists, hair-stylists, secretaries, and travel agents. I began teaching there in January 1984. Once again, I was assigned to teach typing, as well as shorthand.

Honestly, I was hopeless at both. I have dyslexia and am probably one of the most disorganized people you could ever meet. My shirt never stays tucked in for long, and my chinos are fraying at the hem. I lose everything, especially my glasses. My handwriting is large, crooked, and never travels in a straight line.

Years later, when I became the president of a global nonprofit, visitors to my gorgeous corner office on Wall Street sometimes asked me whose child had been scribbling with a Vis-à-Vis marker all over the pieces of paper on my desk. I would have to sheepishly explain that the child was me. I started using Vis-à-Vis overhead markers as a teacher to write on transparencies, and they are still my favorite pens.

As a teacher, to say I was rumpled would have been kind. Marilyn Sanders, the neat, well-dressed supervisor of typing and short-hand classes at Jane Addams, couldn't stand me.

Marilyn was a slim white woman in her early forties married to an African American businessman. If she had been a nice person, I would have looked up to her as a role model because she was incredibly organized and smart. Marilyn quickly proved to be a master of humiliation, however, and I became her favorite target.

Typing and shorthand were her areas of expertise. They were not mine. I found shorthand impossible to comprehend, let alone teach. I read all the literature assigned to me and tried very hard to absorb it, but I just couldn't make shorthand stick in my brain. As for typing, it took me thirty minutes to type a simple business letter that was not riddled with mistakes. I never was able to learn how to properly format anything.

There were nineteen teachers in Marilyn's department, all women except for me. When we gathered for staff meetings, Marilyn would point at a chair in the back corner, far from everyone else, and command me to sit there. Then she would display my smudged, sloppy work in front of my colleagues and declare, "He can't even do this."

Marilyn took enormous delight in quizzing me about shorthand at staff meetings. She would hold up a page of shorthand notations and point to one, asking me to tell her what it was. After letting me stutter and attempt to guess for a while, Marilyn would snarl, "It's a LATCH." The other teachers would titter as I sank further into my dunce's corner.

Shorthand was on its way out. Perhaps that was what gave Marilyn her vicious edge. But I didn't know that. I thought I was letting everybody down, most of all my students, who apparently needed to be fluent in shorthand and ace typists to have any hope of employment after graduation.

I felt horribly inadequate and guilty, except when I was in the classroom. The kids loved me. Luckily for me, the school's principal, Pat Black, also liked me—and really disliked Marilyn.

Pat was five foot six and stocky, with a kind Irish face, a broad smile, and dark blonde hair that she always wore in a ponytail secured with a huge grosgrain ribbon clip. I think she had one in a different color for every day of the week. Pat strode down the school hallways and into every classroom like a professional wrestler, with her shoulders pulled back and such a strong, powerful gait that you could feel her energy shake the floor. She was a natural, unflappable leader. I have always tried to emulate her.

From the day I entered Jane Addams, Pat and I had a strong rapport that Marilyn and the other teachers seemed to resent. Pat thought I had a gift for teaching and always looked after me.

Marilyn, in contrast, was itching to fire me. Whenever Pat was away from school for the day, Marilyn would call me into her office. She would shake a piece of paper at me and demand, "What's this?"

She made me so nervous that I couldn't think straight. I would finally squeak out something like, "Uh . . . a piece of paper?"

"This is your shorthand lesson. LOOK AT IT! No one can understand this!"

I would cringe, apologize, bow, and scrape. Marilyn would sigh, roll her eyes, and tell me to pack my things and get out.

Marilyn fired me four times. When Pat would return to school the next day and learn that I had been fired, she would be infuriated. Pat would write poor Marilyn up for some infraction. Then Pat would call me at home and hire me back.

By this time, I had moved from my cute and relatively clean one-bedroom apartment in the West Village to a complete rathole in the East Village. I had closed my import-export business to focus on teaching, and the East Village was the only Manhattan neighborhood I could afford on my teacher's salary.

I lived in a sixth-floor walkup at 432 East 14th Street between First Avenue and Avenue A—one of those old-fashioned tenement apartments with splintering wooden floors and a bathtub next to the kitchen sink, covered by a board that doubled as a countertop. The first time I opened the refrigerator, the smell of something rotting hit me in the face so hard that I shut the door and never opened the refrigerator again.

There was a hole in the kitchen floor big enough that if I didn't step carefully around it, I would tumble into the apartment below. To remind myself to avoid the hole, I put duct tape around and over it. When friends came over, I warned them not to step on the tape because it was covering a hole into the next apartment. My visitors would look at me like I was insane. If anyone started to open the refrigerator, I would run over to hold the door shut and say, "Oh no, I haven't bought anything. Let's go out to eat!"

I feel embarrassed even thinking about it.

Filthy air streamed through a broken window in the bedroom during the winter. The place was freezing in the winter and sweltering in the summer.

I often thought, "I should get that window fixed." But I was so exhausted when I got home from teaching, and traveling by subway from the East Village to the South Bronx and back, that I never found the energy to contact the landlord and harass him into fixing it. I just slept on the couch.

Despite my exhaustion, I tended to sleep fitfully because my mind was racing with ideas about teaching. When I woke up at night, I would scribble lesson plan ideas and insights with my favorite green Vis-à-Vis marker on the wall above my makeshift bed.

When Pat would call to rehire me, I would be lying on that ratty couch in my horrible apartment, staring up at my notes and feeling sorry for myself for being such a failure.

The fourth time Marilyn fired me, Pat called me at home, per usual. But she didn't hire me back. She asked me to come meet with her in her office.

This is it, I thought. She can't protect me anymore.

When I arrived the next morning, Pat said, "Look, Steve, I don't think teaching typing is the best use of your abilities. I've got another idea.

"I've got twenty-three special ed kids who have done things so illegal that I can't bring them back into Jane Addams. They can't be let back into *any* New York City public school because they've committed violent crimes like assaulting a teacher, bringing guns to school, setting a girl's hair on fire . . ."

To the shocked look on my face, Pat responded calmly, "You'd be surprised how often a kid will set another kid's hair on fire.

"Anyway," Pat continued, with a dismissive wave of her hand, "these are children who have severe emotional outbursts. Although they can't be allowed back into Jane Addams at present, they still have the legal right to an education. Would you be interested in taking them as a class to an offsite program?"

Many school administrators would have not given these children a second thought, but Pat Black was too principled for that. She was determined to make sure that all the children in her charge received the education to which they were entitled by law.

"We could find a city government building and set you up with a classroom there," Pat said. "The students will earn special ed diplomas if they stay in the offsite program. I want to at least give them a shot at graduating, although given their track records I'm not hopeful that any of them will.

"Your goal is to save one of them," Pat added.

What choice did I have? It was either accept this crazy assignment or lose my job. I knew Pat was trying to save me just as much as she was trying to save these kids.

I plastered an eager smile on my face and said, "Yes, of course, I'll give it my very best!"

CHAPTER 5

WE CAN BE HEROES

"We can be heroes just for one day. We can be us just for one day."
—DAVID BOWIE, BRIAN ENO, "Heroes" (1977)

Pat Black found space for me and twenty-three special ed students who had been expelled for violent crimes at the New York City Department of Buildings' Bronx Borough Office.

The Department of Buildings (DOB) enforces the city's building codes and zoning regulations. The DOB also issues permits, licenses contractors, responds to structural emergencies, and handles inspections for more than one million buildings. Each borough has its own DOB office, where all housing-related records in the borough—property deeds, construction permits, complaints, violations, etc.—are stored.

The Bronx Borough Office was in an enormous limestone

office building at 1932 Arthur Avenue that took up nearly an entire city block. A cursory glance at Google reviews today for the Bronx Borough Office, which is still at 1932 Arthur Avenue, yields such comments as:

> *"Would rate zero stars if possible. Worst-run department of all time."*
> *"This place sucks."*
> *"I don't know why everyone who works here be hating."*

The more things change, the more they stay the same.

Each massive, dimly lit floor of the Bronx Borough Office was crammed with dust-laden metal shelving units that seemed to go on for miles, stretching into darkness. Manila folders brimming with paper records were jammed tightly into the shelves. Eccentric clerks shuffled around all day filing each individual paper that arrived—and the papers never stopped coming. These clerks were lifers, wandering among the filthy shelves for thirty-odd years, searching for the correct folders in which to file every piece of paper that crossed their desks.

It was a job that would destroy anyone's sanity.

Once a month, the clerks gathered to verify that they had properly filed every single one of their assigned papers. Inevitably, it would be discovered that some papers were missing, causing a flurry of activity rather like a fire drill. The clerks were summoned to gather in their fourth-floor war room, which they called "The Temple."

As I was exploring the building one day, in order to get the lay of the land before bringing in my class of miscreants, I was invited to witness this sacred meeting by an elderly clerk I had met. This fellow was severely humpbacked and had crooked, bulging eyes. He spoke in a slow, halting monotone. I couldn't help but nickname him "Igor."

Igor shuffled up to me and droned, "Steve. We're having . . . a staff meeting. The Temple. Could you . . . come down? Provide . . . some leadership."

"Well," I replied, "I'm not a clerk."

"Come down!" Igor barked as he turned on his heels. Startled, and also curious, I followed Igor into the elevator and rode with him to the fourth floor, marveling at the sticky piles of dandruff on his decrepit black suit jacket. I nervously brushed at the shoulders of my own suit jacket, where I knew dandruff also tended to accumulate. We exited the elevator and Igor scuttled into the gloom. I trailed him closely, a little spooked.

My asthmatic lungs slammed shut as we crept down a narrow hallway created by two rows of incredibly dusty shelves. The shelves were so close together that our shoulders banged against the files, kicking up mushrooming clouds of decades-old dust. I quickly took a whiff from the inhaler I kept in my pants pocket.

Finally, we arrived at a small corner room.

"Why is this called The Temple?" I asked Igor.

"The paperwork . . ." Igor groaned, "is the heart . . . of the city's . . . housing."

The clerks were seated around a table. They had the thin pale skin and weak blinking eyes of creatures who had spent their lives in semidarkness. One clerk had stringy, gray hair that fell to his shoulders and long yellowing fingernails. Another was a bald little person with a wrinkled face like a Shar-Pei.

Shar-Pei took the lead at this meeting, pounding his small meaty fists on the table and screaming, "Where! Is! The! Paaaaaaper!"

I felt deeply impressed with the importance of our mission.

Clearly, these papers were vital to the inner workings of New York City, the greatest city in the world. This was serious shit. Not a single paper can be lost, or we will not know where people are living, or who owns what building.

One of the younger clerks gingerly raised a skinny blue-veined hand and ventured hesitantly, "I mean . . . don't we have duplicates?"

Shar-Pei fixed him with a death glare, shrieking, "We must have the original! It is our job to provide backup!"

I nudged Igor and whispered, "When was the last time we were called upon to provide backup?" I was really getting caught up in my role as a clerk.

Igor didn't say anything for around thirty seconds. I could see the wheels turning behind his jaundiced eyeballs. Finally, he muttered, "Nineteen . . . sixty . . . three. Right before . . . the president . . . was . . . assassinated."

Each clerk clutched a black folder labeled with his name. It contained the papers he was to file.

Shar-Pei announced, "First, we check the folders!"

All the assembled clerks opened their black folders and searched until one clerk brandished a slip of paper and cried, "Here it is!"

All the other clerks responded as a Greek chorus, with great enthusiasm and relief, "THERE IT IS!"

This tremendous fuss, I came to realize, was about a piece of paper that no one would likely ever seek again. The Department of Buildings was the dead end for these records. Files went in, but they never came out. No one asked for a backup file from the Department of Buildings. Or at least no one had since before President John F. Kennedy's assassination in 1963.

Nonetheless, on the sixth floor, there was a gigantic open administrative area dotted with metal desks at which 180 female typists sat typing triplicate copies of every single paper that came in before handing the original and its copies off to be filed. I was never able to discern any logical reason for this effort.

The sixth floor was easily the size of the main floor of the New York Public Library. This is where I was sent to teach twenty-three special ed students who had been judged too threatening to let back into a public school.

We were assigned to a large conference room enclosed by floor-to-ceiling glass walls smack in the center of the floor. It felt like we were inside one of those life-sized dioramas at the American Museum of Natural History on 79th Street.

The first thing I did was to try to set up some semblance of a classroom. There were no desks in our room, but there were several long tables, and I managed to round up enough chairs for the kids. Pat Black sent a truck over with some chalkboards and whiteboards on stands. I set those up at the front of our makeshift classroom.

Pat had given my new class an important-sounding name: The Offsite Special Ed Dropout Program. On the first day in our new classroom, I wrote it on the chalkboard and declared to my students, "We are going to become the number-one program in the country. All of you are going to graduate. All of you are going to have businesses. We are going to become legendary!"

Slouched in their chairs, the students eyed me dubiously. One girl stuck her hand in the air.

"Yes, Shana?" I responded eagerly. From reading her file, I knew that Shana was an intelligent girl with an aptitude for writing, who had been expelled for stabbing another girl during a fight. My speech had clearly inspired Shana. I felt so encouraged.

"But then shouldn't it be called the 'Anti-Dropout' program?" Shana drawled, snapping her gum.

In a way, I discovered on that first day, we had found the perfect home. No matter what insane noise my new students made, the typists never looked up from their desks. Apparently, the clacking of their typewriter keys and the thick glass walls surrounding our classroom muted our racket.

At any given moment, for example, my student Loran would yell, "Ahhhhhhhhhhh!" for fifteen minutes straight while rhythmically punching the back of another kid's chair in some kind of fugue state. Anton enjoyed spitting beatbox rhythms into his fist, whether I was talking or not. That prompted Victor to launch into speed rapping, chattering as fast as he possibly could.

Victor was about five foot six with glossy brown skin, curly black eyelashes, and a very engaging smile. He looked so friendly that it was hard to believe he had spent a month in notorious Bellevue Psychiatric Hospital for biting through a female student's cheek.

I asked Victor how he could have done something so awful to that girl, leaving her with a permanent scar on her face.

"I loved her so much it drove me crazy," Victor replied with a wink.

We were supposed to begin each school day at 9 AM. Given the violent records of my new students, it was no surprise that none of them arrived by nine. Lamont and Estelle had each set other students on fire. Mateo had shot and injured another student. Anton had served a year in the notorious Spofford Juvenile Detention Center in the Bronx for killing another teen in a fistfight, before being released on a technicality.

I had three students, actually, who had done time at Spofford.

Spofford made Rikers Island, where I taught years later, look like a Sunday school picnic. With walls covered in peeling sheets of lead paint, Spofford was a hellhole where juveniles were forced to defecate in public. They were stashed in the Solitary Housing Unit, or SHU, for the smallest infractions, and they were criminally underfed. "To be given no more meat" was a common directive for the treatment of juveniles in the SHU.

All of my offsite students had experience working for drug dealers. All of them. Fort Apache ran on drug money. It was common for people to use bags of crack or heroin to buy groceries or wash their clothes at a Laundromat. The dealers, unlike legal employers, were eager to hire local teens and teach them a trade.

Teens in Fort Apache lived in constant fear of being beaten, jailed, or shot, whether they participated in the drug trade or not. They were in survival mode. My students were on edge, quick to react violently to any perceived threat.

I knew from my previous efforts teaching at-risk children that their hypervigilance made it difficult for them to concentrate on school. Tying lessons to entrepreneurship seemed to cut through the stress and grab their attention. Before I could try that, however, I had to get them to show up.

I had one incentive that lured my students to the Department of Buildings that first week. Most of them straggled in between 11 and 11:30 AM for the free lunch.

Lunch was delivered especially for us from Jane Addams. The typists were not supposed to know about this, so the delivery man would sneak the box into a side room. Once lunch had been safely delivered, I would wipe the back of my hand slowly across my face. That was my secret signal to the class that lunch had arrived.

We would amble slowly over to the room, trying not to draw attention to ourselves, and slip inside to have our lunch. Jane Addams usually sent over sandwiches with cartons of milk, or sometimes hot food.

I immediately noticed that these kids had atrocious table manners. They all chewed with their mouths open, talking loudly. None of them had learned how to properly use forks, knives, or napkins. Earvin ate spaghetti, for example, by shoving his mouth into his plate and hoovering up noodles. Victor would spill milk on the table and make a big display of licking it up as if he were pleasuring a woman. When we had soup, it was the worst. You could hear slurping all the way to the restroom down the hall.

The first lesson I attempted to teach, therefore, was on table manners.

"Let's pretend," I told the class, "that we have been invited to London to receive a special award from the Queen of England, and we need to work on our manners."

That just made everyone laugh, which inspired Anton and Earvin to see who could burp the loudest, in order to make everyone laugh more. I was tearing out what was left of my hair.

Our saving grace was the typing pool supervisor, a wonderful African American woman in her fifties named Miss Archibald. Miss Archibald was single, childless, and devoted to two things: the Department of Buildings and her church. She radiated an unshakeable serenity.

Miss Archibald was very Christian, very loving, and she took to my students like crazy. To her, they were a delightful surprise. From the moment she met them, she expressed great love for them, enveloping them in motherly hugs whenever they would let her.

During that first week, at least one of my students would go over to Miss Archibald's desk and talk to her every day, sometimes for hours. The students confided in her, sharing things they never told me. She became our de facto class counselor. She constantly let my students know that she believed they would contribute to society in some meaningful way. I cannot overestimate the positive impact that kind of belief has on a troubled child.

In desperation over my inability to improve my students' table manners, I asked Miss Archibald for her advice. As luck would have it, she had worked in a fancy restaurant years ago, where she had learned exquisite table manners. She actually taught classes in table manners at her church's summer camp.

For the rest of the week, Miss Archibald met us for lunch in our secret room. The students were enthralled by her elegant manners and her sensitivity in addressing their issues. My own table manners improved as well, as I learned to chew my food thoroughly and enjoy it instead of wolfing it down.

If I had any hope of luring my students to stay for more than just a free lunch, however, I had to improve our environment. We were serenaded by the muffled clickety-clack of 180 typewriters. Our makeshift classroom consisted of glass walls, gray tables, uncomfortable metal folding chairs, a chalkboard, and some whiteboards. I decided to lean on the elementary teacher's trick: make the classroom a fun and stimulating learning environment.

The first thing I did was print out my favorite poem, "Invictus" by William Ernest Henley, and tape it on a glass wall. At home, I pumped myself up every morning by reciting this poem as I stood before my dingy bathroom mirror struggling to knot my tie properly. The powerful cadence and sturdy conviction of "Invictus" shoved aside my daily sense of dread and filled me with courage and a sense of purpose. Or at least enough courage to face another day.

Out of the night that covers me
Black as the pit from pole to pole
I thank whatever gods may be
For my unconquerable soul

In the fell clutch of circumstance
I have not winced nor cried aloud
Under the bludgeonings of chance
My head is bloody, but unbowed

Beyond this place of wrath and tears
Looms but the horror of the shade
And yet the menace of the years
Finds and shall find me unafraid

It matters not how strait the gate
How charged with punishments the scroll
I am the master of my fate
I am the captain of my soul

I gave my new students copies of "Invictus" and announced that I expected them to memorize it by the end of the semester. Each day when they arrived, they were to touch the poem on the wall with their eyes closed and think about it for a moment. Initially, the kids rolled their eyes at my request, but I noticed them doing it. I hoped "Invictus" would become a comforting daily ritual for them, too.

Every day, I taped more quotes and speeches to the glass walls, so that everywhere the students looked, they would find something inspirational to read.

I printed out Churchill's famous 1941 speech "Never Give In, Never, Never, Never," and posted it, highlighting my favorite passage:

> *There was no flinching and no thought of giving in; and by what seemed almost a miracle to those outside these Islands, though we ourselves never doubted it, we now find ourselves in a position where I say that we can be sure that we have only to persevere to conquer.*

"We have only to persevere to conquer." That was the lesson I wanted to impart to these kids who lived in a war zone.

Some quotes I wasn't technically supposed to have in a public school—but then again, we were no longer in a public school.

> *Dear God, give me an unremitting sense of purpose.*

> *Dear God, I don't ask you to make my life easier but to give me the strength to face all my trouble.*

I also posted Psalm 23 on the ceiling:

> *Yea, though I walk through the valley of the shadow of death, I will fear no evil, for you are with me.*

Being a Unitarian, I had no particular religious axe to grind. I simply wanted my students to become familiar with the great literature of courage for which people have lived and died.

I also taped up the Declaration of Independence and the Bill of Rights. I taped up Martin Luther King's famous "I Have a Dream" speech. I read King's stirring words aloud to my students and told them, "This is why you learn to write. So your words can change the world."

I added motivational phrases I had absorbed while growing up, like "Quitters never win, winners never quit," and (Churchill again) "The pessimist sees difficulty in every opportunity. The optimist sees opportunity in every difficulty."

I posted (and read aloud) my favorite passage from "The Charge of the Light Brigade" by Alfred, Lord Tennyson:

"Forward, the Light Brigade!"
Was there a man dismayed?
Not though the soldier knew
Someone had blundered
Theirs not to make reply
Theirs not to reason why
Theirs but to do and die
Into the valley of Death
Rode the six hundred.

Being someone who is inherently untidy, however, I quickly turned our classroom into a makeshift mess of smudged papers and badly written signs taped crookedly to the walls. It looked like a third grader had been let loose with access to a Xerox machine, Sharpies, and Scotch tape. The kids would walk in, raise their eyebrows, and shake their heads.

This was not the effect I was going for. It was time to call in a ringer.

Lucky for me, I met a wonderful elementary school teacher on the subway. Nancy taught kindergarten and first grade. I told her I was teaching an offsite special ed program for children who had been kicked out of high school. I asked if I could hire her to help me transform our classroom, and she said yes, thank goodness.

We spent a weekend decorating the classroom. Whatever fairy-dust magic elementary teachers have that I don't have, Nancy had it in buckets. She went to Kinko's and printed the fifty quotations, speeches, and math equations I had chosen in bright bold colors and a variety of fonts.

I brought in a ladder and Nancy directed me: "This goes here," and "that goes there," and "Steve, that is *not* straight."

When my students wandered in on Monday, the room looked beautiful! Nancy had helped me create an incredibly colorful, stimulating environment. No matter where you looked, even if you were spacing out in class, your eyes would fall upon something interesting, uplifting, or inspiring. The students were fascinated and walked around looking at everything.

Nancy and I had hung a mobile of the solar system from the ceiling. There was a chart taped to the ceiling showing the major constellations, like Orion and the Big Dipper. We posted the periodic table of the elements and the multiplication table. We also taped a color chart to the wall because, surprisingly, most of these teenagers didn't know their colors. They could name basic colors like red, blue, yellow, and green, but it seemed no one had taken the time to teach them colors like magenta or turquoise.

I assigned each student a color. I placed a huge globe in the center of the room. On my table in front of the classroom were boxes of pushpins in different colors. The students got pushpins in their assigned colors to mark any places on the globe they wanted to go. I asked the students to move their pushpins to a new place every day. Nearby was an atlas where they could look up the places they had selected and learn more about them.

Since the classroom was a large glass box, basically, with a door to my left as I stood at the front, Nancy suggested that we use the two back corners of the room and the corner to my right to create three distinct spaces where students could hang out. To my right, we stacked a dozen of my favorite art books on a small table and covered a larger table with art supplies—sketchbooks, tempera paints, crayons, colored pens. We posted one rule: CLEAN UP AFTER YOURSELF.

In the far-right corner, we piled a table with books I had brought from home, paperbacks and hardcovers by Charles Dickens, Langston Hughes, Ayn Rand, Mark Twain, Malcolm X, James Baldwin, and many more classic authors. Nancy contributed several novels by Judy Blume.

The far-left corner table held my favorite math and physics books. I became fascinated by physics at an early age and wanted to share my passion for it. This might sound over the top for a special ed class, but I wanted to surround my students with ideas and subjects to which they had not yet been exposed. I wanted them to understand that knowledge is power and scholarship is a beautiful thing.

My second rule, after the rule requiring the students to touch "Invictus" when entering our classroom in the morning, was that once a day they had to walk around and look at everything in the room.

The third rule was "no violence or threat of violence." This classroom was to be a safe space.

Each day after lunch, I herded everyone back to our classroom. I was initially dismayed by the glass walls surrounding us. I soon realized, though, that my students were behaving better than they might have otherwise, because they were not shut up in a walled-in classroom with me. They knew they were being observed.

I think the fact that they had an audience made them want to look good.

The first assignment I gave every day was the Do Now. This was a short quiz testing the class on one thing we had learned the previous day.

I had developed the Do Now technique while teaching at Boys and Girls High. The minute the kids walk in the door, give them a problem to solve. Don't give them a chance to look around, start goofing with each other, or zone out.

My offsite students would dig into the Do Now as if they were studying at Oxford. They put on quite the show for the typists, who, frankly, rarely looked their way.

With Pat Black's blessing, I decided to rename the offsite class the "South Bronx Entrepreneurship Education Program." I purchased two dozen simple black cloth messenger bags. My kind friend Larry Stanton, who owned a printing shop in the South Bronx, printed "South Bronx Entrepreneurship Education Program" on each bag in bright blue letters, without charging me a penny.

Inside each bag, I placed a composition notebook, a pen and pencil, a plastic ruler, a calculator, a blue ledger book, a receipt book, play money, a paperback dictionary, and a copy of the positive-thinking classic *Think and Grow Rich* by Napoleon Hill.

I gave one bag to each student and said, "This is your briefcase. Do not lose it. Bring it with you to class every day."

They oohed and aahed over the bags. As I handed them out, I said, "Look, a lot of stuff has happened to you. Most of it wasn't your fault. I've read your case files and many of you have had lives out of a Dickens novel. Here's your chance to start over."

Victor's hand shot up. "What's a Dickens novel?"

I came in the next day with Cliff's Notes for *Oliver Twist*, *David Copperfield*, and *Great Expectations*. We read them out loud. My purpose was not to encourage my new students to pity themselves but rather to view themselves as strong, successful survivors of profoundly challenging circumstances.

I wanted them to have a sense of how hard their lives were. Nobody had ever told them that. Before I could hope to teach these children, I had to address the dearth of positivity and encouragement in their lives. I had to help them become the heroes of their stories.

"You are *heroes*," I told them, "and we are going to become the number-one class in this country in something. We just have to figure out what that is.

"In my view," I continued, "it should be entrepreneurship, because that way each of you can start your own business and earn money legally from your unique skills and talents."

This was finally my opportunity to test my theory that teaching entrepreneurship could light a fire for learning in even the most challenged students.

I had my lab and my subjects. I was determined to go for it.

CHAPTER 6

I'M SORRY ABOUT YOUR MOM

"Dear Father in heaven, I'm not a praying man, but if you're up there and you can hear me, show me the way."
—George Bailey, *It's a Wonderful Life* (1946)

Miss Archibald, Our Lady of the Typing Pool, also made it her mission to protect my offsite students from the wrath of the bureaucratic sticklers at the Department of Buildings.

Almost every morning, the elevator bell would ding, and a doddering old clerk who bore a strong resemblance to Albert Einstein, save for the clerk's vacant expression, would emerge and moan, "There was a young man getting off on the fourth floor. The fourth floor is a secure, classified area. I have to call the FBI. The CIA. This is unacceptable."

Miss Archibald had been dealing with this clerk for twenty years. She always handled him so kindly, thanking him for alerting her to this dangerous situation, assuring him that the proper authorities would be notified, and gently guiding him into the elevator and on his way back down to the fourth floor.

Such odd behavior made it clear that those assigned to the Department of Buildings had something in common with me: they had failed downward and finally landed at a job from which they were unlikely to be fired, because no one in his right mind would want it.

One typist, Janeen, seemed to be an exception to this rule. Janeen was a tall African American lady in her forties with beautiful high cheekbones. She sat near the windows, far away from the other typists, who were mostly gathered in the center of the room. Janeen had long, glossy black hair topped with a pouf of teased bangs. She wore power suits in bold colors like fuchsia and orange. Janeen stood out in delightful contrast to the clerks, who dressed either in head-to-toe black or in clothes of indeterminate colors that had faded to gray.

The older boys in my class found Janeen very attractive. They flirted with her outrageously, saying things like, "Oh my God, you look so hot today. I'd love to take you down to the fourth floor back where Abraham is and get nasty with you."

Abraham was the ancient clerk with the hotline to the FBI and CIA.

I tried to get the boys to cut it out, but Janeen didn't seem to mind at all. She laughed and flirted back with them.

I looked forward to seeing her every day, myself. She looked like a real businesswoman from *Working Girl*, one of my favorite movies.

One afternoon, Janeen rose abruptly from her chair and began running laps around the perimeter of the typing floor in her high heels, shouting, "My church pastor has got to go! He has been rude to the whole church! He didn't go on the fishing trip with Jerome!"

I was shocked. She had clearly lost her mind. Not one of the typists paid any attention. They remained hunched over their typewriters, tapping away.

I ran out of our classroom after Janeen, motioning for my students to sit still. She was moving at a fast clip, but I finally managed to flag her down.

"Janeen!" I implored her. "Is there any way I can help you?"

Janeen stopped for a moment and stared at me, wild-eyed and completely gone. She broke into a run again.

Miss Archibald came over to me and put her hand on my shoulder.

"Oh, don't worry about her, Steve," Miss Archibald murmured reassuringly. "She's been doing this once a month for seventeen years. It only lasts for about five minutes."

Miss Archibald clucked and shook her head. "And it's always about that darn fishing trip with Jerome."

Before I could get back to my classroom, I saw my student Miguel, a devout Jehovah's Witness, lumber toward Janeen clutching the Bible he always carried in his backpack. Miguel was five feet tall and round as a beach ball. He walked with a pronounced limp because his right leg was six inches shorter than his left leg. Miguel wore an orthopedic shoe with a thick platform on his right foot.

The first day Miguel walked into class he gave me a huge smile, and I immediately sensed his basic decency. Miguel had been expelled from Jane Addams for defending himself against a bully named Earvin by throwing a table at him, breaking several of Earvin's ribs. That fight got Miguel expelled for "excessive force" and brought Earvin into my offsite program as well.

"Genesis! Psalm Four! I wish to call your attention to the Lord's word!" Miguel shouted as he trundled after Janeen waving his Bible.

Miguel apparently thought Janeen was on the run because she was filled with the Holy Spirit and had become what Jehovah's Witnesses call "a force for God." He seemed to view Janeen's breakdown as an opportunity to join her in preaching the gospel.

As Janeen emerged from her manic state, she looked startled to see Miguel chasing her. Janeen stopped and stared down at him, puzzled.

"Miguel!" she exclaimed. "Go sit down. You are making a spectacle of yourself!" Janeen seemed to have total amnesia regarding her own mad dash around the room.

Miguel looked dismayed. "Oh! You mean . . . we're not talking about God now?"

"Oh no, no, no, Miguel," Janeen tut-tutted. "This is inappropriate. Please go sit down." I followed her as she guided Miguel back to our classroom and into his seat.

Miguel looked perplexed as he stuffed his Bible into his backpack.

I suppose I ran after Janeen because I had spent my childhood running after my mother.

Nancy Mason Mariotti was a gifted special ed teacher who bonded particularly well with troubled students. She became well-known for her ability to reach the most difficult children in the most disadvantaged schools in Flint. She always told me, and all her students, "You are the hero of your story." Without that belief in yourself, nothing else matters.

Growing up, I struggled in school. I had a gift for mathematics, but I also had dyslexia and attention deficit disorder, which made reading, writing, and absorbing information very challenging for me. My mom and dad always kept it positive, no matter how poorly I was doing in school. They steadfastly encouraged me to believe that I could learn, and that I *would* learn. Even though I was an academically challenged kid, they inspired me to envision myself as a success, as a hero. If I had grown up like my student Mariana, who was living in a group home in Fort Apache because her father was dead and her mother was addicted to crack and dying of AIDS, I never would have made it.

In 1957, I was four years old, riding on my father's back as we bicycled down a pretty suburban road in Ann Arbor on a crisp fall day. My mom followed closely behind us on her bike.

My dad noticed a pile of bricks jutting into the road and swerved to avoid them. My mother hit the bricks and flew over her bike's handlebars, striking the pavement headfirst. Tragically, this was long before the first bike helmet was invented by Bell Auto in 1975.

My father told me later that he was sure she had died instantly. He jumped off his bike, with me still clinging to his back, and raced over to my mother. She was barely breathing. We waited for an ambulance for what felt like an eternity. Mom was finally rushed to a nearby hospital.

We were lucky that day. My mother survived. She was stitched up at the hospital, treated for a concussion, and released.

Over time, her scar faded, but signs of brain trauma emerged. My mother had fits of rage and sadness that terrified me. Before an outburst, she would exhibit physical warning signs—a flushed face and a look of surprise. Within moments, her face would turn bright red and she would begin screaming verbal abuse at whoever was nearby. Usually, it was me or my little brother, Jack; sometimes my father.

Over the next decade, her outbursts became more intense, lasting an hour or two. In the summer, she would run to the coat closet, put on three or four heavy coats despite the humid Midwestern heat, and take off running out of our house and down the street.

I would follow her, pleading with her to come home. She would turn on me, screaming, "Leave me alone!"

Finally, I would give up and run back home, burying myself in a book or television program to hide from the fear and humiliation I felt.

Soon the phone would ring, and a kindly neighbor would let me know that my mother was "having a bit of an episode."

"I'll be right there," I would answer politely. I would dash over to find my mother going to the bathroom in the neighbor's backyard.

I quickly learned that the best way to handle her in these moments was to show no sign of embarrassment. Just simply give her a hug and say, "Let's go home, Mom."

She would daintily take my hand as if she were the Queen of England and stand up. Together, we would make our way back home; me in shorts, dirty tennis shoes, and a baggy T-shirt, struggling to carry a pile of coats, and my mother in a nice dress and heels. Although the circumstances were painful, I felt proud to be able to escort her safely up the street.

We learned that her special ed students also recognized the signs that my mother was feeling ill. They handled her outbursts by surrounding her, giving her hugs, and telling her that they loved her. Luckily, perhaps because of her deep commitment to teaching and her students, her outbursts in school were rare and fairly mild. She began taking medication in 1967 that seemed to help and probably saved her career.

Unbeknown to us, however, a brain tumor was slowly growing. On May 17, 1985, nearly three decades after her bike accident, the tumor drove my mother into a seizure in our living room.

Jack, who was sitting with her watching television, rushed her to the hospital, where doctors discovered a mass growing underneath the original point of impact on her skull.

Surgery was scheduled for the following Thursday. I flew to Michigan and waited anxiously with my father and brother at McLaren Hospital for the surgeon to emerge. He told us that the tumor was benign, but the size of a man's fist.

"We will have to wait and see how she responds to the surgery," the doctor said.

When my mother awoke, she seemed fine except that she could not move her right leg. She looked up at me like a child with her round and chubby face and murmured, "What am I going to do if my leg is paralyzed?"

"It's temporary, it'll be fine," I reassured her, and then I left the room, with tears streaming down my face.

I stayed in Michigan through the weekend. During that time, my mother and I made up and acted out plays, as we often had on long winter afternoons when I was a child. Her favorite was one in which she played the patient with the brain tumor, and I played a nurse who was going to have to operate on her because the surgeon had skipped out to play golf.

"Now where on *earth* did I put that textbook on how to do brain surgery?" I exclaimed, as I minced around the room. My mother laughed and laughed.

We talked about my childhood and hers, and I learned so much about her and my maternal grandparents. It was the most magical time my mother and I ever spent together.

Unfortunately, I had to return to New York to resume teaching. Within a week, my father called to say that Mom had had another seizure. I flew back to Michigan and went straight to her hospital room. She held my hands, and we told each other our favorite jokes and giggled together.

As I walked out of the room to get some water, she began struggling loudly for air. Lights were blinking on the machine attached to her bed. Nurses and doctors came running down the hall and into her room, waving me out of their way. They raced her bed out of her room and down the hallway into another room. My father and I ran behind them, until a door closed in our faces.

We stood waiting until a young doctor came out to tell us that she had slipped into a coma. Since the doctors thought she might eventually emerge from the coma, a feeding tube was threaded down my mother's throat into her stomach. She was transferred to a nursing home in Grand Blanc with a ward devoted to housing comatose patients.

I don't remember going to the airport or saying goodbye to my father and brother. I just remember sitting numbly on the plane, feeling dead inside.

Back in the South Bronx, I felt more urgency than ever to honor my mother's teaching legacy, but I was still struggling to find my way. At least I had discovered that the city's poorest kids were as fascinated by money and business as I had been growing up in a middle-class suburb.

Starting in grade school, I always had some little business going, from mowing neighbors' lawns to washing cars and selling golf balls. My businesses helped me overcome my tremendous shyness and awkwardness. They got me out talking to grown-ups and other kids. I learned how to negotiate and sell, and I made money, which filled me with pride and a sense of self-sufficiency.

Nothing makes you feel more like a man than being able to buy your own Hershey bar.

I was eager to get my offsite students excited about entrepreneurship. I knew it would help them learn.

Pat Black had given me carte blanche for this program and told me to ask for whatever I needed. I doubt she imagined when I asked for a VHS player, a projector, and a portable screen that I would show movies every day, but for a couple of weeks, that is exactly what I did. In part, this was my cheap ploy to get the students to stay after lunch. But I also hoped to instill in my students a sense of how heroes behave, so that they could become the heroes of their own lives.

I turned to the movies that had inspired me and made me feel that I could choose a higher road and become the hero of my life. Movie heroes like Luke Jackson, played by Paul Newman in *Cool Hand Luke*, and inner-city teacher Mark Thackeray, portrayed by Sidney Poitier in *To Sir, with Love*, had inspired me to stand up to Ford's moral failure in doing business with South Africa's apartheid regime. They had helped me overcome my terror and become a teacher after I was mugged.

I hoped these heroic characters would help my students, too.

During those two weeks, we watched a classic movie every afternoon: *The Bridge on the River Kwai*; *To Sir, with Love*; *High Noon*; *Rocky*; *Roman Holiday*. None of my students had seen or heard of these great films.

By that time, I had gotten used to the difference in our movie-watching cultures. In suburban theaters in Michigan, if you talked during a movie, you were shushed. If you kept it up, an usher would tap you on the shoulder and escort you out. Not so in New York. City kids *participated* in a movie. They laughed; they made loud cracks and comments. I didn't mind, actually. It was really entertaining.

After each movie, we would talk about it for at least an hour. I encouraged my students to view themselves as heroes faced with challenging circumstances and choices between good and evil, just like the protagonists in those films.

I certainly was not at the top of my career at the time, and my students were not at the top of theirs. We had both been kicked out of Jane Addams, to be honest. We were in the same boat. So, I suggested that we recreate ourselves.

"I want you to pretend that you've all won a scholarship to be here," I said. "I'll pretend, if you pretend, and then let's just act like that."

I truly believe that watching those films began to change their behavior. Our movie run brought us together as a class. It also helped us connect with the employees on our floor.

Initially, the clerks and typists continued to ignore what was happening behind our glass windows. But one morning I arrived a bit early, at 8 AM, and found a gaggle of clerks and typists inside our classroom, exploring the quote-filled walls and learning corners with awe and delight on their faces. It was very touching. I showed them around with pride. Soon I noticed them peering between the posters taped to our walls, watching the films with us. This helped break the ice between my students and the clerks and typists. They had something to talk about—movies.

The final movie I showed at the end of this two-week stretch was my favorite film, *It's a Wonderful Life*, the story of an entrepreneur.

My students loved *It's a Wonderful Life*. They thought crabby old villain Mr. Potter was hilarious: "Look at that old guy in the wheelchair!" They made fun of Jimmy Stewart's mush-mouthed way of speaking. They were joking away until the film's last forty minutes, during which they went stone-cold silent.

When the bell rang and the angel got his wings, they were all crying.

We spent the next week playacting *It's a Wonderful Life* as our first lesson on entrepreneurship. I printed out dialogue from the film and brought in play money so we could act out different scenes. Anton jumped at the chance to play the villainous Mr. Potter, even though he was wildly miscast, being six foot two, very plump, and always smiling. Victor had Jimmy Stewart's drawl down cold. He was on fire to play George Bailey, although Victor would have been better cast as Mr. Potter.

Victor was a relentless smart aleck and a drug dealer. He could be charming and delightful, but he also had a dark, intimidating side. One day, Victor brought $18,000 in hundred-dollar bills to class, wrapped in a rubber band. He pulled the stack of cash out of his pants and counted it out on the table over and over again, gloating, "I am the richest fifteen-year-old motherfucker in the world!"

Estelle, who was sitting next to him, rolled her eyes.

I walked over to Victor and snapped, "Get up."

Victor just grinned up at me.

"Get up," I repeated forcefully. "Now."

Victor stood up, clutching his money. I took him by the elbow and firmly steered him out of the classroom and into our lunchroom. I didn't know if I was supposed to report this incident to the police or not, given that having money is not technically a crime, but I had to do something.

"Don't you ever bring that kind of money into this classroom ever again," I warned Victor sternly, letting him see how angry I was. "Put it away. Now. And I'd get out of the drug industry if I were you," I added, "because you're going to wind up in prison. Or dead."

Victor just shrugged and flashed me a sly grin as he tucked the fat wad of cash back down his pants.

When we staged *It's a Wonderful Life*, Victor did an uncannily good job of playing George Bailey. I could only hope that some of Bailey's innate goodness was rubbing off on Victor.

The class and I really delved into *It's a Wonderful Life*. I explained that George Bailey was fighting for his values and his small business's survival. He felt hopeless and desperate enough to consider suicide, yet he found the inner strength to save his family, his business, and his town. He was transformed from ordinary man to hero.

I told my students: "George Bailey is an entrepreneur. This gives him a lot of freedom and also lots of responsibility. He's running his own company, he gets to be his own boss, but when his absentminded uncle accidentally misplaces eight thousand in cash—and Mr. Potter steals it—it's George's responsibility alone to solve the huge problem this causes for the company."

This enabled me to discuss the advantages of keeping one's cash in a bank. Instead of in one's pants, for example.

We also discussed the fact that *It's a Wonderful Life* was not a success when it was released in 1946. It was a flop that almost ended director Frank Capra's career. I used this information as an opportunity to teach the concept of breaking even and how to calculate break-even points.

The break-even point for *It's a Wonderful Life* was $6.3 million, I explained, a figure it never came close to achieving in its initial release. Now that my students were used to looking at a screen in class, I used an overhead projector with transparencies to teach the break-even formula and demonstrate the calculations.

"Here's an example of a product that failed when it was released," I said. "It got horrible reviews and did not sell enough tickets to break even, yet today it is considered one of the top American films of all time. *It's a Wonderful Life* became a Christmas classic, earning millions from annual television screenings."

That got us talking about how sometimes a business that you create may fail.

"As Henry Ford famously said," I told the class, "'Failure is simply the opportunity to begin again, this time more intelligently.'" That quotation went up on the wall, too.

Watching and acting out *It's a Wonderful Life* with the class gave me courage, and I believe it gave my new students courage, too. It set the tone for the class with an entrepreneur's story that brilliantly expresses the tribulations and triumphs of owning a business. For the rest of our time together, every Friday afternoon was movie time.

Next, I focused on developing some routines to increase the sense of safety and security in our classroom.

As soon as each student arrived in the morning, I walked him or her around the room, pointing out different sayings and speeches on the walls and asking questions. Then, I would walk the student to a table and pull out a chair. I treated each kid like royalty. When I did this, the student would usually giggle with embarrassment. It *was* a bit ridiculous, but my goal was to change how these teens thought about themselves.

They had been labeled failures, just like me. They had been

treated rudely by teachers in front of their peers, as I had been humiliated in front of my colleagues by Marilyn Sanders. My goal was to reprogram my students' subconscious minds with the thought, "I'm special, and I have the right to live a normal, good life."

I also banned nicknames in our classroom. This was not a popular rule, but I insisted upon it, because I did not want my students to be prisoners of their nicknames. Loran, for example, was nicknamed "Shootem" because he had shot another student at Jane Addams in the foot. That was not a name I wanted programming his subconscious mind on a daily basis.

Every morning, I wrote a Do Now on the board. The students were required to tackle it as soon as they sat down. Each item taped to our walls was numbered. A Do Now might be: "Find #19. Which one of the rights in the Bill of Rights do you think is most important? Write one paragraph explaining why."

We were just starting to build some cohesion as a class when the first fight erupted.

———

Whether Mariana was inside or outside, she never took off her bulky white parka. She wore it over a too-big T-shirt and baggy jeans held up by a belt with a large rhinestone-skull buckle that had some rhinestones missing.

Mariana had been emancipated by the state and lived in a group home nearby. She walked to class and always arrived by 8:30 AM. She and I developed a special bond because most of the other kids didn't arrive until nine thirty or ten. I had given up on punishing them for arriving late; it didn't have any effect.

Mariana was lively and interested in everything. She would walk around the room and pepper me with questions about the pictures of Martin Luther King, Octavio Paz, and Robert Kennedy. She was thoroughly bilingual and quite intelligent.

Mariana told me she was nine or ten when she noticed her mother acting erratically and realized that drugs were to blame. Her mother often neglected to feed Mariana, her sister, brother, and two half-brothers.

"I remember passing out because I was so hungry," Mariana told me.

Mariana ran away at twelve and lived in a homeless shelter until she was accepted into a Lutheran Social Services group home at thirteen. Astoundingly, through all this Mariana continued going to school.

On her birthday, Mariana told me she had memorized all ten of the math equations I had posted at the front of the room. I invited her to write them on the chalkboard in front of the class. She did, flawlessly, and we gave her a big round of applause.

Sometimes, Mariana's mother would show up at the classroom to beg for money. Her mother was painfully thin, with the purple Kaposi sarcoma blotches characteristic of advanced AIDS on her face and arms. We would pass a hat around and give what little change we collected to her.

It was heartbreaking. My own mother was still in a coma, so I felt Mariana's pain more than she knew.

After Mariana's mother left one day, Estelle—who always had her winged eyeliner on point and her long nails polished to perfection—popped her gum and drawled, "Gee, what a great mom you got."

Mariana grabbed Estelle by her glossy black ponytail and yanked her up out of her chair. Before I could intervene, Mariana took the chair and whacked Estelle incredibly hard in the torso with it.

I was horrified. Estelle was gasping for air. I thought for sure Mariana had cracked her ribs. I ran to Mariana and grabbed her, but I couldn't get a grip on her slippery puffy coat.

"Let her go!" I yelled at Mariana.

She and Estelle were screaming at each other in Spanish, while Mariana held tight to Estelle's ponytail. Mariana kept wriggling out of my grasp and punching at Estelle, who had flown into a rage and was punching back. I kept trying to restrain Mariana, but she was insanely strong, flooded with adrenaline and rage.

Thank goodness Anton charged over like the Jolly Green Giant. He grabbed Estelle by her waist and lifted her up into the air kicking and screaming, out of Mariana's range.

I was furious at both girls, and I let them know it. From day one, I had regularly stated that there was zero tolerance for violence in my classroom. They both were uninjured, thank God, other than the bruises they had managed to inflict on each other.

I called the police. The girls were immediately sent home, accompanied by officers. Before the girls were escorted out of the classroom, I spoke sharply to Mariana and Estelle: "You have abused each other and your fellow students with your violent behavior. If you are not both here at eight AM sharp tomorrow, I am going to have these officers come back and arrest you for assault. I will gladly testify against you and make sure you go to jail."

At this, both their eyes grew huge. I had come to learn that if you are a low-income teenager in New York City, you are already marked for arrest. The police in the South Bronx harassed at least one of my students on their way to or from our classroom every single day.

I would normally never threaten my students with the police, but I was furious—and worried. Every kid in this classroom had a history of violent behavior. I knew that if I didn't quash this fight forcefully, our classroom would never be a safe space.

Mariana and Estelle both showed up at eight the next morning. I had arrived early and asked the one and only security guard at the Department of Buildings to come to the classroom. Malcolm was thrilled, since he spent his days sitting at his desk, bored out of his mind. There really wasn't anything of value to guard at the DOB. Malcolm wore a uniform, though, and was a muscular, imposing fellow. He served as the authority figure I needed to stress the seriousness of the situation, although in actuality he had zero power to do anything.

This is where the playacting we had done after watching *It's a Wonderful Life* came in handy. I told the girls that we were going to playact the previous day's incident until we got their conflict worked out nonviolently.

I had a photo of Mahatma Gandhi with me, which I taped to the wall. I gave Estelle and Mariana a brief talk about how the Indian activist had used nonviolent protest to send British colonists packing and achieve India's independence.

"All right," I announced, "now we are going to recreate exactly what happened yesterday, minus your unacceptable violence. I will play Mariana's mom. You are not to touch each other. If you do touch each other, I'm going to have fun testifying against you, and you are going to serve a year in prison."

I was bluffing, but I was very angry and determined to prevent any additional violence.

"Mariana," I added, "you have nothing to be ashamed of. As you know, AIDS has made a lot of people very sick through no fault of their own."

As we played out the scene, Mariana and Estelle started

shouting at each other in Spanish again. Malcolm stepped forward to make sure they didn't touch each other.

We replayed the scene at least nine times until finally Estelle changed her words. In English, she said to Mariana, "I'm sorry about your mom."

Mariana burst into tears. I handed her some tissues, and she blew her nose and wiped her eyes. When she regained her composure, Mariana mumbled, "Thank you."

I had to hand Estelle some tissues, too.

Estelle had been in foster care most of her life and had probably never been treated with respect. How would she know to treat someone else with respect?

This fight helped me realize that many situations that landed at-risk teenagers like my students in prison for assault or worse could be prevented. So many conflicts that escalated into violence could be defused or avoided altogether if they practiced simple things like making eye contact and saying "thank you" or "excuse me."

Or, "I'm sorry about your mom."

CHAPTER 7

THE BROKEN TYPE-WRITER ROOM

"The world breaks everyone and afterward many are strong at the broken places."
—ERNEST HEMINGWAY, *A Farewell to Arms* (1929)

After the fight between Mariana and Estelle was resolved, I turned my attention back to developing a curriculum for the offsite class. The pressure was on for me to step it up, because each week my increasingly diligent pupils were arriving earlier.

When I first started teaching this program, students wandered in around 11 AM, mainly to get lunch. My bone-rattling subway ride from the East Village to the South Bronx took more than an hour, and I was never good at getting up early. I was always tardy. It hadn't mattered before, but now, when I arrived at eight thirty, half the class would already be there.

The kids also stopped leaving early. Suddenly, my job was a lot more demanding.

I was really excited about this development, though. I used my long, lurching commutes to brainstorm lesson plans, which I scribbled with my favorite Vis-à-Vis marker in the sketchbooks I carried in my briefcase. I knew I had to develop a daily and weekly routine for the class to keep the momentum going and myself organized.

I hoped things were turning the corner not only in my classroom but also in Michigan, where my mother was showing signs of emerging from her coma. My father was extremely excited. He was convinced that the love of his life was about to return to his side, and they would live the rest of their lives happily together.

My brother and I were more cautious, yet still optimistic. I longed to look into my mother's eyes again and tell her all about my students and my newfound passion for teaching. I knew she would be thrilled.

For now, though, the doctors said she needed rest, so I stayed in New York and focused on developing my classroom routine.

Every morning, after the students completed the Do Now assignment, I required them to write for ten minutes in their private journals. These were the composition books I had put in their briefcases. I told the students that they could write whatever they wanted, and that I would only read their journal entries with their permission. No matter what they wrote, they would earn an A as long as they wrote for ten minutes.

My goal was to get these special ed kids writing by removing any shame they had about their underdeveloped abilities. I also wanted them to discover that journaling was a safe and healthy way to vent their frustrations without harming other people or themselves.

My next step was to get the students to compose simple, short memos. I explained that the memo is the foundation of business communication, used to convey information quickly and concisely. I kept the memo format on the board at all times:

To:
From:
Date:
Subject:

I assigned one memo every day for the students to write to me, on a wide variety of simple topics, such as:

What is your favorite movie and why?
What are your worst faults? How do you intend to improve them?
What are your strongest assets? How could you use them to start a business?
Describe three goals you have for this month.

The only memo rule was "no run-on sentences." I drilled it into the students constantly to keep their sentences short and easy to understand. I was obsessed with conciseness and refused to accept any memo longer than three hundred words. I announced that I would give either an A or F grade after only one reading. The memo had to be clear. If I understood the memo, it got an A. If I didn't understand it, it got an F.

"You want to communicate your ideas clearly, in simple,

easy-to-understand language," I explained. "This is how you will communicate with your boss when you get a job or with your employees when you run a business."

My students were put at ease because I was teaching them that the goal of writing was clear communication, not flowery expression. Removing academic language from our classroom and replacing it with businesslike language seemed to calm these teenagers down. It made them more willing to try the assignments. They were much more comfortable attempting "memos" than "essays" or "papers." And they were motivated because I had given them a real-world reason for these exercises.

My favorite memos to read were the students' responses to "How would you improve this class?" At first, their responses were smart-alecky:

> *Get rid of the teacher.*
> *Get rid of fat-ass Anton.*

After a few weeks, they began writing more thoughtful responses like:

> *Give us more time to work on assignments.*
> *Allow us to pick our own team members when we work in groups.*

I did give them more time in class for Do Nows and other assignments. I did not allow the students to pick their own team members, since I wanted them to learn to get along with a wide variety of people.

Sometimes the kids' memos hit a little close to home:

Wear nicer clothes to class. You're our leader.
Make the room neat before we come to class. It's a mess.

It was painful for me to read the memo about my clothes, but Estelle was right. I read her memo out loud and resolved in front of the class to do better. I reminded the class of the value of clean, well-fitting clothes in making a positive impression, using my tendency to wear stained chinos and stretched-out sweaters as examples.

To discuss the memo asking me to clean up the room before the students arrived, we held what we called a "face-off." This was a one-on-one debate between me and the student who had written the memo—Shana, in this case. The winner was selected by the class with a show of hands.

First, Shana read her memo out loud asking me to clean up the room before class started each day.

I read my memo in response: "I suggest that whoever enters the room first, whether it is the teacher or a student, cleans up the room. The students have a much closer commute to our classroom than I do. They should take equal responsibility for keeping it neat."

I won that face-off by a show of hands!

I also allowed students to write memos to me protesting any grades they thought were unfair. I did this to teach my students how to advocate for themselves with authority figures in a calm, reasonable manner.

There are few things so satisfying as hearing another person say, "You're right. I may have been wrong." I wanted my students to have this experience when they truly deserved it.

As Winston Churchill once said to a woman who was berating him for changing his position, "When the facts change, I change my mind." That was another quote added to our classroom wall.

I wanted the class to understand that it is a sign of strength to be willing to change your mind, and that it is important to be open to what other people have to say. I believed learning this could help inoculate them from getting into the stupid—yet potentially deadly—fights that arise on the streets out of sheer obstinance.

If you listen to your opponent's point of view, sometimes that is enough to get your opponent to relax and stop wanting to pound your face in.

———————————————

One weekend, three of my students were in the wrong place at the wrong time—hanging out near some young men who were pelting cars with rocks and eggs on the Grand Concourse in the Bronx. Carlos, Lamont, and Mateo were running away from the situation when they were stopped by a patrol car. The officers were convinced that my students were the vandals and took them into custody.

While held in a cell together, the boys requested a pencil and piece of paper from the guard. As he eagled-eyed them to make sure they didn't stab anybody with the pencil, they composed a memo so simple and convincing that they were released. Here is how I remember it:

To: Officers Malone and Natchez
From: Three 12 graders at Jane Addams high school
Date: June 1, 1985
Subject: the arguments for our innocence

As you know we got arrested for throwing eggs and rocks at cars on the grand concourse. Although we saw this illegal activity happen we did not do it and we tried to stop it by yelling at the guys who were doing the throwing at the cars.

We thought they was going to hurt someone or get somebody killed maybe even a kid.

Instead of stopping they start throwing rocks at us and start to charge us. We ran when they came close to us. That is when your car and siren and the other car and siren pulled up. If you think back we was the three in the front you saw first. Running not throwing things and when you yelled we put our hands up so you would know we was trying to help. The other kids that are in some gang all ran but you arrested us. We are innocent and trying to be good citizens.

Twenty minutes later they were released to Lamont's mother, who was the first to arrive.

When I heard this story Monday morning, I was both proud and horrified. The incident reminded me of what my pupils were exposed to when they were not in school. If they had dealt with the police in their previous verbal style of monosyllables and profanity, their story might not have had a happy ending.

———————

In general, if my students came to class and they tried, they earned A+ grades. But if they were rude to me or other students, or made *any* threats of violence, they received automatic Fs.

These were children with serious emotional problems who were used to being rude and making violent threats. I decided to create a system that would enable them to get some space and calm themselves down when they needed it, without disrupting the class.

At any given moment, without having to ask permission, a student could raise one finger to be excused to go to the bathroom. The student could raise two or more fingers to break away from the class and spend time in any of the three corners of our room that Nancy and I had set up. Two fingers signaled the art table directly to my right. Three fingers meant the corner table in the far-right corner piled high with novels and biographies. Four fingers indicated the far-left corner, which contained the math and physics books. Raising five fingers enabled the student to leave the room altogether, for any reason.

The students were not allowed to leave our floor, however, and they could not leave the building. I made it clear there would be serious consequences, including expulsion from the program, if they left the floor or the building.

The next thing I did that worked out surprisingly well was to ask the typists if any of them would like to mentor a student. Sixty of 180 typists volunteered. That still brings tears to my eyes!

I have to give credit for their largesse to Miss Archibald, our champion at the Department of Buildings. Miss Archibald was always elegant, polite, and classy. She nodded and smiled and patted people on the shoulder. That was how she kept the typing pool running smoothly. We had never, ever heard her raise her voice.

When we first invaded the sixth floor, the typists complained about us to Miss Archibald every day. We were too noisy. Why did we get to eat lunch in a special room? A kid had left his trash on the floor. We were using up all the toilet paper. Etcetera.

One morning, about a week after we had moved in, I was astonished to hear sweet, kind Miss Archibald shouting at the top of her lungs. My students ran to our glass walls, and I poked my head out of our classroom door. What could possibly be going on?

"These chiiiiildren are here to be helped!"

Miss Archibald was preaching like the reverend on a Sunday morning.

"They are OUR children! YOU are to help them in wha-teeeeever way you can. Period!

"If you want your union rep to come in, Yolanda," Miss Archibald intoned, lowering her right arm like a boom and point-ing her index finger at a middle-aged typist quavering in her desk chair, "HAVE HIM COME IN."

Jesus had spoken through his vessel.

From that moment on, the typists were nicer to us. Some even said hello to the kids in the morning and seemed to enjoy having the energy of young people in their midst.

Nonetheless, I was surprised and moved by the typists' incredi-bly kind response to my request for mentors. I asked each volunteer to tell me some subjects she felt strong enough in to tutor a child, and I assigned each student to a couple of mentors.

These mentors became valuable adjuncts to our program. Often, kids wind up in special ed not because they are unintelligent but because they are missing a key bit of knowledge that is pre-venting them from progressing with their peers. Sometimes, seri-ous learning issues arise simply because a child missed the first two weeks of school, never learned one or two basic concepts, and is too embarrassed to let the teacher know.

I had students who thought they were hopeless at math when they had simply never memorized the multiplication table. They were missing that crucial bit of information the rest of us take for granted because a parent or teacher took the time to drill it into our heads. I used our mentors to help fill in such gaps.

Gladys, for example, was a typist who had gone to City College and was good at arithmetic but had dropped out in her freshman year to have a baby. I would send a student to sit with Gladys for forty minutes, and he would come back knowing his multiplication table cold.

After the students wrote in their journals each morning, we read one page out loud from a book that promoted the power of positive thinking, such as Napoleon Hill's *Think and Grow Rich*, which was in every student's briefcase, or *The Power of Your Subconscious Mind* by Joseph Murphy.

Think and Grow Rich, which was first published in 1937 by The Ralston Society and has sold more than 100 million copies worldwide, is one of my all-time favorite books. Early in the book, Hill tells the story of his son, Napoleon Blair Hill, who was born without ears and had very little hearing. The elder Napoleon was determined to help his son succeed despite this handicap. Since this was one of my favorite stories in the book, I volunteered to read it to the class.

> *I sold him the idea that when he became old enough to sell newspapers (his older brother had already become a newspaper merchant), he would have a big advantage over his brother, for the reason that people would pay him extra money for his wares, because they could see that he was a bright, industrious boy, despite the fact he had no ears.*
>
> *When he was about seven, he showed the first evidence that our method of servicing his mind was bearing fruit. For several months he begged for the privilege of selling newspapers, but his mother would not give her consent. She was afraid that his deafness made it unsafe for him to go on the street alone.*
>
> *Finally, he took matters in his own hands. One afternoon, when he was left at home with the servants, he climbed through the kitchen window, shinnied to the ground, and set out on his own. He borrowed six cents in capital from*

the neighborhood shoemaker, invested it in papers, sold out,
reinvested, and kept repeating until late in the evening. After
balancing his accounts, and paying back the six cents he had
borrowed from his banker, he had a net profit of forty-two
cents.

When we got home that night, we found him in bed
asleep, with the money tightly clenched in his hand.

When I finished reading this passage, there was not a dry eye
in the classroom. My students, who had all been told they were
disabled in some way, seemed deeply touched by this heartwarming
story of grit and determination.

Each morning, I invited students to volunteer to read out loud.
Some, like Victor, were eager to do so, but others ducked their
heads and never raised their hands. Their obvious anxiety told me
that these were my functionally illiterate students. They were too
embarrassed to attempt to read aloud in front of their peers.

Frankly, I was surprised that anyone in the class could make
it through a single page of *Think and Grow Rich*, because I had
read their test scores. None had tested above second- or third-grade
reading levels.

This perplexed me, so I called up Bella Frankel, a reading
expert who had taught special ed in public schools for forty years.
Bella was a gregarious lady in her early fifties with frizzy red hair
and a bellowing laugh. Like Pat Black, she was a natural leader who
radiated confidence and positive energy. I met Bella when we both
taught at Jane Addams, and she had taken a liking to me. I often
called her when I was stuck on a teaching problem or needed a little
bucking up.

This time I asked Bella, "What's the secret to getting special ed
kids to read?"

"Well, Steve," Bella said, "it depends on the child. Some kids are so behind that you have to sit with them with a dictionary and flash cards every day and teach them three to four hundred words, period. They need to memorize that basic reading vocabulary before they can read anything.

"With most kids, though," Bella continued, "you have to find out what their interests are. If they're interested in something, they'll make the effort to read about it."

Bella also recommended that I allow students to underline words they did not know and help them look those words up in the dictionary. She suggested that I have them write one paragraph each day about what they had read.

It came out in the media around this time that American towns were building prisons on their outskirts based on the percentage of their young adult population that read at the second-grade level. They were using literacy rates to forecast their prison business, counting on the school-to-prison pipeline that destroys the lives of so many low-income youths.

Shocked by this news, I did a little digging and uncovered staggering statistics from the United States Department of Justice that remain relatively unchanged today. Approximately 85 percent of all juveniles who interface with the juvenile court system are functionally illiterate. More than 60 percent of all prison inmates in the US are functionally illiterate. More than 70 percent of inmates in America's prisons cannot read above a fourth-grade level.

According to the DOJ, penal institution records over decades indicate that if inmates receive literacy tutoring in prison, they have only a 16 percent chance of being incarcerated again. If they receive no literacy tutoring, their recidivism rate climbs to 70 percent. In one report, the DOJ stated: "The link between academic failure and delinquency, violence, and crime is welded to reading failure."

If I had a sense of mission before, it was nothing compared to how I felt after discovering this information. I was on fire to get my students to read.

———————————————————————

I spent a lot of time trying to figure out my students' interests in order to encourage them to read. I brought in Marvel comics, which are definitely not written at the third-grade level. I brought in an auto repair manual from my days at Ford. I didn't understand a word of it, but Mateo was obsessed with cars and read it cover to cover.

I also brought as many rags-to-riches entrepreneur books as I could find, like *Ragged Dick; or, Street Life in New York with the Boot Blacks*, and *Rough and Ready; or, Life Among the New York Newsboys* by Horatio Alger Jr. My students loved Alger's smoking, gambling street urchins. All the Alger stories became hits in our classroom.

Anton read every Judy Blume novel that Nancy had contributed to the books corner. I never asked him why. I was just glad he was reading.

I asked the mentors of the children I had identified as functionally illiterate to work on reading with them for a half hour daily. I taught the typists Bella's flash-card method so they could help their students develop a fundamental reading vocabulary. Working with their mentors improved the reading level of most of these students significantly, along with their confidence.

Earvin, however, refused to even try.

Earvin stalked around with his fists clenched and his shoulders up around his ears. He had been kicked out of Jane Addams for beating up and robbing other students, and for the fight with Miguel. Earvin read at the first-grade level.

I could not get Earvin to work on his reading with his mentor;

he was too ashamed. I was worried that if his literacy did not improve, Earvin would be unable to make a living legally and would wind up in prison for assault or worse.

One day, I gave Earvin a children's book and sent him to sit at a table in a small room where broken typewriters were stored, waiting to be fixed.

"Go in there and read this book out loud," I told him. "No one will be able to hear you. Underline any word that doesn't sound right when you say it or that you can't figure out how to say. When you're done, I will come sit with you and we'll go through the book together."

An hour later, Earvin poked his head out of the broken typewriter room.

"Mr. Mariotti, I'm ready," he called.

I quickly scrawled a memo topic on the board.

"Write a memo answering this question, please," I instructed the class.

I grabbed a chair and went to sit with Earvin amid the piles of broken typewriters.

As he haltingly attempted to read to me, I discovered that Earvin did not know how to pronounce words like "engine," which he sounded out as "en-gin" with a hard *g*, or "rocket," which he sounded out as "roh-ket." Earvin knew the alphabet and he understood how to string letters together to form words. His reading vocabulary was extremely limited because no one had shown him how to pronounce many simple words. He would sound words out, not recognize them as part of his oral vocabulary, and become very frustrated.

Earvin was smart, though. Once I showed him how to correctly pronounce "engine," for example, he did not forget it.

Over the next few weeks, Earvin spent hours in the broken

typewriter room reading out loud and underlining words in the books I gave him that he did not know how to pronounce. His reading vocabulary expanded rapidly. It was thrilling for me to witness his progress as we sat together each day reading aloud. Within a month, Earvin's reading level rose from first grade to sixth grade. After a few months, he was reading at ninth-grade level.

Much of successful teaching is finding ways to help students past the fear of being humiliated for not knowing something, as my mother had so often done for me when I was a child. The broken typewriter room became a no-judgment sanctuary for my students.

"This is where the broken typewriters get fixed," I told them. "Whatever you are struggling with academically, you can take it in there. Go ahead and talk to yourself. No one will hear you. When you talk out loud, you can hear what you're thinking. That often helps you correct your mistakes."

Once a student like Earvin was feeling confident enough to try working with a mentor, I would send one of the typists into the broken typewriter room. In this way, we solved many reading and math problems that these special ed students had.

There is something freeing about being left alone to make your mistakes in private. Then, when someone who cares about you comes in and says, "Okay, seven plus nine is not seventy-nine. Let's talk about that. Why do you think seven plus nine is seventy-nine?" you may be ready to accept some help.

I began sending Loran to the broken typewriter room whenever he had one of his "Aaaaaaah!" spells. Loran loved spending time in there. I knocked on the door one day and when he let me in, I discovered that he was teaching himself how to fix the typewriters. He had discovered four things that typically caused breakdowns: dry ribbons, dirty keys, locked carriages, or stuck paper-release levers.

I was amazed and said, "That's all it is?"

"That's all it is, Mr. Mariotti!" Loran exclaimed with a happy grin.

Loran started charging the typists $1.25 for every typewriter he fixed.

It was clear to me that my students had been mismeasured and their potential had been ignored. For the most part, these were normal children who had gotten stuck in special ed for behavioral problems. People treated them like they were dumb, so they behaved that way.

I was determined that they would not become prison fodder.

My students were making real progress. I prayed that my mother was also progressing back home.

One afternoon in May, however, Miss Archibald came bursting into our classroom.

"Steve," she cried, "your father is on the phone. He says it's an emergency!"

Deep down, I knew what my father was going to tell me. In a moment of weakness, I actually considered not taking the call. Only the loving strength that radiated from Miss Archibald gave me the courage to follow her out the door.

I walked silently behind Miss Archibald down the long corridor toward her office. The deafening clickety-clack of 180 typewriters mercifully drowned out my thoughts, and for that I was grateful.

Miss Archibald gave me the phone and took my hand, holding it quietly as I listened to my father struggle through his tears to tell me that my mother had sunk into what her doctors were calling "a long-term coma" and "a vegetative state."

I spoke to Jack, as well, who reassured me that she was not in any pain and confirmed that there really was no more hope left for us.

"I am so sorry, Steve," Miss Archibald murmured as she gently took the receiver out of my hand and hung up the phone. For a moment, I saw my mother's unconditional love, which was solely responsible for any virtues I had managed to develop, shining through Miss Archibald's soft brown eyes.

I wiped my own eyes with the tissue she gave me and thanked her. As she opened the door to her office, and I began the long walk back to my classroom, I felt my heart break.

CHAPTER 8

CAN YOU HIT ME AGAIN?

"Our greatest glory is not in never falling, but in rising every time we may fall."
—OLIVER GOLDSMITH, *The Citizen of the World; or, Letters from a Chinese Philosopher, Residing in London, to His Friends in the East (1762)*

My father continued to cling to hope that my mother would emerge from her coma. He refused any discussion of taking her off life support. Jack oversaw her move into the long-term care unit of the nursing home in Grand Blanc. He encouraged me to stay in New York and look after my students.

"There's really nothing you can do here," Jack said quietly when we spoke on the phone.

I knew my mother, too, would want me to focus on my special ed kids. At night, though, I slept fitfully on my beat-up couch, tossing and turning, hearing her voice. In the morning, my face would be wet with tears I didn't remember crying.

At the Department of Buildings, I continued to focus on getting my students to think positively and view themselves as heroes. That was something profound my mother had done for me.

One day, perhaps because death and loss were weighing heavily on my mind, I asked the students to write their own obituaries. It was a rather morbid exercise, but I wanted to know how they envisioned their futures. The results were very sad.

Victor wrote: *I'm going to die at 21, probably shot.*

Shana wrote: *I die at 19 in a drive-by.*

Anton wrote: *I get stabbed in a fight when I'm 20 and I die.*

Mariana wrote: *I get mugged for my sneakers and shot.*

I was horrified. These teenagers saw no futures for themselves. I had no idea their lives were this imperiled.

"View me as God," I sternly admonished each student who turned in a grim obituary. "God does not approve this obituary. Try again." Teachers were not supposed to mention God in the classroom, but I was too upset by what I was reading to give a damn.

I made each student rework his or her obituary until it contained a storyline that represented a fulfilling life, like "I got married and had two children," or "I started a successful business and became a millionaire." As "God," I gave an A to pretty much any obituary better than: I get shot and killed at 21.

Once they had begun to imagine different endings for their

lives, I asked the students to write down five life goals and share them with the class. Their goals were heartbreakingly normal: "get married," "have children," "own a house," "become head of my neighborhood soccer club."

To drive home the value of positive thinking, I brought in my Polaroid camera. I took each child's photo twice. For the first photo, I asked the student to think about something sad or depressing. This led to some very dour expressions!

Then I said, "Okay, for your next photo, think of something positive and give me a big smile."

I had a chipped front tooth that I couldn't afford to get fixed, so I was embarrassed to smile myself. But I would crack a big grin and that would make them laugh. The fact that I had an embarrassing problem and was willing to smile anyway seemed to encourage them to smile for their portraits, too.

I posted the two different photos of each student side by side on the wall, so they could see the huge difference that a shift in their thoughts made in their external expressions. I explained that their facial expressions would have a huge impact on whether people react to them positively or negatively.

"I want you to start looking at yourself in a different mirror," I said.

Every morning, after we read from *Think and Grow Rich*, we played a few rounds of the negotiating game. I developed this game as part of an entrepreneurship-based curriculum that was slowly forming in my mind.

I would bring in a simple product, like a tie, and split the students into two groups. I told one group they could not sell the tie for less than a dollar. I told the other group they could not buy the tie for more than ten dollars. Then I let them loose to negotiate with each other until they reached a price that satisfied both seller and buyer.

First, though, I had to get across the concept that negotiation is about compromise, not about beating or intimidating your opponent into submission. I read the students a great story from Herb Cohen's bestseller *You Can Negotiate Anything* that illustrates this point.

A brother and sister are squabbling over how to divide the last quarter of a pie. Just as the boy gains control of the knife, their mother arrives on the scene.

"Hold it!" Mom says. "I don't care who cuts the pie, but whoever cuts it has to give the other person the right to select his or her piece of pie."

To protect himself, the boy cuts the pie into two pieces of equal sizes.

The moral of the story is that if two people shift their focus from defeating each other to defeating the problem, everyone benefits. The best negotiations are those in which both parties are satisfied because they have reached a "win-win" agreement.

"You could beat up your opponent and just take the tie," I told the class, "but that person will never do business with you again. Success comes from *repeat* business. You want to win over a customer so he or she comes back to you to buy more."

The negotiation game taught my students the value of choosing voluntary exchanges over involuntary exchanges, such as mugging someone or selling rocks to crackheads who were helpless to stop buying them.

Some of my students had significant selling experience—in the drug trade. They quickly learned that negotiating with non-junkies was an entirely different experience, requiring listening, patience, and politeness. It was not a quick or easy hustle, but it was safe, legal, and more emotionally rewarding.

I taught key negotiation tactics like letting the other person name a price first, listening before speaking, and using silence as a tool. The students got these tactics down fast! These children had already negotiated with angry landlords and pissed-off gangbangers. They were constantly navigating dangerous situations on the street and negotiating for their safety. They were naturals!

Pat Black had given me eleven video camcorders. We were constantly filming. We filmed and then watched our entrepreneurship games every day. The kids were allowed to film themselves anytime they wanted. If they wanted to film another student, however, they had to obtain written permission from that student using a simple release form that was always on my desk. They were not allowed to show a film of another student outside of class.

My hope was that my students would see themselves more clearly on camera and begin to adjust their behavior. To my surprise, they turned the camcorders on me a lot, which really helped me become a better teacher.

It was also how I learned for the first time that my right eye twitches when I am tired or stressed. I never knew I had this tic until my students filmed me. We were watching a tape one day, and I said, "Wow, look! I've got a twitch in my eye!"

The students cracked up.

Shana exclaimed, "Mr. Mariotti, how could you not know that?"

That evening I called my best friend from Flint.

"Did I have an eye twitch back in high school?" I asked him.

"Yeah, Steve! We thought you knew that!" he laughed.

I declared Thursday goal-setting day. Every Thursday, the students had to write down their goals for the week and report on whether they had achieved the goals they had set the previous Thursday. A goal might be: "read one book," "memorize the multiplication table," "be on time for class," or "don't curse." The students could work in teams or alone on their goals. If they wanted to share their goals, they could tack them up on our goal board.

I would share my goals for the week, too. My goals usually included "be on time for class" and "don't curse," also.

After we had written down our goals, we meditated on them. I asked the students to close their eyes and envision themselves achieving their goals. Then I went around the room and had each student hold out his or her right arm.

I pressed gently on top of the student's forearm and said, "If you really believe in your goal, keep your arm firm. If you *really* believe, I won't be able to press your arm down."

This is applied kinesiology "muscle testing," which a New Agey girlfriend had shown me. If you don't truly hold the energy of believing in your goal, your arm will drop when pressed, but if you do genuinely believe in your goal, your arm will stay firm.

Applied kinesiology has been debunked scientifically, to be honest, but it provided a concrete little exercise the students and I could do together to strengthen our resolve.

Friday was money day. On Fridays, all we talked about was money and how to make it. I made it very clear that no student was allowed to miss money day. It helped that I always showed a movie on Friday afternoons.

Every Friday morning, after the Do Now, our reading, and playing a few rounds of the negotiating game or the sales call game, we worked through balancing my checkbook. I wanted to teach my pupils basic life skills, and my messy finances were as good a place to start as any. I used the overhead projector to show them how to reconcile my checkbook.

Each week, we also worked through a simple income statement for a make-believe small business. I taught concepts like cost of goods sold, profit, and loss. We calculated net profit, return on investment, return on sales, and other financial ratios. It was a great math workout!

Tying math lessons to money worked well, but none of my students had any legally obtained money. None of them even had bank accounts.

I decided to apply for a grant from Trickle Up, a nonprofit giving people in third-world countries fifty-dollar microgrants to start small businesses. To my amazement, I received a small grant from Trickle Up to open fifty-dollar savings accounts for each of my students. At the time, I was the only person in the United States whom Trickle Up had financed.

Our first field trip was to a local bank, where we opened a savings account for each student. The only rule I set—which was probably illegal—was that students could not withdraw any money from their accounts without my permission.

Luckily, they believed in my phony prohibition, because my goal was to take the class on more field trips—to the wholesale district in Midtown Manhattan. I was planning to have them use their savings to buy goods wholesale that they could resell for a profit.

First, though, I had to track down overworked, drug-addicted, or absent parents and get them to sign permission slips. I decided to create one permission slip that would allow me to take each student on one field trip per week for one year. Teachers are supposed to obtain one permission slip per student for every field trip, but once again I rationalized that since we weren't actually "in" the school system, I could bend the rules.

To develop relationships with the parents, I instituted a rule that I had to speak to every student's guardian or parent once a week. I got to be friendly with the parents in this way and could tell them how their children were doing in class. A couple of students, like Mariana, didn't have available parents. In those cases, the students had to call me once a week after school or on the weekend for a little chat.

I also decided to have dinner with one student's family every few weeks. I planned to bring general-purpose field-trip permission slips and get the parents to sign them. I figured I would offer to bring Chinese food, since some of the families were subsisting on very small incomes.

I had discovered just how poor some of my students were when I naively and arrogantly decided to lecture the class one day on healthy food choices.

Estelle's hand shot up. When I called on her, she said, "How we gonna eat good if we ain't got no money?"

"How are we going to eat *well*, if we don't *have* any money, Estelle," I corrected her. Then I asked, "How bad is it? You get a good lunch here. What do you eat for dinner at home?"

"Lots of times we ain't got nothing but peanut butter at my house," Anton said.

"I'm on food stamps," Mariana chimed in, "and it's not enough to live on."

Other students nodded their heads in agreement.

"Hell, not me!" Victor shouted. "I can get whatever I want! Food, snatch, weed, any thang!" He pulled a roll of cash out of his pocket and waved it around.

"Put that away, Victor," I snapped, "and know that you are risking your life, your freedom, and your soul for that money."

"You need money though," Mateo piped up, "'cause without money you can't do nothing. No food, no clothes, no girlfriend, no movies, no nothing."

I didn't know what to say. The thought of my students going hungry made me feel sick. I nodded my head silently in agreement that poverty is torture.

The first home I went to for dinner was Shana's. She lived in a sixth-floor walk-up on 106th Street. When we arrived at her apartment door, it took immense effort to push it open. Once we squeezed inside, I saw why.

Shana's mother was a full-on hoarder. Old newspapers, magazines, and folded-up cardboard boxes were stacked in columns until they touched the ceiling, creating narrow passageways through the apartment. There were mountains of clothes, toys, books, and stuffed-full trash bags. The apartment reeked of stale garbage.

Now I understood why Shana often arrived in our classroom in the same clothes she had been wearing the day before, and why I sometimes found her sleeping on the sidewalk outside of the DOB when I arrived in the morning. She didn't want to go home.

After we exchanged pleasantries, Shana's mother motioned for us to clamber up a garbage-bag mountain, using an aluminum ladder. The three of us ascended the ladder as if nothing were amiss. We sat down on the mountain, with our heads grazing the ceiling.

I opened cartons of Chinese food I had brought, and we quietly ate our steamed chicken, broccoli, and rice.

I noticed that I was sitting on a *Look* magazine from 1968. As I shifted off of the magazine, in order to try to read the cover, I realized I was starting to wheeze, no doubt in reaction to the unbelievable filth of the apartment.

I have had asthma since I was four years old. I still remember that first nighttime attack as a child and how panic-stricken I felt when I couldn't breathe for the first time in my young life. My quick-thinking mother saved my life by rushing me into the bathroom and turning the hot water on full blast to create a cloud of steam, while my father called our family doctor.

I am usually good at coping with my asthma, but this attack at Shana's home was coming on rapidly, robbing me of the ten to twenty minutes I usually had to take medication and mentally prepare. Worse, for some dumb reason I had forgotten my inhaler.

My inflamed lungs filled with mucus, making it impossible to suck in any air. I slowly listed sideways until I was lying down on the mountain. I was mortified that this was happening. Unable to talk or even cough, I felt increasingly desperate. Trying to breathe was agony.

I could feel my face swell and knew it was turning purple as I struggled to breathe. I heard my raspy gasps for air. They sounded very far away. Humiliation washed over me at the realization that I was about to die atop a pile of trash.

Shana, who had seen me use my inhaler in class, immediately took charge, screaming to her mother that I was having an asthma attack. Shana's mother pulled out an inhaler and put it to my lips, pressing down as I tried with all my might to inhale the magic mist that would save my life. Apparently, she had asthma, too, which was not surprising given the state of her apartment.

Seeing that I was unable to inhale the mist, Shana's mother

pulled a green-and-blue box of Primatene tablets out of her jacket. I have never been so glad to see something in my life.

Those remarkable pills always worked immediately for me. They are so powerful, in fact, that pharmacies started keeping them behind the counter, because teenagers discovered they could crush and snort the tablets to get an intense high from the ephedrine in them.

Shana lifted my head up and helped me swallow two tablets with a tiny sip of tea. She gently laid my head back down. The next moments were pure torture. I still could not breathe and was filled with anxiety that the medication would not work for me in this filthy environment.

After what seemed like a lifetime, the pills kicked in. Suddenly, my lungs cleared and I sucked in a cool, delicious rush of oxygen. Fear of death was replaced by the euphoric feeling of every cell in my body sending a thank-you to God and Primatene for another day of life. It was a moment of incredible relief that I will always remember.

Shana and her mother slowly lifted me up, carefully cradling my shoulder and neck. They were so gentle with me as they helped me swallow another pill.

I called the fire department and Shana's school therapist the next day, out of concern for Shana and her mother's health. That caused a terrible fight between Shana and her mother, who wasn't too happy with me after that.

Luckily, I had already gotten her to sign the permission slip.

Upon hearing that I had gone to Shana's for dinner, Victor promptly invited me to his home. I was pleasantly surprised. I hadn't taken Victor for a warm and fuzzy guy. Maybe he was starting to take a liking to me.

In reality, I soon discovered, Victor had invited me for dinner because his mother's boyfriend had moved into their apartment. Victor hated the boyfriend—a nice man who worked for the municipal government—and had thrown a bunch of his clothes out the window. Victor got it into his mind that if I came over and demonstrated support for Victor against this man, Victor's mother would get rid of him.

Victor and his mom lived in the projects on Third Avenue. A marine's kid brother had been shot and killed on the project playground recently. The marine was given a furlough to attend his brother's funeral, and went to the playground to visit the spot where his brother had died. He was questioning some children about his little brother's murder when someone slipped behind the marine and shot him in the back of the head.

It was that kind of neighborhood.

Victor's home was cozy, though, with comfy floral couches and a Formica dining table. We had a lovely meal together, although Victor started glowering as soon as he realized I had no intention of helping him throw the boyfriend to the wolves.

Victor softened up, though, as I told his mother what an intelligent young man I thought he was. I sang his praises regarding how much his reading, writing, and math skills were improving.

After dinner, Victor said to me, "I'll show you the roof, the view is really nice." We climbed the piss-stank stairs to the roof and shoved open the heavy door.

"Wow!" I exclaimed, as I took in the glittering buildings and sucked in some relatively fresh air. "It really is pretty up here!" I could even make out a few stars in the sky.

Right then, we were jumped by three huge dudes in dark sweatshirt hoodies, baggy jeans, and pristine white sneakers. Two of them grabbed Victor, ripped off his sneakers, and sent them sailing over the edge of the building. Then they flipped Victor upside down and hung him over the edge by his ankles.

Victor's assailants shook him eight stories above the unforgiving pavement, bellowing, "Where's our money, motherfucker?" and "Who the fuck you think you're fuckin' with, bitch?"

The third guy, a dead ringer for bodybuilding rapper Melle Mel, wrapped a meaty hand around my upper arm and pointed a knife at my face.

My knees buckled.

I begged them to let us go. I was crying and carrying on. "I'm his teacher! For God's sake, let him go! I'm his teacher!" I could hear my voice become increasingly hysterical and high-pitched, as if it were something outside myself I couldn't control anymore.

"Shut the fuck up, white boy!" my captor growled in a deep baritone. He tilted his head and two more men emerged from the shadows, grabbed me by the ankles, and hung me over the side of the building next to Victor.

I immediately pissed my pants.

They laughed and started swinging me side to side, banging me into Victor.

Lights, street, sidewalk, buildings swirled around me. I puked in what felt like slow motion, watching my vomit spiral through the air and into the night.

Victor, meanwhile, was laughing his fucking ass off. Cackling away as if being swung to and fro while hanging by his ankles from the roof of the projects was the funniest damn thing that had ever happened to him.

One of his tormentors yelled, "Gawd, motherfucker, your feet stink!"

The thugs all burst out laughing. The two holding Victor pulled him back up onto the roof. The other guys hauled me up as well and dropped me in a pile on the roof. They proceeded to punch Victor in the gut and kick him in front of me.

Desperate to stop him from being murdered, I started up with the begging and pleading again: "Victor, tell them where the fucking money is! Please let us go, please. I'm his teacher. I just came for dinner. Please! What can I do? Victor! *Tell them where the goddamn money is*!"

I have zero bravery in these situations. I was ready to say anything. I would have given up D-Day. Victor, in contrast, silently smirked at his attackers while they beat him.

Two men moved toward me again. They dragged me to my feet and over to the edge of the roof. "We're gonna drop him," one said to Victor.

"Okay! Okay!" Victor shouted. He gestured toward the decrepit wooden water tank on the roof. The men who had been beating Victor yanked him up by his arms and dragged him to it. Victor felt around under the tank. He pulled a tiny screwdriver out of his pocket, unscrewed a wooden panel under the tank, and pulled out a thick stack of cash in a ziplock baggie. He dangled it by one corner with a shit-eating grin on his face.

Melle snatched it from his hand.

"Can we go now?" Victor said sarcastically.

Melle pulled brass knuckles out of his pocket and slid them onto his right hand. "All right," he grunted, "but this is so you don't forget us." He threw a haymaker at Victor that cut a gash across his left eyebrow and knocked him to the ground. Blood poured down Victor's face.

"Awww, that felt good!" Victor yelled as Melle and his crew stalked toward the roof door. "Can you hit me again?"

I ran to Victor and helped him stand up. I put his arm around my shoulder and staggered with him to the door and back down the stairs to his mom's apartment.

"Who are those guys?" I demanded. "We've got to call the police!"

"If you wanna call the police, Mr. Mariotti, that's fine," Victor mumbled, "but I'll be dead by morning."

Back at the apartment, Victor's mother cleaned his nasty cut in the kitchen, fussing about his "nonsense." After I cleaned myself up in the bathroom, the boyfriend poured me a stiff drink.

Two months later, gang members executed the entire family that lived on the floor above Victor's apartment. Victor came to talk to me about it. That was the only time I ever saw him rattled. It was the only conversation we ever had when he wasn't joking around and being a smart aleck.

"Their blood was dripping down the walls in our living room, Mr. Mariotti," he told me. "My moms had to clean that up."

CHAPTER 9

THEY DON'T PAY YOU FOR THAT

"I shoot an arrow into the air, where it lands I do not care, I get my arrows wholesale!"
—CURLY HOWARD, *Cactus Makes Perfect* (The Three Stooges, 1942)

The South Bronx was a dangerous place in the 1980s, divvied up between gangs loosely affiliated with either the Bloods or the Crips. These subgangs had names like the Wild Cowboys or the Maceteros. Every housing project was infiltrated with its own drug-selling organization that ran the corner operations and executed street justice. A drug-selling corner went for $15,000 to $20,000. Taking a hit out on someone cost around $3,000.

Sometimes, as a special treat, I took my students to lunch at a nearby diner. I stopped that after we witnessed two shootings.

We were walking down the street around noon when a guy walked up to another guy and shot him in the leg. According to my students, this was common punishment for an unpaid debt. The kids thought nothing of it. They discussed the caliber of the gun and speculated as to whether the shooter was a Blood or a Crip.

A few weeks later, I took them out for lunch again and the same damn thing happened.

There was a loan shark on every corner in neighborhoods like Fort Apache. The astronomical interest these moneylenders charged was called "the vig," also known as "juice," "the cut," or "the take." "Vig" comes from the Russian word for winnings, *vyigrysh*.

If you borrowed a thousand dollars from a loan shark on Monday, you would owe two thousand a week from Monday, four thousand two weeks from Monday, and so on. It was easy to get into serious trouble very fast.

I was fanatical in impressing upon my students, "Never, ever borrow money from a loan shark. No matter what. They may seem very friendly, like all they want to do is help you. But if you miss one payment, they will break your leg. If you miss two payments, they will kill you."

I wasn't telling my students anything they didn't already know. The entire city was rough back then. People were murdered in broad daylight on 14th Street in Manhattan. You took your life into your hands just walking around.

Nonetheless, I knew I had to show my students the world beyond Fort Apache if I was going to inspire them to give entrepreneurship a try.

My girlfriend, Janet McKinstry, came up with the idea for a

field trip to the Midtown Manhattan wholesale district. She had helped me with the grant proposal to Trickle Up, too.

I fell for Janet at West 4th Street Saloon, where I went for dinner every day after school. I was a fan of the place for two reasons: free popcorn and beautiful waitresses.

West 4th Street Saloon was always hopping with actors and actresses. It was a hangout for John Belushi, William Hurt, Melissa Gilbert, Ray Sharkey, and many other faces I recognized from film and television. The restaurant was owned by actor Dylan McDermott's father, Mac McDermott. Mac was married to playwright Eve Ensler, who had a huge hit in the nineties with her episodic play *The Vagina Monologues.*

Every day after class, I caught the graffiti-adorned 2 express train at Prospect Avenue in the Bronx and rode it twenty stops to 14th Street–Union Square. There, I grabbed the F train for a quick one-stop ride to West 4th Street and Sixth Avenue.

At the time, subway train exteriors blazed with incredibly colorful "burners"—elaborate spray-painted murals created by graffiti artists. Some of these artists, like Fab 5 Freddy and Lady Pink, went on to well-deserved gallery exhibits and long careers. The interior walls of the subway cars were covered with complex tags scrawled with thick black, red, or green markers. If you looked carefully, you could make out the names of artists like Dondi, Zephyr, Julio 204, or SAMO, the tag used by painter Jean-Michel Basquiat.

The Bronx was the epicenter of train "bombing," as painting a car was called, thanks to Pelham Yard at 1483 Waters Place, where several hundred subway cars were stored at a time for inspection and repairs, making them irresistible targets for local artists.

In 1985, the New York City Transit Authority began an intense campaign to eradicate graffiti from the subway with increased security at the yards and stiff penalties. In 1989, the last graffitied train was removed from service, and with it, in my humble opinion, went a bit of New York's flair.

After climbing the steep stairs from the West 4th Street station to the street, I would walk west for a couple minutes to West 4th Street Saloon, on the corner of West 4th and Jones Street. I would arrive around 4 PM and work on my lessons plans until six.

I loved the restaurant's rough-hewn wooden tables, made smooth and glossy by decades of hands passing over them. I would grab a big bucket of salty popcorn, spread out my notebooks, and pore over my lesson plans, scribbling notes in my childish scrawl as I shoveled handfuls of popcorn into my mouth.

At six, I would have a burger and a couple of beers. Then I would walk across town to my East Village hovel, feeling pretty good about life.

My favorite waitress and aspiring actress at West 4th Street Saloon was Edie Falco. I asked her out every Friday, and every Friday she replied, in that now-famous deadpan voice, "I don't think so, Steve."

Edie's best friend was another waitress named Janet, who took a keen interest in my work. Janet was tall and slender, with snow-white skin, long black hair, and blue eyes. She would stand behind me, look over my shoulder, and say, "Hmm, I would teach it this way!"

I was thirty-four and Janet was only twenty-one, but she had a knack for organization that proved invaluable to me as I slaved over my lesson plans.

One Friday, I noticed that Janet seemed irritated when Edie and I were engaging in our weekly ritual. So, I asked Janet out instead, and she said yes.

In September, Janet and I explored the Midtown Manhattan wholesale district, also known locally as the *tchotchke* district. This was
where street vendors, souvenir stores, and cheap clothing stores
bought their wares in bulk at big volume discounts.

The wholesale district ran north to south from around West
30th Street to West 20th. It was bounded by the Flatiron Building
on 22nd and Fifth Avenue and by Madison Square Garden on 32nd
and Seventh Avenue.

Wholesale businesses placed signs in their windows that read
"To the Trade," "Wholesale Only," or "Solo Por Mayor." You could
also spot wholesalers by their gaudy window displays of hair orna-
ments, perfume bottles, toys, costume jewelry, batteries, sunglasses,
T-shirts, and socks. Wholesalers near the Garment District sold fab-
ric in bolts and notions like buttons, thread, appliqués, beads, and
rhinestones.

I searched for wholesale stores that sold inexpensive items by
the dozen, such as hair combs, trendy earrings, or pens. If a wholesaler sold anything I thought my students might be able to resell at a
profit to friends and family, I added it to my short list. I introduced
myself to store owners and explained that I would be bringing students from the South Bronx Entrepreneurship Education Program
to their stores to purchase wholesale goods for resale.

Meanwhile, Janet helped me get each student set up with a tax
ID number, which was not an easy task. Pat Black gave us access to
the student records we needed to obtain Social Security numbers
and other information.

I used Trickle Up grant funds to order business cards for the
students with their names and tax ID numbers printed on the front,
along with:

South Bronx Entrepreneurship Education Program
Jane Addams Vocational High School
This student is purchasing goods wholesale for resale.

The back of the card displayed my name and title as director of the program, and my phone number.

Since Friday was our weekly money day, I scheduled our first field trip to the wholesale district for the first Friday in October. The plan was to let the students buy a few things and try to sell them over the weekend. We would reconvene on Monday to discuss their experiences, go over their record keeping, and create simple financial statements.

We left at 2 PM on Friday for 30th and Broadway. For a surprising number of my students, this was their first trip out of the Bronx, and they were beyond hyped up. Just keeping them in their seats on the subway was a major challenge.

By this time, thank God, Pat Black had assigned a para to my offsite program. "Para" stands for paraprofessional educator. When I was growing up, we called them teacher's aides.

My para, Luisa, was twenty-seven and had moved to New York from Puerto Rico a few years prior. She was fluent in Spanish, but her English was not very strong. She could barely write in English when she began working in my classroom. Nonetheless, she helped me in a thousand ways every day.

Luisa was a genius at keeping my rowdy bunch in line by admonishing them in rapid-fire Spanish like a strict but loving mother. On Thursdays, when we set our goals, she shared hers, as well. Luisa's were to lose fifteen pounds and become fluent in speaking and writing English. I am proud to report that when she moved on from my classroom and became a full-time teacher two years later, she had achieved her goals.

Luisa even applied what she learned in our program to starting her own clothing business. She made women's clothes and eventually got her monthly gross income up to $3,000. She was a great role model for all the kids.

In spite of my preparations and Luisa's help, though, our first trip to the wholesale district was kind of a disaster. Most of the students lost their inventory or gave it to friends over the weekend without even trying to sell it. I saw this as a positive, though. It gave me an opportunity to explain to them how tough entrepreneurship really is.

"When you see the gentleman running the bodega in your neighborhood," I said in class the following Monday, "have some appreciation for how much money he had to save up to buy all that inventory. He went to a wholesaler to buy every can of cat food and every package of toilet paper, just like you did. Think about how hard he works every day to sell his goods at a profit so he can support his family. He has to think about what the people in your neighborhood need, and what they will buy. He has to figure out what prices they will pay. You have to do exactly the same thing.

"That business owner is a hero in your community," I declared. "How can you be a hero in your community? What could you buy from a wholesaler in midtown that your friends or family in the Bronx would love to buy from you? You know them better than anyone else does. You have unique knowledge of what your market wants."

My students hung on every word.

We faced some challenges with the wholesale store owners initially, though.

During our second Friday field trip, Shana sauntered into a

wholesale store on 32nd and Broadway that sold inexpensive earrings and necklaces. Shana had short-cropped hair and wide shoulders. She favored baggy jeans, extra-large polo shirts, and the big
puffy sneakers in vogue at the time. She walked with an exaggerated
drop-and-dip swagger, like a tough teenage boy.

The Pakistani owner started yelling, "Get out! Get out of my
store! Get out!"

I was standing on the sidewalk when I heard him shouting.
I quickly opened the door. Shana darted past me muttering, "He
thinks I'm some kinda thief, Mr. Mariotti."

I got really angry. I charged into the store and yelled, "I find
this very discourteous! I find this racist! Are you the store owner?
I am the director of the South Bronx Entrepreneurship Education
Program and you just ejected one of my students!"

It was not one of my finer moments. I was on my high horse.
I didn't think to ask Shana if she had shown her business card. Of
course, I found out later, she had lost her card.

"Oh!" the owner cried, giving me a big smile. "Is this the teaching program? I've heard about it! Please, your student can come
back in. My apologies!"

I was still furious, imagining how hurt and upset Shana must
be. I figured I would have to go after her and work hard to convince
her to reenter the store.

To my surprise, before I could go back outside to look for
Shana, she strolled back into the wholesaler's on her own, totally
calm. She introduced herself to the shop owner, who politely
showed her around so she could make her purchases.

This was when I knew that no matter what happened in Shana's
world, she would never give up.

That incident helped me realize how strong my "disadvantaged" students really were. If a store owner had yelled at a prep

school student like that, I would have probably had to scrape the kid off the sidewalk. My students, in contrast, could handle rejection and were not easily rattled. They had courage, heart, and grit. They were willing to try and try again.

What more does an entrepreneur really need?

The wholesale district was also a great lab for my students to test our classroom lessons on negotiation and basic economics. They began to understand that prices are subjective, determined by supply and demand.

I instructed the kids not to bargain with the wholesalers until we were accepted in the district. By our third trip, I gave the students permission to bargain. They went to town, using tactics they had learned from playing the negotiating game in class. They would do things like walk into a store, pick up and examine an item, put it down, and walk out as if they were not interested in it. Then they would walk back in slowly. Invariably, the wholesaler would lower the price per dozen.

The students also learned how to return any damaged items they discovered in their bulk purchases.

"As long as you keep your receipt," I told them, "you have the power to return any damaged merchandise. But you must be polite."

After we had visited the district a few times, the wholesalers were very nice to my students and were willing to take returns in exchange for store credit. I loved seeing students labeled special ed function at such a high level in the real world.

Maurice was the first student to make a profit from our wholesale field trips. Although he was not one of my worst-behaved pupils, Maurice was belligerent and threatening. He didn't hold conversations; he barked at people.

Maurice loved playing our morning negotiation and sales call games, but he would often lose his patience and start cursing his opponent, getting in his face like a boot-camp drill sergeant.

"Maurice, they don't pay you for that," I would say. "You're not going to make any money for that. Back down."

My constant refrain in class when we played these games was: "They don't pay you for that." I said it every time a student got frustrated and devolved from behaving like a professional business-person to saying things like, "Motherfucker! Kiss my ass!"

My students began to learn that it is the simple, small inter-actions with other people that create success. Being on time, being friendly, wearing clean clothes, saying "thank you" and "you're welcome," making eye contact, shaking hands, keeping your word when you make a deal. These behaviors make you money.

I boiled all these behaviors down to one phrase, "They don't pay you for that," because being poor is hell. When you are poor, you feel angry, you feel like a failure, you can't sleep, you don't eat well, and you think about nothing but money.

In the wholesale district, Maurice invested twenty dollars in a dozen pairs of sunglasses. Within a week, he had sold out, doubling his money. Maurice discovered that he had unique, valuable knowl-edge he could use to create profit. He knew exactly what styles his peers in the Bronx would be eager to buy. He was able to determine a price they would pay that still gave him a solid profit.

Maurice's entire demeanor changed once he realized I wasn't kidding about "They don't pay you for that." He evolved from angry and threatening to conversational and polite. He learned from our daily games and his selling experience that in order to succeed in business, he was going to have to treat people politely, not snarl at them or try to intimidate them with his body language.

Maurice learned to assert himself non-aggressively by selling.

He was also making money, which reduced his stress level. A very decent young man began to emerge.

Soon, Maurice was averaging sixty dollars per week in his spare time through sales. It was thrilling to witness the increase in his confidence and self-esteem. His success inspired the other kids to take our wholesale field trips more seriously and search for products that they could sell successfully, too.

On Monday mornings, we conducted a debriefing meeting, which I called our *kaizen* circle, after the Japanese business term for "continuous improvement."

In Japanese businesses, I explained, kaizen circles are sacred spaces into which no blame is allowed. Every person in the circle is empowered to make suggestions without being subject to criticism.

We would sit in our kaizen circle and discuss Friday's wholesale buying trip and how sales had gone over the weekend. We dug into how the students could improve their negotiating, selling, and marketing skills. We talked about the importance of not acting over-eager when purchasing wholesale, for example, and the importance of being friendly to store owners and sales prospects.

The value of friendship came up a lot, because my students had been ostracized by their peers for being labeled special ed. They had very few friends, if any. Selling was giving them a viable reason to reconnect with other teenagers and start conversations.

Every single one of my students also became friends with the wholesalers. If a kid was sick and missed our weekly trip, the wholesalers would ask me, "Where's Tyrone today?"

I thought it was beautiful that my students were connecting with these hardworking adults, who were wonderful role models. The wholesalers were primarily immigrants. They were bootstrapping entrepreneurs, operating in a neighborhood that was also plagued with drug dealing and gang activity.

I required each student to track their wholesale purchases and sales using the accounting ledgers in their briefcases. I was obsessive with my students about record keeping, because in actuality I am terrible at it.

I bragged to my students repeatedly: "I keep track of every cent I spend!"

That was one of the great fibs in the history of the world.

They eventually caught on that their teacher was somebody who was constantly struggling. I lost at least one thing a day—and still do! For a brief, glorious time, however, I had them convinced that I was a brilliant and consistent record keeper.

I was a stickler about making them keep accurate records for every item they bought at the wholesalers and every penny they earned. The students had one hour each Monday morning before our kaizen circle to use their records to create their weekly income statements.

"As entrepreneurs," I explained, "the income statement is your scorecard."

The wholesale price of the items the students were selling was listed on their income statements as "cost of goods sold." I encouraged the students to keystone, or double the price of their wholesale goods, to create their selling price. Cost of goods sold was then subtracted from the selling price to calculate gross profit.

A student's income statement might show $19 in sales, for example, with cost of goods sold of $8.50. Her gross profit, therefore, would be $10.50.

The students were also required to calculate return on investment (ROI) as a percentage, using the formula profit/investment × 100, or "What you made over what you paid." For the student with $19 in sales and $10.50 in gross profit, her ROI would be 55 percent. Not too shabby!

Watching kids who had been expelled and labeled special ed calculate return on investment every Monday was an exciting validation of my theory that entrepreneurship education could unlock the potential of at-risk youth.

In the kaizen circle, the students presented their income statements and reported on how their efforts to sell their products over the weekend had gone. We analyzed why some products had sold and some had not.

The kids were very good at sharing their ideas with each other and figuring out their markets. Honestly, I often sat there in awe of them.

Miguel had purchased a dozen chain necklaces that he had been unable to sell. He passed them around the circle.

"The clasp is too small," Anton pointed out, struggling to open it with his huge fingers.

Fashionable Estelle picked up one of the chains. Instead of struggling with the tiny clasp, she made a lariat knot in the chain when she put it around her neck.

"Just tell everybody this is the cool way to wear it," she told Miguel. "Like, you bought it downtown, and everybody downtown is wearing it this way."

Miguel nodded, smiling. The following week Miguel reported that he had sold out his new "cool" style.

My goal was for each of them to find their "self-seller." A self-seller, I explained, is a product so good that it sells itself. As General Motors founder William C. Durant famously said, "The secret of success is to have a self-seller, and if you don't have one, get one." Durant was from my hometown of Flint, Michigan, I told the class, and I shared his story.

From 1878 to 1886, Durant tried several careers, including selling insurance and real estate. Nothing really took off. The young entrepreneur had yet to find his self-seller. When he was twenty-five, however, Durant hitched a ride to work with a friend. He noticed that his friend's new horse-drawn buggy from Coldwater Road Cart Company rode more smoothly than any buggy Durant had ridden in before.

Durant's friend explained that the smooth ride was due to a new spring design. Durant was so impressed that he traveled to Coldwater, Michigan, the very next day to attempt to buy the design. The owner was willing to sell his buggy design for $1,500. Durant insisted that the deal include the patent for the springs.

When Durant made the deal, he didn't have $1,500, but he didn't let that stop him. Durant borrowed $2,000 from the Citizens National Bank in Flint and made two sample buggy carts. He demonstrated one cart at the Tri-State Fair in Madison, Wisconsin. Within a week, Durant had orders for six hundred buggy carts.

By 1893, Durant's original $2,000 investment had grown to $150,000. By 1901, his company was the biggest buggy manufacturer in the country.

In 1904, the Buick Company approached Durant about its still-experimental horseless carriage, the "Buick." Durant had a gut feeling that the Buick was another self-seller. At the 1905 auto show in New York, Durant "sold" 1,108 Buicks even though the company had only manufactured thirty-seven. By 1906, the Buick Company was worth $3 million.

In 1908, Durant bought Buick and several other automobile manufacturers. He gathered them under the name General Motors. General Motors was the world's largest automaker from 1931 through 2007—and it all started with a self-seller.

I should have remembered Durant's advice, I told my students, when I started selling products for my import-export business. One of the first products I tried to sell, I explained, was a bicycle lock from Taiwan. I was representing the lock exporter.

After many phone calls, I finally secured a meeting with an importer who would have ordered thousands of locks. My commission on the sale would have been $5,000 per month.

The importer picked up one of the locks and yanked it as hard as he could.

It broke, and I was shown the door.

The class found that story absolutely hilarious.

After several weeks of trial and error, many of the students had found their self-sellers. Ruben, for example, started a trend among his friends and classmates for funky patterned socks he bought for $3 per dozen from a wholesaler. Ruben sold the individual pairs for $2.50 each. This was tangible success and money in his pocket for a kid who had previously experienced very little of either.

Other students were still searching for their self-seller. Victor, for example, walked into three or four wholesale stores and came right back out.

"Why did you walk out?" I asked him.

"I can't sell that shit in the hood. It ain't in fashion," Victor replied.

Victor had a real knack for business. He understood that it didn't matter how cheap something was; if it wasn't on trend, he wasn't going to be able to sell it to his friends.

Finally, Victor found a wholesaler who was selling something that caught his eye: shearling sheepskin coats. These coats had become very popular in the rap scene. Eighties rap artists like

Run-DMC and the Fat Boys wore them with tracksuits, thick gold "dookie" chains, and Adidas "shelltoe" sneakers. Victor built up a good business buying sheepskin coats wholesale in midtown and selling them to B-boys in the South Bronx at a nice profit.

I saw a softer side of Victor emerge as he began to experience some legal business success. He was passionate about music and wanted to start a record label, perhaps even a clothing line.

"I feel like there's a bigger world out there beyond the South Bronx," he told me, as he shared these dreams, "and that I can be an entrepreneur and make a lot happen."

It was good to hear that Victor had a goal beyond the drug trade, which, frankly, offered no future beyond prison or death. I felt glad that exposure to entrepreneurship was helping him envision a better life.

In the 1980s, Midtown Manhattan was far safer than the South Bronx, but it was still more dangerous than it looked. I found out firsthand that tchotchkes were not the only things sold wholesale in the district. Massive drug deals went down there as well.

There were wholesale stores not only on the ground floors of the buildings but also on second and third floors. I sometimes took a few kids with me into the buildings to visit different kinds of businesses and meet the owners. Most store owners were very friendly to us.

One Friday afternoon, I was exploring the district with Victor and Miguel. We must have been near the border of the Diamond District, because I noticed one building had a sign for Diamond and Gold Jewelry "To the Trade" on the third floor.

We entered the building and rode a creaky old freight elevator up three flights. We walked down the hallway toward a door that

I assumed was the entrance to the wholesale fine-jewelry business. Without knocking, I opened the door.

Victor, Miguel, and I stood in the doorway gawping at glistening white bricks of cocaine neatly wrapped in plastic and stacked in pyramids on long wooden tables.

The street value of just one kilo of uncut coke at the time was around $20,000. We were looking at probably a million dollars in illegal drugs. Six or seven men were counting piles of cash. Black assault rifles were strewn on the tables.

Some of the men were speaking rapid-fire Spanish to each other; my best guess was that they were Colombian. Others looked to be West African and were murmuring in heavily accented pidgin English. The Colombians were dressed in dark trousers and linen *guayabera* shirts. The West Africans were wearing jeans and brightly colored dashikis.

An elegant Latino who reminded me of Omar Sharif stepped to us immediately and placed his assault rifle's barrel against Victor's temple.

I almost started crying. I knew the shot was going to blow through my head, as well, since I was standing next to Victor in the doorway, with Miguel to my left.

Thank God Miguel is short, I thought. The blast will miss him.

Then I realized they would never let Miguel live either. Not only was I going to die, I was getting two students killed because I stupidly walked through the wrong door.

As we already know, I am not cool under pressure. The moment that assault rifle went to Victor's head, I nearly lost control of my bowels.

Freaking Victor, though, was cool as a cucumber. He started chatting to these guys about *his* drug business!

"Yo, man, I'm a distributor up in the South Bronx, maybe y'all can be my new supplier!"

Victor was very picky about what he bought wholesale, so he was thrilled to have stumbled upon the distribution chain for some primo cocaine.

Miguel began babbling in Spanish.

I put my hands up.

Then, to my horror, Miguel took a step *toward* the dealers, waving his South Bronx Entrepreneurship business card in his plump little hand.

I reached out to grab him. To stop him from moving toward the men and the guns. Miguel dodged my grasp and took another earnest step toward his imminent demise.

Miguel was the sweetest kid in the world. He had suffered a lot in his young life, enduring multiple surgeries for his uneven legs. He had been bullied for being overweight and "slow."

I couldn't bear the thought of his life being over already.

But whatever Miguel said to the dealers, they started howling with laughter.

I mean, they were cracking *up*. They were wiping tears from their eyes. The handsome motherfucker holding the rifle against Victor's temple even lowered it a bit, he was laughing so hard.

"*¡Vámanos!*" somebody shouted, and we took off out the door and tore ass down the hallway.

As soon as we were safely inside the elevator, I turned to Miguel and asked, "What the *fuck* did you say to them?"

"I told them, 'We are on a class field trip!'" Miguel replied, with a big loving grin.

All three of us started cackling like hyenas at that.

When we were back out on the street and I could finally stop laughing, I said, "But Miguel, how did the Africans understand you?"

Miguel looked at me like I was a complete idiot.

"That's why I spoke in English, too, Mr. Mariotti!"

I never heard him speak in English. I had totally blanked out, I guess, from sheer terror.

CHAPTER 10

NOW FOR THE UPSELL

"Courage is fire, and bullying is smoke."
—Benjamin Disraeli, *Count Alarcos: A Tragedy* (1839)

Mariana had moved from her group home into a small apartment in the projects near 167th Street, a few blocks from the offsite program.

This was a very tough neighborhood, and I often worried about her living there alone. But with her puffy white parka and rhinestone buckle as her armor, Mariana passed safely to and fro each day.

When her social worker and I went to Mariana's apartment for dinner, I was amazed by how clean and organized it was. You could tell Mariana hadn't just cleaned up because her teacher was coming over. She cared about her home and kept it nice.

Mariana cooked delicious beans and rice for me and her social worker, accompanied by glasses of sticky-sweet neon-green soda. The social worker was there because it would not be okay for a male teacher to be unsupervised in the home of a female student.

As we walked back to the subway, I marveled at how well Mariana was taking care of herself. The social worker informed me that all my offsite students, including Mariana, were categorized as "disabled." This designation enabled them to receive Social Security disability benefits.

I did not believe Mariana or my other students were incapable of working, and I did not want to see them waste their lives in a welfare system that would never let them save enough money to rise out of poverty. I became very motivated to get all the students part-time jobs, so they could gain work experience and have a shot at not being dependent on disability checks for the rest of their lives.

Every day after class, I shepherded small groups from the class to Arthur Avenue, a busy Italian American thoroughfare in the Bronx lined with shops, restaurants, and markets. It took seven weeks of daily effort, but all the students got part-time jobs.

This wasn't entirely a success story, though. Some kids got into conflicts at their jobs or struggled due to learning issues.

Celia, for example, had difficulty with sequencing tasks. This is a common learning problem that was affecting her working memory and ability to recall information and actions in an effective order. As a result, Celia could not remember the steps for making a hamburger at McDonald's, no matter how she tried.

Celia was tall and skinny, with unusually long arms. Her hands dangled to her knees, and she had slightly webbed fingers, crowded teeth, and a concave chest. She was bullied relentlessly for her odd looks and spoke a bit haltingly due to a brain injury that had occurred at birth. Nonetheless, she was a sweet and funny girl. I knew she could succeed at something.

Making hamburgers was not it, however. The poor manager called me over three times.

Finally, I said to him, "Well, she does have a problem with sequential learning, so maybe that's why she's struggling with following the steps."

"Steve, why on earth didn't you tell me that?" the manager exclaimed. "I would have assigned her a different job."

He added Celia to the restaurant's cleaning crew. She did very well in that role and was able to keep her job.

That McDonald's manager taught me an important lesson I have never forgotten. You cannot cover up any actual disabilities that special ed children may have. Instead, you have to understand, and be honest about, their strengths and weaknesses. At the same time, having a disability does not necessarily mean that a person cannot work and be a wonderful contributing member of society.

Many of my students caught the work bug. They enjoyed earning money and feeling the sense of pride that having a job provides. I considered that real progress.

Thinking about Celia now, I believe she may have had a severe case of Marfan syndrome, a genetic disorder that affects the body's connective tissues, leading to unusually long limbs. An arm span longer than a person's height is considered a positive indicator of Marfan syndrome.

I wish I had known of this disease when I was Celia's teacher. I doubt she was being treated for it. With early diagnosis, medications, and careful monitoring, people with Marfan syndrome can achieve normal life spans. Without intervention, sadly, their life expectancy may only be around forty years due to the strain the disease places on heart valves and blood vessels.

Although Celia was succeeding at McDonald's, other students still mocked her relentlessly. They were merciless. Victor, for example, would bend his knees so deeply that his hands brushed his calves and stagger around imitating her.

One day, Victor came to class wearing fake arms from a Halloween costume with big floppy hands that hung down to his ankles. To her credit, even Celia laughed at how absurd he looked.

Celia's personal hygiene issues did not help matters. Her body odor was quite strong. The other kids held their noses when she walked by. They called her "monkey" and "gorilla." I got really fed up with their bullying.

One day I snapped, "You're all making fun of Celia, which I find to be inappropriate and cruel. But when we get on the special ed bus, you all lie down on the floor so nobody will see you. It looks like I'm the only one riding the special ed bus!"

They cracked up at that, of course. It was pretty funny, actually.

"Quiet!" I shouted. "But then you come in here and humiliate Celia," I continued. "How can you live with yourselves?"

The class fell silent. Victor and Earvin, two of Celia's biggest tormentors, stared at their sneakers.

I decided to bring in some Bibles and read short passages every morning to drive home to these teenagers the evils of bullying and the benefits of compassion. I agree with separation of church and state wholeheartedly. I knew I was not supposed to be reading from the Bible in a public school program, but I was desperate to stop this bullying of Celia. Most of my students had gone to church with a relative at least a few times, and some went every Sunday. I hoped that their familiarity with religion might work in my favor.

I rationalized once again that since we were not actually in a public school classroom, I could bend the rules.

I also taught the class the word "empathy" and explained what a valuable tool empathy is for the entrepreneur.

"You can't sell if you don't have empathy," I said. "As an entrepreneur, you must be able to empathize with your customers in order to figure out how your product or service can meet their needs. You must try to feel what they are feeling in order to approach them and pitch them effectively."

I broke it down in very simple terms: "If you do not cultivate empathy, you will not make any money with your business."

One day, I shared with the class that I was teased mercilessly in junior high school because I was smaller than the other kids my age.

"They called me Mouse," I told the class. "I couldn't stand it! That stupid nickname followed me to high school. My entire freshman year, everybody called me Mouse."

"Your voice does get kind of squeaky sometimes. Like, when you're mad!" Shana said. The class laughed.

"Yes, Shana, thank you ever so much for pointing that out," I replied sarcastically.

More laughter.

"So you can imagine how squeeeeaky I sounded when I was a freshman!" I said, playing along. Then I grew serious again: "That's why I know how awful it feels to be bullied—and why I want you to stop bullying each other."

"Did you ever get them to stop calling you Mouse?" Lamont asked.

"Um, yes, yes I did," I said, suddenly realizing that maybe this was not the best story I could have chosen to tell.

"How?" Lamont wanted to know.

"Ah, well . . . on my sixteenth birthday I decided to start

punching anyone who called me Mouse right in the nose," I admitted reluctantly.

"Oooh, Mr. Mariotti!" Estelle shouted. "Oooh, you got some hood in you!"

"That is not a course of action I am recommending to you!" I stated firmly, to more whoops and hollers from the class. "I got into several fights before the kids at my school finally stopped calling me Mouse."

"But they stopped, yo!" Lamont said.

"Yes," I winked, "they sure as hell did."

After we had been reading from the Bible and talking about empathy and compassion for a couple of weeks, I announced that we were going to create "personal balance sheets."

The students were already familiar with balance sheets. They knew that assets were listed on the left, balanced by liabilities and owner's equity on the right. Most of them could recite the balance sheet formula:

Assets = Liabilities + Owners' Equity

I handed out blank balance sheet forms and asked my pupils to write down their assets as a human being on the left, and their liabilities as a human being on the right. Next, I asked each student to stand in front of the class and read his or her assets out loud. I told them they could also read their liabilities if they wanted, but they did not have to do so. I felt very proud listening to them share assets they probably did not realize they had before entering this class.

Victor read from his list, "I'm funny. I'm smart. I'm good at understanding what my market will buy. I'm good at rapping."

Earvin said, "I work hard in class. My reading has improved a lot because I worked at it."

Celia murmured shyly, "I'm nice. I share my things with my sister. I like to work at my job and make money."

To my surprise, each student also chose to share his or her liabilities. And to my surprise, every child, except for Miguel and Celia, included "lack of empathy" as a liability.

Everybody loved Miguel because he was kind to everyone. He was extremely empathetic. When Miguel read his liabilities, he said, "I have a serious weight problem and one leg is six inches shorter than the other."

"Why is that leg shorter, Miguel?" I asked.

The story Miguel shared broke open our hearts. Miguel told us that he had been born with uneven legs. As a child this disability had caused him to break his shorter leg several times, making it even shorter each time it was surgically repaired.

"It kept snapping in the same place," Miguel told us, as we winced in response. He revealed that he had spent an entire year in a body cast that extended from his neck to his ankles. Miguel described in vivid detail how itchy and miserable that was.

He told us that he spent much of that year confined to a hospital bed near several other children in full-body casts. Rather than ask us to pity him, Miguel had us howling with laughter with tales of how late at night, when the nurses were half asleep, the body-cast kids played "roller derby."

"You rock side to side until you get your bed rolling on its wheels," Miguel explained. "Then you ram your bed into the other beds!"

When we finally stopped laughing, Miguel added somberly, "It's my worst nightmare to ever be in a cast again."

Miguel had been mocked and bullied by his classmates, too, but that day I saw tears in my students' eyes as he opened up so humbly about his suffering.

"Now that you know Miguel's story, and the importance of empathy, will you ever bully him again?" I asked.

Several students shook their heads no.

"Now what about Celia?" I asked. "Do you think you could work on your empathy and stop bullying her, too?"

Victor raised his hand.

"Yes, Victor?" I said.

"I would like to apologize to Celia for bullying her," he said quietly.

"That is wonderful, Victor!" I enthused. "Celia, is that all right with you?"

Celia nodded with a bashful smile. To my amazement, Victor went over to Celia and bent down to give her a hug as she sat in her chair.

With that, the entire room turned into some kind of revival meeting. Kids were crying and hugging and apologizing to each other. I was crying! That was the day we all became genuinely devoted to one another.

—————

Despite our newfound connection, however, it was not long before we had a frightening incident.

Guns were a constant presence in the South Bronx. I reminded the class regularly that a gun brought into our building would result in immediate expulsion, and that the police would be notified, without exception.

Any violence was grounds for expulsion, so I was startled one afternoon when Victor slammed his chair to the ground and lunged at Mateo, a thin Latino kid who had never seemed threatening or intimidating to me.

I charged in between Mateo and Victor and wrestled them into separate corners. I yelled at Mariana to run downstairs and get Malcolm the security guard.

I was furious at Victor, certain that he was the aggressor. He was hopping up and down in his corner, talking ninety miles a minute like he always did, pointing at Mateo and yelling, "Motherfucker, goddamn motherfucker, he got a fucking shotgun!"

Mateo was cursing, too, shouting, "Motherfucker, suck my dick, shut the fuck up!"

I had learned that such words are almost always said right before somebody gets killed. It was always "suck my dick" or "motherfucker." Those words mean, "I'm going to kill you."

I spun around on Victor.

"Shut up, Victor! If you continue to say that Mateo has a gun, the SWAT team will be here in no time. If you are lying, you will have committed perjury!"

That was a big rule in my classroom: no perjury. Most of my students had seen the inside of a courtroom and understood that perjury was a serious crime.

"I ain't lying, Mr. Mariotti! I ain't lying!"

I grabbed Victor by the arm and marched him into our lunchroom, which also served as our detention hall. He was still swearing and carrying on. I shoved him into the room, shouting, "Stay in there and do *not* come out!"

By this time, Malcolm had arrived on the scene. He frisked Mateo and found no weapons.

I was furious at Victor. I stormed back into the detention room and barked, "We didn't find a gun on Mateo! I need to know! Are you telling the truth?"

Victor yelled, "Yeah, motherfucker, I told you he got a sawed-off shotgun!"

"He doesn't have it. And don't call me motherfucker!" I snapped as I was about to slam the door shut.

"It was in his coat!" Victor shouted. "He put it in the fire escape."

I ran for the fire escape as though somebody's life depended on it. I was zooming around corners like the Tasmanian Devil in a Bugs Bunny cartoon. I got to the "Exit" sign and flung open the door. A beat-up sawed-off shotgun was leaning against the wall.

I was afraid to touch it. It looked like it could go off at the slightest provocation. I tore back to the typist room and searched for Miss Archibald. I grabbed her and told her to call the police and not let anyone near the fire escape.

I returned to the classroom and approached Mateo, who was cowering in the corner with Malcolm standing over him.

"Mateo," I said, "Victor has accused you of having a weapon, which is very, very serious."

Mateo started to cry. He admitted he brought the gun to school because he had been threatened by some Bloods on his way home the prior evening.

"Mateo, I'm sorry, but I have called the police," I told him.

That only made Mateo cry harder.

I felt terrible for him, but I said, "Mateo, you have to go with Malcolm down to the security office to wait for the police. I understand that you say you were threatened, but you can't bring a weapon into a classroom and around other innocent people."

Sadly, Mateo was expelled from the offsite program.

Not only was this incident a disaster for Mateo, it was a setback to my plan to get my offsite students back into Jane Addams, at least part-time.

I met with Pat Black regularly and kept her apprised of our progress. She agreed that if there were no more violent incidents going forward, in April we could make a presentation to her, Jane Addams's head of security, and the Bronx school-district superintendent.

This was hopeful news. Theoretically, every one of my students had now worked a job, although some had lost theirs or were hanging on by a thread. Every kid was selling a product and writing a business plan. They all could express positive, well-defined short- and long-term life goals.

All my students were in counseling for their emotional problems. I got to know their therapists well. One of them said to me, "Steve, whatever you're doing, keep it up. It's working."

The students had improved their reading, writing, math, and interpersonal skills significantly. I thought we could put together an impressive presentation and maybe, just maybe, get them back into school.

We worked hard on our presentation for a month—taping it, watching it back, tweaking it. Each student got two minutes to present a business plan and one minute to screen a videotaped commercial for his or her business.

Some of the students' ads were really funny. Miguel, for example, made a commercial for his business teaching English to people from Puerto Rico who had moved to New York—but he deliberately filmed the entire ad in very dramatic, over-the-top Spanish.

Maurice and Anton topped everyone, though, with their hilarious ad for a fake business called Camouflage Fashion Wear.

The video opened with Maurice speaking directly to the camera as he pimp-walked along 149th Street, one of the most dangerous blocks in Fort Apache. Maurice was decked out in a blue T-shirt, a blue baseball cap, and blue jeans. He leaned on a blue cane as he strutted and swaggered toward the camera.

Blue was the Crips' gang color. Crips was short for "cripple," because the Crips used canes as props for their exaggerated pimp-walk and dance moves. They also used their canes as weapons—smashing victims across the face, knocking out teeth and breaking noses.

The Crips originated in Southern California back in 1969. By the early 1980s, however, they were making significant inroads into the South Bronx, which was controlled by the Bloods. The Crips wanted a piece of the lucrative crack cocaine business run by the Bloods. Deadly turf wars broke out between the Crips and the Bloods, as their subgangs, called "sets," battled for control of crack and heroin distribution on every street corner and inside every housing project.

"Yo, man," Maurice said into the camera, "one of the most important decisions you're ever going to make is what gangbanging set you're going to join."

He put up one hand. "I know! It's a hard decision. Your parents, your friends, pushing you this way or that."

The camera panned up all six feet, two inches of Anton smoking a gigantic fake bong made of tinfoil. Anton was playing Maurice's dad and was decked out in a blue tracksuit.

"Son, what is your decision?" Anton demanded between tokes. He started beatboxing and rapping, "You gots to be a man! Make up your mind! Where you gonna go after special ed, the special special ed?"

The camera swung back to Maurice, who declared, "We all

have to be or not to be, and so I chose my father's path. I joined the Crips." He cracked a huge smile, showing off teeth he had stained blue by swigging some food coloring off camera.

"That way," Maurice said, "I have a better chance of getting into Sing Sing, not a second-rate max like Green Haven or Sullivan. Those are bullshit places where you learn nothing at all about advanced gangbanging. I chose the Crips—like many of you homies—to help build my résumé so I can achieve my long-term career goals.

"Now you know," Maurice continued, "joining the Crips is no joke because those damn Bloods will kill your ass if they see you wearing your colors or throwing up your signs." Maurice made the Crips' hand sign, curling his thumb toward his fingers to form a *C*. "We have to protect ourselves, which is why I developed Camouflage Fashion Wear."

Maurice stepped off camera for a moment and returned wearing a red T-shirt, a red cap, and red pants. The camera then pulled back to reveal Victor and Earvin, strutting toward Maurice decked out in head-to-toe red. All three hugged and displayed the Bloods' hand sign, curling their index and ring fingers toward their palms to create a *B*.

Maurice turned back to the camera and stage-whispered, "Now for the upsell." To Victor and Earvin, he said, "Yo, homies, check this!"

Maurice took two pairs of red sunglasses with red-tinted lenses out of his pocket.

"These will go perfect with your outfits. Man, you will be the first to be truly wearing *all* red—and protecting your eyes, too!"

The two "Bloods" eagerly bought the sunglasses for twenty dollars a pair. They swaggered down the block wearing their red sunglasses, laughing and high-fiving each other.

The camera closed back in on Maurice, who said, "Now for the fun part. Watch this, my Crip brothers." He quickly stepped off camera a second time. When he returned, he was wearing all blue again.

Maurice waved down Victor and Earvin and hollered, "Bloodies, look a-here!"

Victor and Earvin turned around and stared Maurice down for several seconds, long enough for viewers to think they were about to witness the beatdown of a Crip by two Bloods.

"Just want to invite you to my house this Sunday for cookout!" Maurice yelled.

"Sure, Blood!" Victor and Earvin shouted back. "See you there!"

They turned and swaggered off screen.

Maurice whirled back to the camera and donned a pair of red sunglasses.

"That's the kicker, yo," he said. "You can make real money selling these shades to other gangbangers, and they'll see *everything* as red!"

"To all you Crips and homies," Maurice declared, "visit Camouflage Fashion Wear and pick up a dozen pair of red sunglasses at wholesale price today. You will double your money selling to other gangsters, guaranteed, or I will give you your money back!"

Maurice grinned widely as the camera zoomed in on his blue teeth.

All kidding aside, my students had come up with a variety of interesting business plans. Earvin, who was obsessed with cars, wrote a plan for an auto repair business. It was likely the first time he had ever imagined a career for himself outside of mugging people and beating them up.

I found it very interesting that all my Latino students wrote plans for import/export businesses. They each strongly believed that their community would buy a type of food, or some article of clothing that they could import.

Ruben was from a town in Oaxaca, Mexico, where beautiful embroidered dresses were made and shipped all over Mexico. No one was bringing them to the United States, however. I figured he could buy the dresses for two or three dollars and sell them for ten.

"No," Ruben insisted when we were working on the financial projections for his business plan, "I can buy a dozen from Mexico for three dollars."

At the time, I didn't believe him, but Ruben was right. He knew his markets. The huge disparity in wages between Mexico and the United States devastated my hometown in 1985, when General Motors closed its Flint factories and shifted automobile production to Mexico, throwing thirty thousand people out of work.

On a rainy April day, the offsite class and I crammed into Pat Black's office at Jane Addams High to make our presentation. The burly head of security did not seem pleased to see us, but at least he was there.

Our presentation went extremely well. Pat, the school-district superintendent, and even the security director were impressed with the improvements my students displayed in reading, writing, math, and in their behavior and hygiene. I felt so proud of the class that I was trying not to well up with tears.

Nonetheless, the road was not entirely clear for the students to return to the school. Some were still selling drugs, and there was that incident with Mateo and the shotgun. I had also confided in Pat about the run-in with gang members on Victor's roof. She convinced me that we had to file a police report about it, although we were careful to impress upon the officer how much danger Victor and his parents would be in if the police were not extremely discreet.

Pat was fond of Victor, who had a special rap song he always burst into whenever he saw her. The song was titled "MissBlackStopFuckinWitMe!" but Victor spit the words out so fast that Pat never did understand what he was saying.

"That is so *good*, Victor!" Pat would always say. "You are so *talented*! Keep it up with your rapping!"

To this day, Pat still asks me, "What was that rap song about that Victor always sang when he saw me?"

"I have no idea!" I always respond.

Ultimately, the security director offered a compromise: I could bring eight students per day back into the school. They would be allowed to attend classes for three hours per day. They would also open and run the school store from 11 AM to 1:15 PM every day under my supervision. My para, Luisa, would run the classroom at the Department of Buildings when I was at Jane Addams.

I was satisfied with this compromise. My mission was to return these teens to normal life and help them build solid futures. Attending classes with their peers, even part-time, and working in the school store was a great start. The store was also the perfect lab for my ongoing exploration of the power of entrepreneurship education. I felt very excited for us to embark upon this new adventure.

CHAPTER 11

MRS. SPRATT

"There are two great days in a person's life—the day we are born and the day we discover why."
—Anonymous

The special ed department had always run the school store at Jane Addams, so I was quite familiar with it. I felt confident that my offsite students could run it very well, due to the real-world experience they now had in buying, selling, and keeping good records.

What I hadn't figured on was Mrs. Spratt, the school secretary, who sat right outside the school store in a cubicle. She was white, around fifty, with dark brunette hair. Like my supervisor, Marilyn Sanders, Mrs. Spratt was very slim and always impeccably dressed. She also shared Marilyn's mean streak.

At the end of each day's selling period, we counted up the school store inventory and turned over our accounting report and cash to Mrs. Spratt. Mrs. Spratt was incredibly rude to my students and refused to speak to me altogether. She was part of the cadre of teachers who had snickered at me during departmental meetings while Marilyn Sanders waved my stenography lessons around and made me feel like a dunce. These ladies thought they had gotten rid of me. Now, I was back, with troublesome students they thought they had gotten rid of, too.

To make matters worse, the South Bronx Entrepreneurship Education Program had received some exciting media attention. The *Daily News* ran an article about the program with a photo of me and some of my offsite students. We were also written up in the *New York Times*.

If these teachers had disliked me before, they *hated* me now. Returning was very awkward. It didn't help that their jobs were starting to become obsolete. Typing was being replaced by word processing. Stenography was fading away as computers entered the workplace.

Mrs. Spratt made me so nervous that I would send one of my students to give her the money and reports when we closed the store each day. Sometimes she didn't even speak to the child or say thank you. She would stick out her hand without looking up from her desk and snatch the cash and accounting report. She treated both me and my students with contempt bordering on hatred.

My students noticed right away that they weren't getting to keep any of the money they were earning at the school store. They wanted to go back to the wholesalers. I had a mini-revolt on my hands.

"Look," I told them, "sometimes you have to make compromises to achieve greater goals—such as graduating from high school. This is also giving you work experience you can put on your résumés to get better jobs. I want you to get a taste not only of business ownership, but also of what it's like to work for someone else."

I approached Pat about starting a profit-sharing program for the students who worked in the school store. After all, they had a point. They were doing all the selling and pocketing none of the profit. Unfortunately, Pat told me there was no way she could authorize this.

I was left to wonder once again: Why don't our public schools teach our low-income youth how to earn money? We fail to do so, then we imprison them if they resort to drug-dealing, robbery, or prostitution.

The school store was a terrific lab for my class, though. By observing the students interacting in a working environment, I discovered new things about them.

Miguel, for example, adamantly refused to wait on customers, so his job was to advertise the store and clean it. I thought perhaps Miguel was embarrassed about his weight, or about the platform shoe he wore to compensate for his shorter leg.

One afternoon, a teacher walked into our store and bought five steno pads at eighty-five cents each. Only Miguel and I were standing by the store counter. Miguel knew our policy was to avoid making customers wait, so he reluctantly handed the steno pads to the teacher.

I watched Miguel fill out the sales slip. He began to fidget.

"What's wrong?" I asked.

"Nothing," he muttered, dropping his pen on the ground. Miguel picked up the pen and stood up, turning toward me.

"Mr. Mariotti, can I talk to you?"

"Sure," I said.

Miguel walked over to me. "I can't multiply," he whispered.

"What?" I exclaimed, taken aback. I knew Miguel was a bit slow at math, but I had never noticed that he could not multiply.

We walked back to our customer together, and I completed the sales slip.

After the teacher left, I said, "Miguel, you have to learn to multiply. If you can't multiply, people will think you're dumb and you won't be able to function in most jobs."

Miguel looked like he was going to cry.

"Hey," I reassured him quickly, "I have my faults, too."

Miguel smiled and said, "Yes, I know. You're untidy."

"Yes, yes, I am. Now, why can't you multiply?"

"I don't know," Miguel replied, looking genuinely perplexed. "Nobody ever showed me."

"Oh, come on!" I exclaimed. "Really?"

"Really, word up!" Miguel declared.

Learning is like a big pyramid of building blocks. For the learning disabled, some blocks near the bottom of the pyramid are missing. All the other blocks that would normally fall into place are either left out entirely, or are shoved in wrong.

Before I could help Miguel, I needed to determine which blocks he was missing. First, I had him try to multiply 696 × 24.

"I can't do this," he mumbled, but I forced him to try. I had to figure out if he didn't know his times tables or if he didn't understand how to carry numbers.

Sure enough, Miguel could put the numbers in the right places, but they were always the wrong numbers. He understood the mechanics of carrying numbers, but it was clear that he didn't know the multiplication table. Instead, he was trying to calculate 4 × 6, for example, by adding up four six times in his head. That is why it took him forever to solve a math problem.

I was so excited for him. Dear Miguel, I can get you out of

special ed. All it takes is three hours of memorization and you will be free.

I wrote out the times table: $1 \times 1 = ?$, $1 \times 2 = ?$, etc.

Miguel watched me intently. "I never seen this before," he muttered.

"Okay, let's see what you can do," I said, pushing the long rows of numbers over to him.

Miguel leaned on the glass counter, his legs dangling in the air. He began solving the problems. Up to $5 \times 5 = 25$, he was perfect. But the sixes were a disaster. As soon as he hit $6 \times 3 = 18$, Miguel was completely lost.

Miguel was missing some fundamental blocks way down at the base of the math pyramid. What person could multiply without having memorized the multiplication table?

I wrote out the rest of the sixes:

$6 \times 4 = 24$
$6 \times 5 = 30$
$6 \times 6 = 36$
$6 \times 7 = 42$
$6 \times 8 = 48$
$6 \times 9 = 54$
$6 \times 10 = 60$

I pushed the piece of paper in front of Miguel and said, "Take ten minutes to memorize this."

Miguel stared intently at the numbers in front of him. He grimaced and squirmed and trembled. All the while, he remained perched on the counter, his round stomach squashed almost flat, his feet off the floor. It must have been a comical sight: Miguel trying as hard as he could to memorize the sixes, and me rocking back and forth in front of him, my eye twitching, my shirt half untucked.

There is no way I can accurately describe my intensity. I was on the verge of complete success as a teacher, about to raise the math level of a special ed kid by six years in one lesson. Miguel must have sensed my overeagerness because he started to twitch, too. He totally lost his concentration.

I resorted to bribery.

"Miguel, close your eyes. I'll give you fifty cents if you can get the sixes correct."

He recited them correctly, except for 6 × 8, which we ignored. I placed two quarters on the counter with a satisfying *click, click.*

Miguel stood up, stuck out his chest, and announced, "I don't need no money, Mr. M, for learning what I should already know."

I felt embarrassed. Miguel saved me by picking up the quarters and putting them in his pocket. "But it is very nice," he added with a bright smile.

"Here's another fifty cents to memorize the sevens," I said, reaching into my pocket. I was warming to my role as briber.

"No," Miguel stated firmly.

"Look at it this way," I argued. "All I care about is showing that I can teach a kid with a learning problem how to multiply."

Miguel thought for a moment, and then he said, "Mr. Mariotti, you keep your money. I'll learn it just because I should. Then you can say you taught it fair and square."

I almost fainted. How could anyone think this young man was dumb?

We were solving problems inside the school store, but we had not made a dent in the Mrs. Spratt issue. I did not want her treating my students poorly for one more day.

Back at our DOB classroom, I called a kaizen meeting.

I told the students, "I've got a serious issue, and I'll tell you what it is. I don't have tenure, which means I can be fired at any time."

Mariana piped up, "Is that why you got sent home four times last year?"

Nothing got past them.

"Yes, Mariana, that is why. I was sent home because I'm not a good typing teacher. And no matter how I try, I just can't learn stenography. Plus, I'm not organized and I talk to myself. In the teacher meetings, I tend to daydream and not pay attention."

"We know all that about you," Anton said.

The other students nodded. Truthfully, many of them could outperform me in a business environment, and I thought it was good for them to know that.

"We need to find a way to turn this situation with Mrs. Spratt around," I continued. "Can you help me?"

We spent an hour talking about it and came up with a strategy. I had learned that her birthday was coming up in a week. We decided to throw her a surprise birthday party.

"Okay," I said. "I'll get a nice cake and some ice cream. What should we get her for a present?"

"She loves that skinny pen," Estelle observed.

Mrs. Spratt was indeed obsessed with her long, thin calligraphy pen, which she dipped into an inkwell on her desk. Her penmanship was beautiful, and she used her calligraphy pen to handwrite memos to the other teachers. Mrs. Spratt had mentioned in a meeting that she had always wanted to be an artist, and her memos really were works of art. When she was writing them, she had a dreamy half smile on her face and almost looked pleasant.

"Great!" I exclaimed. "We'll get her one of those!" The students each chipped in a dollar. I went to a stationery store and bought her a lovely calligraphy pen for around twenty-five dollars.

I also visited my buddy Larry Stanton, the printer, and had him print this on the front of a pretty blue T-shirt:

Mrs. Spratt
Vice President of Finance
Jane Addams High School Store

The morning of Mrs. Spratt's birthday, eight students and I arrived early to set up her surprise party. We put her cake and present in the school store and arranged some decorations. Soon we heard the brisk click of Mrs. Spratt's heels on the linoleum. Per usual, she marched straight toward her desk without acknowledging me or the students.

I nudged Ruben and whispered, "You're on."

Ruben was the one student in our program that Mrs. Spratt almost liked. Ruben was openly gay and obsessed with fashion. He was short, with caramel skin and jet-black hair he wore swept up in a pompadour. Ruben knew how to sew, and tailored the sleek shirts and high-waisted trousers he favored so that they fit him beautifully. He always looked very elegant.

In short, Ruben was the antithesis of my rumpled, messy self, so Mrs. Spratt tolerated him. Since she refused to speak to me, it fell to Ruben to turn the school store's earnings in to her each day. Sometimes, I would actually hear them chatting.

One afternoon, I heard Ruben and Mrs. Spratt laughing hysterically. Ruben called out, "Mr. Mariotti, you gotta come see this!"

I was so scared of Mrs. Spratt that I felt nervous, wondering, "Is this a trap?" That woman never laughed. I could only imagine that if she were laughing now, it had to be at my expense.

All the other kids dropped what they were doing in the store and trailed after me. They were apparently very curious to see how any interaction between Mrs. Spratt and me might turn out.

Ruben and Mrs. Spratt were standing near the window behind her cubicle giggling up a storm. We huddled in behind them and peered out the window, too.

Down on the street, a drunk man was urinating onto the school building at length, blissfully unaware that from all four stories of the school, students and teachers were looking out the window at him. There must have been three hundred people watching him pee while he swayed back and forth, trying to not fall over.

He was so indifferent to this fact that we all burst out laughing. Howls of laughter echoed throughout the school.

That was the only time I ever heard Mrs. Spratt laugh.

———

On her birthday, Ruben's job was to lure Mrs. Spratt into the school store. I poked my head around the corner to watch the action.

Ruben entered her cubicle and said, in his most charming voice, "Mrs. Spratt, I've got a question about how to do the accounting for a returned item. Could you please come into the store to help me?"

"Oh, all right," Mrs. Spratt huffed with an exasperated sigh. She pushed away from her desk and followed Ruben into the store with an exceptionally crabby look on her face.

Miguel and Anton had attached a huge rolled-up banner above the door to the store. As soon as Mrs. Spratt walked in, they released it. The banner read "Happy Birthday" and, as soon as it came down, we all started singing, "Happy birthday to you!"

Mrs. Spratt looked utterly gobsmacked.

Ruben picked up the sheet cake off the store display counter and carried it over to Mrs. Spratt. Her name was written on the thick white icing in blue curlicue frosting.

When we stopped singing, Ruben motioned to Mrs. Spratt to blow out the candles on the cake, which she did. We all clapped and cheered.

Then Ruben announced: "Mr. Mariotti would like to say a few words."

"Happy birthday, Mrs. Spratt!" I cried. "I would like to thank you for being our treasurer. We wouldn't be able to run the school store without you. We've all learned so much about accounting from you. I've personally learned a great deal from you!"

I handed Mrs. Spratt the T-shirt and her birthday present, and added, "We want you to have these gifts to show our appreciation for what a great executive you've been."

When Mrs. Spratt unwrapped her present and saw her beautiful new pen, she started to cry.

From that moment on, Mrs. Spratt was our biggest advocate. She even began standing up for me in our staff meetings. Mrs. Spratt told the other teachers how well my class and I were running the store, and what good work I was doing with the special ed students. Eventually, in large part thanks to Mrs. Spratt, the other teachers in our department began to be kinder to me and smile and greet me in the hallways—even Marilyn Sanders.

Ten years after I left Jane Addams High, I ran into Mrs. Spratt on 8th Street in the West Village one Saturday afternoon. She was carrying a bunch of shopping bags and was wearing khaki trousers, loafers, a navy blazer—and the T-shirt we had given her for her birthday.

"Judy!" I called as I rushed toward her.

"Oh my goodness, Steve Mariotti!" she replied with a genuinely happy smile. Then she looked down at her shirt.

"I didn't even realize I had this T-shirt on," she harrumphed. "I don't think of it as a special T-shirt!"

That was the kind of person Mrs. Spratt was—and always would be.

It moved me so much that she had kept our gift all those years that I gave her a big hug anyway, and she just had to deal with it.

CHAPTER 12

TOUGH LIKE A MOTHER

"Under certain circumstances, urgent circumstances, desperate circumstances, profanity provides a relief denied even to prayer."
—MARK TWAIN, *Mark Twain, A Biography* (1912)

C.J. Meenan was the Pied Piper of Jane Addams High. Students literally followed this lanky, long-haired teacher in droves down the hall shouting his name. That was how I met him.

I had been teaching at Jane Addams for about a week when one afternoon I heard loud chanting coming from the hallway. I poked my head out of my classroom. A tall white guy in a suit was walking backward down the hall, waving his arms as if he were a conductor

179

and the fifteen teenagers following him shouting "C.J.! C.J.! C.J.!" were his orchestra. His feathered sandy-blond hair, which made him look like the singer for a seventies soft-rock band, only added to the theatricality of the moment.

I sought him out in the teacher's lounge the next day. I had to know his story.

C.J. told me he was the son of the maintenance engineer at Jane Addams. His mother was a secretary in the maintenance department. C.J. had grown up in New Jersey, though. He went to a Catholic high school that was always nationally ranked number one or two in football. C.J. told me the happiest day of his life was the first day of football practice because he got injured, and the trainer told him, "I hate to break this to you. You can't play football."

"I turned away and pretended to cry—like Danny DeVito—and he bought it!" C.J. told me, flashing his mischievous grin.

C.J. brought that same irreverent attitude to teaching, and it made him very effective. He was also very compassionate toward his students. He taught me to listen to students and find out what was going on in their personal lives. That was often the key to helping them do better in school, he explained.

I shared with C.J. my experience that exposing low-income students to entrepreneurship motivated them to do better in school. With Pat Black's blessing, we started an after-school club called the "South Bronx Entrepreneurship Club," with an especially vibrant and charismatic special ed teacher named Juan Casimiro. Juan, C.J., and I became great friends. When I left Jane Addams to teach the offsite program at the Department of Buildings—which I dubbed the South Bronx Entrepreneurship Education Program—Juan and C.J. kept the after-school club going.

Once I was able to get my DOB students back into Jane Addams part-time, I strongly encouraged them to join the South Bronx Entrepreneurship Club, and many of them did. The club started racking up some exciting success stories.

Isabel, for example, began a business buying lingerie wholesale and selling it to her friends and family members. She made $10,000 in revenue in one year. Previously, Isabel admitted to me, she had been selling crack after school for one of her drug-dealing cousins.

"I'm making more money now, Mr. Mariotti," Isabel told me, "and I don't have to always be watching my back. I don't feel ashamed no more."

That spring, the South Bronx Entrepreneurship Club held our first business plan competition. We invited local entrepreneurs and community leaders to be our judges. Each student had ten minutes to present a business plan to the judges. This doubled as a great opportunity to introduce students to potential mentors.

A student named Harold, for example, met an attorney who shepherded him through the process of getting a food cart license from the city. Harry's Hot Dogs sold hot dogs every weekend near Yankee Stadium. Harold eventually won a four-year college scholarship to the culinary program at Johnson & Wales in Rhode Island.

José won the business plan competition with a brilliantly simple business called José's Oil Change. José's father owned a garage, and José had become an expert at oil changes. His business plan included a contract for José's Oil Change to handle all the oil changes at his father's garage. José's father also agreed to let José subcontract to provide oil changes for other garages in the neighborhood.

José was very smart and had taken to entrepreneurship like a fish to water. He was incredibly polite and kind. He knew how to listen to others and was ambitious. José had a gift for accounting, as well. At the South Bronx Entrepreneurship Club, we used single-entry bookkeeping, but José taught himself double-entry bookkeeping. I had never seen anyone do that. I believed he would become a successful businessman and a real asset to his community.

José was named South Bronx Entrepreneur of the Year at an award ceremony in the Jane Addams classroom where the Entrepreneurship Club met after school. José looked so thrilled to receive his plaque. He was eager to rush downtown to show it to some friends.

That was the last time we ever saw him.

After the ceremony, José hopped the 4 train from the South Bronx to 14th Street–Union Square. He was climbing the steep stairs from the subway platform to the street, clutching his award, when a pack of teens he didn't know began taunting him about it.

They shoved him.

José tumbled down the stairs. He hit his head and died before the paramedics arrived.

Our entire school was stunned by this news. Children were crying in the hallways. I felt absolutely devastated. I had to force myself not to think about José's callous, pointless murder so as not to be totally destroyed.

In December, we lost another wonderful member of the South Bronx Entrepreneurship Club.

Diego wanted to be a hairdresser. Exposure to entrepreneurship had really gotten Diego fired up about school and encouraged him to dream of a bright future. Due to significant improvement in his once-sullen demeanor and poor reading skills, he had managed to work his way back into Pat Black's good graces and be readmitted into the cosmetology department at Jane Addams.

His dream, Diego told me, was to open the first unisex salon in his neighborhood. "If I can have both male and female customers, I'll have more business and make more money, right Mr. Mariotti?" he said.

Diego was Cuban. He was very handsome and always well-dressed. He wasn't gay, but because of his good looks and his passion for hairstyling, people often assumed that he was. To counter that impression, Diego spoke in a very deep voice. He sounded like Ricardo Montalbán, which was pretty funny, to be honest.

I was so proud of Diego's newfound ambition to become a salon owner. He was on his way to creating a good life for himself. C.J., Juan, and I couldn't wait to follow his journey into adulthood and help him however we possibly could.

One brisk winter afternoon, Diego walked out of Jane Addams and stepped on a young man's foot by accident in front of the man's girlfriend. The man, we found out later, was twenty-three and had just been released from prison. That is an especially dangerous time to run into an ex-con, who is likely to still be on a hair trigger.

The young man took out a knife and slammed it into Diego's chest. Witnesses said the attacker and his girlfriend kept on walking, as if nothing had happened.

Diego bled out on the frozen sidewalk.

My heart broke all over again. I became so depressed that I could barely pry myself off the sofa in my cold apartment in the mornings to go to work. I couldn't find any reason to go on teaching if the good kids, the ones who were learning and growing and eager to succeed, were being murdered.

How could we give awards to our students if they were going to be murdered for walking around with them? How could we encourage them to believe in their futures if an innocent misstep could cost them their lives?

I was seriously considering leaving teaching and moving out

of New York City. I couldn't see the point of staying where the best and brightest of my students were being slaughtered. Yet, I had come to love teaching so much and felt deeply committed to my students. I couldn't go but I wasn't sure I wanted to stay.

I felt agonized. I was in limbo.

Desperate, I booked an appointment with Dr. Ellis, whose "We will flood your fear out of existence forever!" advice had gotten me into this terrible situation in the first place.

"Steve, you can't shove this pain away," he told me. "If you do, you'll stay stuck in this depression, and you'll probably never teach again. You've got to feel the pain."

I didn't want to feel the pain. I didn't want to cry anymore, but that evening I did. I sobbed, and then I beat the crap out of my already beat-up couch. Because after I cried, I got very, very angry.

Once my emotional storm had passed, I became hyper-motivated to do whatever I could to save these children from such horrible fates. I thought about this constantly on my subway rides to and from the South Bronx, and while working and eating dinner at West 4th Street Saloon.

We were graduating maybe ninety teens per year from the South Bronx Entrepreneurship Club at Jane Addams. At this rate, we were never going to make a dent in the soul-crushing poverty and mortal danger millions of low-income youth lived with every day in the United States.

The problem was deeply entrenched and monstrously over-whelming. But my murdered students had made me tough like a motherfucker. They had given me a steel-like resolve to do some-thing significant to help solve it.

It was becoming clear to me that my mission was not merely to teach in the inner city but to teach entrepreneurship there. I believed entrepreneurship education was the key to unlocking the tremendous potential of low-income youth. I also believed that every new legal business opened in a low-income community could help inoculate it against the lure of the illegal drug trade and the scourge of gang-fueled violence.

Unfortunately, the school system didn't embrace my beliefs, despite the evidence I was accumulating that introducing low-income teens to entrepreneurship lit a fire for learning and achievement inside them. The school system's attitude was underscored when an evaluator came to observe my DOB classroom. Pat Black shared the evaluator's report with me. It said my class had "excessive role playing," "too much emphasis on business," and was "too money oriented."

I was sick to death of fighting this mentality. But the report got me thinking: Was there some way outside the school system that I could provide entrepreneurship education to more teens?

A few weeks later, I was eating a burger at the bar at West 4th Street Saloon when I overheard a young investment banker next to me bitching to the bartender about the noise in his hip East Village neighborhood.

"I feel you!" I said, nudging him. "That's why I come here to work!"

He laughed, since the dinnertime volume at the Saloon was beginning to reach a dull roar. We got to talking, and I told him about the South Bronx Entrepreneurship Club, the South Bronx Entrepreneurship Education Program, and how much my students loved learning about small business.

"I need to raise some money!" I shouted. "Have you got any ideas? Are there any companies on Wall Street that contribute to public school programs like mine?"

We were overheard by a fifty-something gentleman standing behind me trying to order a drink. He tapped me on the shoulder.

"You need to start a foundation!" he yelled over the din, add-ing, "I'm a lawyer! I specialize in five oh one see threes!"

"What are those?" I yelled back.

"Come to my office, I'll show you!" he replied, handing me his business card.

His name was Mark Beneson. Mark was short and stocky, with a full head of thick brown hair and tons of energy. I learned during our brief conversation at the bar that his specialty was Second Amend-ment cases and that he considered himself a proud "gun nut."

Mark invited me to his office on Third Avenue and 42nd Street, two blocks from Grand Central Station. I showed up on time for our appointment and was ushered into Mark's office by his secre-tary. It was snowing outside and I was wearing tennis shoes, which were soaked. I must have looked a mess.

Mark was on the phone. He looked up from his desk and glared at me as I dripped melting snow onto his carpet. I stood there awk-wardly while he finished his conversation.

When he hung up the phone, he said, "Why are *you* here?"

"I . . . I thought we had an appointment," I stammered.

"We do not! I am very busy!" Mark snapped.

I apologized and fled his office, feeling extremely discouraged. I trudged down the hallway in my soggy shoes and pushed the ele-vator button. Suddenly, I heard footsteps behind me. It was Mark, running toward me.

Just then the elevator door opened. Mark slammed his arm in front of me to keep me from entering it. For a moment, I thought he was going to beat me up!

"Steve!" Mark panted. "I am so sorry, our appointment *was* for today. I got confused." He escorted me back to his office.

Mark told me I should start a nonprofit foundation to bring entrepreneurship education to low-income youth. He gave me a crash course in how nonprofits operate, explaining that I would be able to use 501(c)(3) tax-exempt status to raise money from donors and build a board of advisors who would help me.

I was thrilled by this idea! I raced home and called Janet. She thought it was a great idea, too. I also talked to C.J. and Juan and got them on board. We couldn't wait to get started.

With my usual flair for the written language, I dubbed my nonprofit the National Foundation for Teaching Entrepreneurship to Handicapped and Disadvantaged Youth—NFTEHDY for short. It was clunky as hell, but I couldn't think of anything smoother that expressed my mission.

A few days later, I was telling my offsite class about my new venture, and sharing with them what I had learned about how 501(c)(3) corporations operate. I wrote the full name of my foundation on the board and began to underline the first letters of each word.

As I was about to underline the H for Handicapped, Shana called out, "Nifty! Just call it Nifty!"

That is how the National Foundation for Teaching Entrepreneurship—or NFTE, pronounced "nifty"—became my organization's original name.

For three months, without ever charging me a dime, Mark helped me with my application to the IRS for 501(c)(3) nonprofit status. When the application was finally up to Mark's exacting standards, we mailed it off to the IRS. I was so excited!

When the first rejection letter arrived from the IRS, Mark called me down to his office. He looked genuinely puzzled as he read the brief, formal rejection letter out loud to me.

"I have never seen this before," he muttered.

I had my own thoughts about what might be going on, but I kept my mouth shut.

Mark immediately got on the phone to the IRS. They told him they would review my application again in six weeks, provided that we made some minor changes involving formatting and reference information. We made the recommended changes and sent the application in again. In two weeks, not six, we received another rejection letter citing more minor issues with our application.

Mark called the IRS and got some input. We edited the application to address the objections and sent it in again. We revised and resubmitted NFTE's application for nonprofit status five times. Each time we received a polite rejection letter from the IRS.

With each rejection, Mark became angrier. By the fifth rejection, he was furious. With me in his office, he called the IRS and demanded to speak to the legal department. Mark paced the floor, working through a series of holds until he got the second-highest lawyer in the IRS legal department on the phone. Then Mark dressed down that IRS lawyer like I had never heard anybody dressed down before.

"I have filed countless successful applications for nonprofit status!" Mark yelled. "This is the only application I have ever seen rejected FIVE TIMES. What the hell is going on?!"

Wow, it's good to have a lawyer, I thought. Mark made Marilyn Sanders sound like a lightweight.

"I have *no* problem bringing suit at this point!" Mark roared.

The IRS lawyer said he would look into the matter and get right back to us.

Mark hung up and flopped down into his cushy leather desk chair. He made a temple with his fingers and lightly tapped them together, musing, "Who do I know at the IRS? Who do I know at the IRS?"

I piped up, "I know somebody at the IRS!"

Mark peered at me quizzically over his bifocals.

"Who the hell do you know at the IRS, Steve?" he said.

It turns out the guy I knew was actually in *charge* of the IRS. I had no idea! Acting IRS Commissioner James Owens was a libertarian free-enterprise advocate from Alabama whom I had met at a conference a few years prior. I warned Mark that he was barely an acquaintance—but I did have his business card in my wallet.

"We are going to call him right now," Mark insisted, handing me the phone. "Call him and don't stop until you get him on the line. Be firm and don't give up. But be nice, especially to his secretary."

To my surprise, I was able to talk to James Owens. I reminded him where we had met, gave him a ten-second pitch for NFTE, and explained that we were having a difficult time obtaining nonprofit status from the IRS.

Commissioner Owens said he would look into it. I felt hopeful that with him on my side this problem would be resolved.

Meanwhile, I learned some disturbing news from a counselor. Earvin had gotten Shana pregnant. She was only sixteen. I was very upset to hear this—and surprised, because there was no love lost between the two of them. I was also pretty sure that Shana was gay.

Earvin was harassing Shana, making it clear that he did not want her to have the baby. At the DOB classroom one day, I was horrified to see Earvin hand Shana a coat hanger and say, "Don't you have to go to the bathroom?" I was furious with Earvin and told him that he was no longer allowed to speak to her.

Shana had really fallen in love with buying and selling. She was paying much better attention in class, as a result. Previously recorded as an "apathetic" student who skipped classes in favor of partying on the streets, Shana was attending class every single day.

She also loved working in the school store. Entrepreneurship lessons were really working for her.

I was concerned about what this pregnancy was going to do to Shana's future. I spoke with Pat Black, who got Shana admitted into a class at Jane Addams for pregnant teens. Shana would be able to attend this program with her baby, increasing her odds of still being able to graduate.

I was not happy with Earvin, though. Worse, every time he walked by me, he socked me on the shoulder. I invariably flinched and he would laugh. His "playful" punches hurt and were getting annoying. The next day, when he raised his arm to punch me in the shoulder, I ducked.

"What the hell are you doing?" I yelled. "Cut it out!"

"You're a pussy," Earvin sneered.

"*What* did you say?" I bristled.

"You act like a bitch. Like you want it up the ass."

"What?! What are you talking about?"

"Your voice, you sound weak. Like a white boy. Next time don't flinch."

It dawned on me that, in some clumsy way, Earvin was trying to teach me something. The next day, when Earvin gave me his usual greeting, I forced myself not to flinch.

"That's better!" he declared, sounding amazed.

"Thanks!" I said.

"You didn't flinch."

"I know. I forced myself not to."

"I can't believe it," Earvin exclaimed. "You're the first white boy that don't."

"Oh yeah?" I replied. "Is that good?"

"Fuck yeah, it is. It'll save you here, man. Can't be no wimp here. It's the South Bronx. You gots to be tough. If you act like a pussy, they'll kill you. They love to see fear. Love it. It's like blood. You act tough, Mr. M, and you'll be safe."

Earvin pulled up his sleeve and showed me three stab wounds on his forearm. He pointed to the dark purple scar closest to his elbow and said, "After this one, I learned not to flinch."

Earvin pretended to hit me one more time. I flinched.

"Try it again," he encouraged me.

Earvin swung at me. I forced myself to remain still.

"You're learning, man," Earvin said, patting me on the back.

Unfortunately, I found out that Earvin was beating up students and forcing them to give him their money. I read him the riot act to stop his bullying, but it was clear from their ongoing anxious reactions to him that he was still harassing them.

Outside the school store one day, I overheard Earvin calling Miguel names and pushing him around. As I was running in to stop this, I saw Earvin slap Miguel in the face. I also saw brave little Miguel stand up to Earvin, yelling, "You are just a bully!"

I barged in and confronted Earvin: "I will be honest with you, Earvin. Miguel is right! You're just a bully and a hoodlum. I am fed up with your behavior. You're banished from the school store and from Jane Addams!"

To my astonishment, big tough Earvin started to cry.

"Miguel is the one who should be crying, not you!" I shouted.

I took Earvin aside and demanded, "Why the hell are you crying?"

"I've been bullied every day of my life," he sobbed.

"That can't possibly be true!" I said, still steamed. I remembered what C.J. always said, though: "Listen, and find out what's going on at home."

So, although I really wanted Earvin out of my sight, I marched him into an office. We talked for two and a half hours.

Earvin took me through a typical week at his home. His older brothers, who had done time for armed robbery and murder, made him wait on them hand and foot and beat him up every single day, several times a day. Earvin told me that he couldn't walk more than a yard without getting socked hard in the arm. That was where he had learned that behavior.

I asked him, "How do they speak to you, like, 'Earvin, could you get me a sandwich?'"

Earvin burst out laughing. "Nah, Mr. M," he replied. "It's more like, 'Get me a fucking sandwich, you fucking motherfucker!'"

The worst part, Earvin told me, was that the beatings were treated by his brothers as a joke. His mother, therefore, did not take him seriously when he tried to complain to her.

"I can't fight back, because it's all one big joke," Earvin sighed.

I decided to go to Earvin's apartment in the projects for dinner to meet his family. I brought Kentucky Fried Chicken at Earvin's request.

The moment I met the two brothers, who were in their late twenties, I understood what Earvin was going through. When they walked into the living room and looked me up and down, appraising me coolly without a flicker of interest in me as a human being in their eyes, every muscle in my body tensed. I felt horrible fear and wanted to leave. I was afraid that I was being set up, with Earvin as bait, for the brothers to beat me up and rob me.

Earvin's mother was very nice, but it was clear that she was in denial. She doted on her older sons. Her live-in boyfriend, on the other hand, seemed as afraid of the young men as Earvin was. If I had to live with the brothers, I would be terrified, too. I looked at Earvin and he looked at me and saw that I understood. We bonded deeply in that moment.

Dinner was fine, partly because the brothers took their meals and left to go eat in their rooms. The rest of us sat at the table and had a nice conversation.

I hated leaving Earvin there. The next day, I called his therapist and the assistant principal at Jane Addams to tell them what I had observed.

Earvin only had a few months to go until graduation. I could only hope that what he was learning about entrepreneurship would help him to earn a living and get the hell out of that apartment.

After our dinner, Earvin chilled out on harassing the other kids. He also appointed himself my bodyguard.

I needed to rent an office for my nonprofit to make it look more legit to the IRS. I saw an ad for an office on 149th Street and Third Avenue for fifty bucks a month. The price was right, so I asked my class, "What's the safest route from Jane Addams to 149th and Third?"

"You can't walk down there, Mr. M, it's too dangerous!" Earvin blurted out.

"In broad daylight?" I scoffed. "Really?"

"That's a killing zone," Earvin said firmly.

He insisted on accompanying me on the twenty-minute walk from Jane Addams to 149th and Third that afternoon. The office was no bigger than a broom closet and up several flights of creaky stairs, but it still made me feel really good to rent it. I was one step closer to having a real nonprofit business.

Shortly thereafter, I heard from Mike Hennessy, the COO of

Fannie May Confections, that he was taking me up on my invitation to visit the South Bronx Entrepreneurship Education Program at the Department of Buildings. I had met Mike at the Association of Collegiate Entrepreneurs (ACE) conference run by Verne Harnish, which I attended every year. Mike was very supportive of what I was doing. I was praying that he would become the first donor to my foundation.

I was very pleased when Mike accepted my invitation to observe my offsite class. He also attended a meeting of the after-school club. After the meeting, I walked him down to my new office. We were accompanied by Earvin and Anton, our bodyguards for the afternoon. Earvin could not have behaved better. He was polite and professional with Mike, like a junior executive. I was so proud of him.

Unfortunately, when we arrived at my office building, I could not get the rusty old front door open. Even Anton couldn't get it open. I felt so embarrassed.

Mike decided not to fund me at that time, which was no surprise given that I couldn't open the door to my own office. But a week later, a hundred boxes of Fannie May chocolates arrived at the DOB classroom for the students to sell.

I was touched by Mike's gesture. Some of the students did very well selling their boxes. Shana, in particular, sold quite a few. Selling is hard, though. Most of the boxes remained stacked in our classroom closet. And we all know how devilishly tempting chocolate can be.

One afternoon, I broke out a box to share with the students after they had been exceptionally good. Oh my God, those chocolates were delicious. The sugar ripped into our veins like crack. After we tore through that box, I went into the closet and brought out another one. The joy of unlimited chocolate overtook us all!

I ate an entire box myself. I think each kid ate an entire box as well. All I can say in my defense is I was thin back then and not so aware of the evils of sugar as I am today.

After that, we were hooked. For the next four days, we held a candy-eating contest at 2 PM each day to see who could eat an entire box the fastest. It was a remarkably effective way to motivate the students to work hard and stay focused all day.

On the fourth afternoon after the chocolates had arrived, a bunch of students were looking at themselves in the mirror that leaned against one of our classroom walls. They were laughing hysterically.

"What's so funny?" I asked. They turned toward me, and their cheeks, noses, and chins were smeared with chocolate. I couldn't help it—I started laughing, too.

"Look at you!" Mariana shouted.

I pushed my way in between them so I could see myself in the mirror.

"Oh geez," I muttered.

My face was covered in chocolate, too.

I ran to the bathroom and grabbed some paper towels so we could clean ourselves up.

This was truly not one of my finer moments as a teacher. Several kids threw up. By the fifth day, we couldn't even look at a box of Fannie May chocolates.

The madness had passed.

CHAPTER 13

SCOTT LA ROCK

"I came with Scott La Rock to express one thing. I am a teacher and others are kings."
—Boogie Down Productions, "South Bronx" (1987)

Several weeks had gone by and, despite Commissioner Owens's promise to look into my 501(c)(3) application, Mark and I had heard nothing from the IRS.

We were sitting in Mark's office, racking our brains about how to solve this problem, when I said, "Hey, do you think Jack Kemp could help us? I know him pretty well."

Mark peered at me quizzically over his bifocals once again. "How the hell do you know Jack Kemp?" he asked.

In 1987, Jack Kemp was the Republican congressman for New

York's 31st congressional district. The district included Buffalo, where Kemp had been a quarterback for the Buffalo Bills.

At the same conference where I had met James Owens, I also ran into legendary economist Milton Friedman. Thirteen years prior, I had been his bag carrier at an event at Hillsdale College in Hillsdale, Michigan. As a twenty-one-year-old econ nerd, the excitement I felt upon meeting my hero was no doubt akin to what meeting Mick Jagger would be like for a normal person. To my amazement, when I reintroduced myself to Dr. Friedman at the conference, he actually remembered me.

After that, I wrote a letter to Dr. Friedman once a year. When I wrote to him that I was teaching low-income youth in New York City about free enterprise, he offered to write a letter of introduction for me to Jack Kemp.

When Congressman Kemp and I first spoke on the phone, he expressed great interest in the fact that I was teaching entrepreneurship to South Bronx teenagers. He wanted to know what life was like for my students in the projects and what challenges they faced. He invited me to visit him at his office in DC, where we spoke for two hours.

Congressman Kemp consistently polled very well in the African American community. Although I didn't know it at the time, he was gearing up for his 1988 presidential bid. That may have spurred his interest in my perspective. Jack told me that he strongly believed in encouraging small-business-formation rates among minorities in order to fight poverty.

Jack invited me to call him anytime, and we spoke often. During one phone call, he asked, "What's the most important thing you're teaching?"

"Vision," I replied. "I'm teaching my students to develop a positive vision for their futures."

"Yes," Jack agreed, "but what I think is equally important is grit. You're teaching grit, tenacity, and a positive attitude. That's all you really need to succeed."

Today, "grit" is a huge buzzword in entrepreneurship research, but Jack Kemp was the first person I heard use it to describe the intangible asset that so many of my low-income students displayed.

I once met someone at a party who was on the Buffalo Bills football team with Jack. "Why was Jack such a successful quarterback?" I asked. I was curious because people used to say that Jack didn't have tons of natural athletic ability, yet he led Buffalo to three consecutive Eastern Division titles and two AFL championships.

"He was tough," Jack's former teammate responded.

"What do you mean?" I wanted to know.

"When you were on the field with him, he would get massacred, but he'd get right back up without showing the agony he just went through," the ex-football player explained. "We were always so inspired by that. And he was never critical. He would never get angry. He was like Joe Montana—same kind of personality and leadership."

That is the kind of leader I want to be, I thought.

———————————

"Good God, Steve!" Mark exclaimed after I told him all this. "Let's call Jack immediately!"

I dialed Jack's office. His secretary told me that he was out but could call us back around 4 PM.

The only time I ever heard Jack get mad was when Mark and I were on speakerphone with the congressman, describing the IRS's ongoing refusal to approve my foundation's nonprofit status. Jack was furious.

"Do not worry," he declared forcefully. "I will take care of this."

Two days later, Mark received a call from Commissioner Owens's secretary, inviting Mark to IRS headquarters in DC to present our case in person. Unfortunately, Mark had to be in court on the day the IRS had offered, so he called me up and told me I would have to go.

"You can do this, Steve," he said. "Dress nicely, speak clearly, shake hands, and look them in the eye."

I was familiar with that advice. I gave it to my students all the time. I borrowed money from Janet to pay for a bus ticket and a new suit.

The Internal Revenue Service Building at 1111 Constitution Avenue NW looked like the grandest post office I had ever seen—on steroids. It was a limestone behemoth, decorated with twenty-four colossal stone columns stretching from the third to the sixth floor. The New York Stock Exchange could probably have fit into its lobby.

Looking up at the massive building I was about to enter, I felt like a speck. I began climbing the wide granite stairs to the entrance, trying not to sweat through my suit in the July heat.

After going through security, I was directed to an office on the fifth floor. There, a secretary ushered me into a rectangular, windowless conference room dominated by a long white table with gray chairs placed neatly around it. I didn't know whether to sit or stand, so I stood, waiting, trying not to bite my nails to the quick.

Within a few minutes, six male IRS agents entered the room, accompanied by a female stenographer. The agents were all white, with tightly cropped haircuts bordering on buzz cuts. They wore crisp white shirts, black or gray suits, and polished black shoes.

I shook their hands firmly and looked each agent in the eye

with what I hoped was a confident but not overeager smile. I prayed the diesel fumes from the bus were no longer clinging to my clothes.

One agent gave my hand a kind squeeze and whispered under his breath, "I'm with you." The others, however, seemed rather chilly, and their greetings were perfunctory.

I stood at the front of the room, practicing my deep breathing, as the agents arranged themselves around the table. As soon as they were seated, I launched into my well-rehearsed pitch. One agent raised a hand to stop me.

"We are familiar with your application, Mr. Mariotti," he stated. "However, this program is aimed at teaching urban minority youth to become better businesspeople. The drug industry is killing the inner cities. We cannot approve a program to train minority youth to become more efficient businesspeople so that they can improve the drug industry."

I knew it.

This was what I had suspected all along. Their reasoning could not have been more racist.

I felt the maddest I have ever been in my life. I grabbed the conference table's edge as hard as I could with both hands to steady myself. I thought of my students and forced myself to keep my cool.

If Victor could laugh while being swung from the roof of his housing project by brutal gang members—if he could say, "That felt good, can you hit me again?"—then surely I could handle six IRS agents who were unlikely to murder me.

If Miguel could charm drug kingpins out of shooting us after we had barged into their midtown safe house, then surely I could convince these dweebs to hand over my nonprofit status.

I also realized that I had failed to adequately explain my mission. That was on me.

"Gentleman," I began, with more resolve than I had ever felt in my life, "I understand your concern. What my proposed foundation offers to the inner city is a compelling alternative to the drug industry. The after-school program we are developing will not merely keep low-income youth off the streets and give them something to do. It will provide them with the knowledge, tools, mentoring, and capital to start their own legal businesses. This will reduce the lure of the drug industry to them."

I didn't give the agents a chance to respond. I was armed with statistics and I was going to use them. I plunged ahead.

"According to Drug Enforcement Administration statistics, the average age of arrest for drug traffickers in 1986 was thirty-five," I continued, "so we have a real chance with teenagers to intervene and teach them how to enter our economy legally. If we do not, I can guarantee you that drug dealers will be happy to teach them how to enter the black market."

One of the IRS agents snorted. "Come on, they won't start businesses!"

"You're right," I agreed. "I estimate that only one in twenty will, but one in twenty is more than double the current two percent business formation rate in the black community."

I saw a couple of agents nod thoughtfully. Maybe I was getting through to them. I swiftly added, "Teaching low-income youth about entrepreneurship also makes them more employable. Imagine hiring a young person who already knows how to read an income statement!"

I dug into my briefcase and pulled out spiral-bound copies of the textbook on entrepreneurship that I had been writing all summer. I passed them around the room.

"Here are my lessons on costs of goods sold, the economics of one unit, return on investment, financial statements," I said. "Imagine two teenagers go on a job interview. One understands and can intelligently discuss all these concepts. The other has never heard of them. Which one would you hire?

"We're talking about making our inner-city youth financially literate so that they can enter our economy legitimately," I concluded, adding firmly, "I can't think of a better way to fight the drug trade."

"Well," said the agent who had been friendly to me, "this certainly gives us a different perspective."

I searched the other agents' impassive faces for a clue to my dream's fate.

"Give us a minute, would you please, Mr. Mariotti?" the agent who had initially interrupted my pitch requested.

"Of course," I replied, gathering up my briefcase and exiting the room. I stood outside the conference room door with my heart pounding, praying my ass off.

Finally, the door opened, and I was motioned inside.

"Congratulations, Mr. Mariotti," the lead agent said, with a polite smile, as he extended his hand for me to shake. "Your non-profit status is approved."

I felt ecstatic on the five-hour Greyhound bus ride back to the filthy Port Authority bus terminal in New York City. Neither diesel exhaust nor the Cheetos breath and rank BO of my seatmate could bring me down. I was the proud owner of a newly minted nonprofit foundation. I was determined to make José and Diego's murders count for something.

The IRS meeting was also my first valuable lesson in how to run a nonprofit: always try to get face-to-face meetings, and always explain NFTE's mission clearly and very positively.

When I got home, I called Jack Kemp's office. He was not in, but his secretary was delighted by the good news. She promised to share it with him.

"Please tell him thank you," I said, "and remind him: Grit! Tenacity! Vision!"

That evening, Jack called and left a voicemail congratulating me and laughing about the message I had given his secretary.

"Now, get this right, Steve," the congressman added solemnly. "Get this right."

Jack's admonition got me thinking: Who might be able to help me get NFTE right?

It was a muggy August afternoon. The air in the East Village was thick as pea soup. Classes did not start until September 8. I had nothing to do but brainstorm.

As I sat sweating in front of my window fan, I thumbed through the grimy index cards in my desktop Rolodex. I started thinking about all the potential donors and advisors I had met since I began teaching.

I first began inviting leaders in the community to speak to my classes at Boys and Girls High in Bed-Stuy in 1982, partly to give myself a break. When a guest came to visit, the students behaved much better, for starters.

One of my first guest speakers was Dan Simmons. He was the older brother of Russell Simmons, who founded Def Jam Recordings in 1983, and Joseph Simmons, a.k.a. "Reverend Run" in the rap group Run-DMC.

Dan was a successful abstract-expressionist painter before his brothers ever became famous. I met him at a church event in Bed-Stuy when I was teaching at Boys and Girls High. Both his parents had been schoolteachers in Hollis, Queens, and Dan had a great deal of respect for educators. To stay in touch, Dan and I had lunch once a year. I made a note to contact him about NFTE.

I knew many business leaders and politicians in the South Bronx because we invited them to Jane Addams to judge our South Bronx Entrepreneurship Club business plan competitions. Pat Black loved that we were networking with the community and bringing wonderful role models to the school to interact with students.

Former Manhattan borough president Percy Sutton spoke to the South Bronx Entrepreneurship Club four times, for example. Percy was also an entrepreneur, heavily invested in the *New York Amsterdam News* and the Apollo Theater. He shared many inspiring stories with the students about being a black politician and entrepreneur in New York City.

Percy's friend David Dinkins was a guest speaker several times, as well. David was one of fifty African American investors who helped Percy found Inner City Broadcasting Corporation in 1971. That was how our pool of guest speakers expanded: a guest speaker would rave to a friend about our program and soon we would hear from a new volunteer.

David Dinkins spoke to students while he was serving as city clerk and again as Manhattan borough president. This was before he became New York City's first African American mayor in 1989. David was always so nice; I knew he would love to hear about NFTE.

Even though I was sweating my face off in my crappy apartment, I started smiling. I had the beginnings of a donor list and advisory board for my nonprofit.

I also thought about the hip-hop artists from the South Bronx who had come to speak to my students and might want to get involved with NFTE. One hip-hop luminary stood out in particular, since he was the first I ever invited to speak to my students in Fort Apache: Scott La Rock of Boogie Down Productions.

Boogie Down Productions was a groundbreaking hip-hop group. La Rock was the DJ, KRS-One was the lyricist and rapper, and D-Nice was the MC. They released their first album, *Criminal Minded*, on B-Boy Records March 3, 1987. The album's single "South Bronx" was the hit of the sticky summer of 1987, blasting from boom boxes and open car windows across New York City.

> *Yo what's up Blastmaster KRS One, this jam is kicking*
> *Word, yo, what up D-Nice?*
> *Yo, what's up Scott La Rock?*
>
> *Yo man we chilling just funky fresh jam*
> *I want to tell you a little something about us*
> *We're the Boogie Down Productions crew*
> *And due to the fact that no one else out there knew*
> *What time it was*
> *We have to tell you a little story about where we come from*
> *South Bronx, the South South Bronx*

When I met Scott, though, he wasn't a star yet. He was a social worker in his early twenties named Scott Monroe Sterling who worked at the Franklin Armory Men's Shelter near Jane Addams. He called me up one day because he had heard about the South Bronx Entrepreneurship Club from some students.

"I'm going to be an entrepreneur," Scott stated, with a nice mix of confidence and humility in his voice.

"That's great!" I enthused. "What's your background?"

Scott told me that he had recently graduated from a college

in Vermont. "But I'm from this neighborhood, the South Bronx," he said. "I'm a social worker and I'm also a hip-hop artist. I deejay every night."

I was not familiar yet with the term "hip-hop," although I knew about rap. I thought Scott had said "bebop."

"You mean, like jazz?" I asked him.

Scott laughed, "Naw!"

"What have you learned about entrepreneurship from being a social worker?" I asked, eager to scoot past my ignorance.

"I've learned to listen," Scott replied.

With that, I invited him to speak to my students, because we were working on active listening as a vital component of selling. I was trying to impress upon the students the value of listening to potential customers—rather than just launching into a sales pitch—in order to discover their needs and sell to them effectively.

Scott came and talked to both the South Bronx Entrepreneurship Club and my DOB class. He was perfect because he had made it to college, yet had decided to return to the hood to build his business.

Standing six foot two, Scott was conservatively dressed and clean-cut, but he had tons of charisma and South Bronx edge. The students loved him immediately.

Scott told us that he had met his business partner, Lawrence "Krisna" Parker, at Franklin Men's Shelter, where Kris was living. Kris's graffiti tag was KRS-One, which stood for Knowledge Reigns Supreme Over Nearly Everyone. Scott said he and Kris had formed a business they called Boogie Down Productions (BDP for short) with Derrick "D-Nice" Jones, a cousin of the shelter's security guard.

In our classroom, Scott drew the BDP organizational chart on the board and explained the different functions that he, Kris, and Derrick were each responsible for in the company.

"We're making an album," Scott declared.

Now that I understood that hip-hop was a new form of music, I was fascinated by what Scott had to say, and even more curious about my students, who seemed to know all about it.

Scott asked the class an interesting question: "Do you think there's a big market for hip-hop?"

"Yeah!" Victor exclaimed. "This is gonna be a huge industry 'cause white people are gonna love it!"

"Nah! You're crazy!" all the other kids disagreed.

But Scott replied, "I think you're right, Victor. They've picked up a lot of other kinds of music from our culture. Why not hip-hop?"

"Isn't hip-hop just a fad, though?" I asked. I had read that in the *New York Times* or something.

Anton, who almost never spoke up in class, declared in his deep baritone, "It ain't no fad! My pops listens to it every night. My mom listens to it all the time!"

"This is a new industry," Scott agreed. "The sky's the limit!"

Scott visited our classroom every couple of months. Each time he came, he had made progress in his career, which was great for my students to see. There was no lesson plan better than for them to observe a young South Bronx entrepreneur building his business.

First, Scott would bring them up to date on Boogie Down Productions. Then, my students would show him how their business plans were progressing. They would share their experiences buying and selling, and marketing their businesses. At the end of Scott's visit, he would always rap for the kids. They accompanied him by beatboxing and drumming on our tables. It was awesome!

Thanks to Scott, I learned how important hip-hop was to my students, and we got to meet other legendary hip-hop artists. As the MC and front man for Grandmaster Flash and the Furious Five, Melle Mel was a pioneer in taking rap from party music to powerful poetry that accurately reflected the desperation and intensity of life on the streets of New York City. Melle Mel came to speak to the South Bronx Entrepreneurship Club. He blew us away not only with his bodybuilder's physique but also with his super-positive attitude and entrepreneurial spirit.

Everybody in the club, including myself, could recite Melle Mel's famous hook from the group's iconic 1982 Sugar Hill Records single, "The Message":

Don't push me, 'cause I'm close to the edge
I'm trying not to lose my head.

We learned that Grandmaster Flash got his start performing in the park on Tinton Avenue and 166th Street, just three blocks north of Jane Addams. He used to run electricity to his speakers from the park bathrooms with an extension cord. I was very impressed with how hardworking and entrepreneurial these rappers were. My students started to think that I was almost cool.

One day, Scott brought some album cover mock-ups to show the class.

"Our album is going to be released in March," he announced. The class cheered.

"Thank you!" Scott said. "We're calling it *Criminal Minded*. Check these covers out and let me know which ones you like best. You guys are my focus group!"

Nearly everyone voted for the album cover that showed Kris and Scott posing with guns, ammunition belts, and a grenade. Only Miguel and I voted against it. As a devout Jehovah's Witness, Miguel was very outspoken against any violent lyrics and imagery in hip-hop. (Victor was a Jehovah's Witness, too. He never missed temple on Sunday. I could never figure that one out.)

"I don't think you should be showing guns when we have too many guns in this neighborhood," Miguel stated.

"I hear you, Miguel," Scott replied earnestly, "I really do. We live with constant gun violence and gangbanging here in the South Bronx. We ain't trying to look gangsta on the cover. We took this pose from some old Black Panther posters. Kris with the ammo belt over his shoulder, grenades on the table—that's a paramilitary revolutionary. We're depicting ourselves as revolutionaries, ready to teach and preach."

Miguel nodded slowly.

Scott was such a positive guy. I wanted his album cover to reflect that, but I also had to admit that he and Kris knew their market far better than I did. As I had always preached to my students, "Your comparative advantage is that you have unique knowledge of your market." Scott and Kris had to use their album cover to capture their market's attention in a big way if they had any hope of being heard.

Scott told the class that he and Kris were mixing a song for the album "to raise the morale of the South Bronx."

One of the students said, "Call it 'Fort Apache'!"

"Yeah, but Fort Apache is negative," Scott responded. "South Bronx ain't!"

The rest is hip-hop history. *Criminal Minded* went gold and eventually made *Rolling Stone*'s list of the five hundred most influential albums of all time.

"South Bronx" was on the radio constantly that summer. Even my friends at West 4th Street Saloon were rocking to it. The fact that I knew Scott La Rock enhanced my cred downtown, too.

Boogie Down Productions was poised to sign a major recording contract with Warner Bros. Records. We were all very excited for Scott and couldn't wait to have him come visit our class in

September and bring us up to date. I was also really looking forward to sharing my vision for NFTE with him.

Throughout that summer, Scott was in touch with Victor, who was working part-time for BDP. Scott was a very positive influence on Victor, and Victor was thrilled to be assisting him in the studio and helping out with marketing. It was Victor who called to tell me that Scott had been shot.

At first, I couldn't make out what Victor was saying. He was talking so fast that I couldn't understand a word, and he kept putting the phone down. I could hear him yelling, "Fuck! Fuck! Fuck!"

Finally, Victor shouted, "It's La Rock, Mr. Mariotti, they shot him! Fuck them fucking motherfuckers, fuck them to hell!"

Scott died on August 27, 1987, at age twenty-five, leaving behind his fiancée and their infant son.

Even though school was not starting for two more weeks, Victor insisted that we gather at the DOB classroom to memorialize Scott. I didn't know how I was going to get permission for this, but I couldn't say no to Victor, who was crazy with grief. My students and I were devastated, even more so when we began to piece together what had happened.

Ever the peacemaker, Scott had been shot while attempting to mediate a dispute between D-Nice and some guys who had jumped D-Nice the previous evening for flirting with one of their ex-girlfriends.

Scott, his manager Scotty "Manager Moe" Morris, and their friend Darryl, a.k.a. "Robocop," drove to the South Bronx in a Jeep Wrangler to help D-Nice find the crew that had assaulted him and negotiate a truce. D-Nice, who later discovered and mentored Kid Rock, finally opened up about the incident on *The Combat Jack*

Show in 2014, saying, "It was really a mission of, like, some peaceful shit. It became violent because of one individual."

Outside a housing project called Highbridge Garden Homes, Robocop, who was six foot five, got into an argument with a member of the crew that had jumped D-Nice. Robocop picked the guy up and body slammed him to the ground.

When someone began shooting at them from an apartment window, Scott and his friends piled into their Jeep to escape. They were speeding away when Scott grabbed his neck and fell forward, his head hitting the dashboard.

Scott's friends raced him to Lincoln Hospital, less than a mile away. Scott was conscious and talking to the doctors when he was brought into the ER. The doctors thought the bullet had merely nicked his neck but they transferred Scott to Misericordia Hospital, an acute-care center twenty minutes north, for exploratory surgery as a precautionary measure. Robocop and D-Nice went to a nearby diner to wait for him to come out of surgery.

Scott died in the operating room. The bullet had penetrated his brain.

I reached out to Miss Archibald, our champion at the Department of Buildings. She arranged for us to be let into our classroom to memorialize Scott.

The afternoon of Scott's memorial, the room quickly filled with teenagers from Jane Addams High. Tears were streaming down their faces. We handed out votive candles and flowers. The kids covered all the chalkboards and whiteboards with messages like "God Bless Scott La Rock" and "South Bronx, South Bronx."

Scott's murder galvanized the African American community in the South Bronx. It was all I heard about for at least six months.

People were extremely upset. They were fed up with the awful violence that plagued their community, destroying their best and brightest.

Scott's partner KRS-One founded the Stop the Violence movement to honor Scott and a young BDP fan who had been killed at a show. KRS-One, D-Nice, and Hank Shocklee also produced the chart-topping twelve-inch single "Self Destruction," featuring many East Coast hip-hop stars, and donated the proceeds to the National Urban League.

The *New York Times* eulogized Scott La Rock with the article "Violent Death Halts Rap Musician's Rise," in which Franklin Men's Shelter director Joseph Eady noted that Scott was not only an up-and-coming hip-hop star but also a wonderful social worker.

"He had a tremendous impact," Joseph said. "He was able to rekindle the hope of those who had lost all hope."

CHAPTER 14

IT'S NOT ABOUT YOU

"Believe in yourself. Believe in your dreams. If you don't, who will?"
—JON BON JOVI

Due to Scott La Rock's horrific murder, the fall semester began on a somber note. But when the IRS letter affirming NFTE's status as a nonprofit corporation finally arrived in the mail in September, I allowed myself to feel a spark of joy.

I believed NFTE was an opportunity to make all these tragic deaths stand for something. Perhaps someday, in some small way, my foundation would help prevent more senseless murders of talented, hardworking young people in low-income communities.

Over the next few weeks, my joy was slowly subsumed by worry. I was the proud founder of a newly minted, yet entirely unfunded, nonprofit. How the heck was I going to raise money?

My students gave me the answer.

One day, I brought several copies of *Current Biography* magazine into the DOB classroom. *Current Biography*, I explained to the class, is published monthly (except in December) right here in the Bronx by the H.W. Wilson Company.

Current Biography provides lively profiles of stars of government, industry, entertainment, and the arts from the United States and around the world. Included are mailing addresses for the offices of some of the most famous people in the world.

"You are going to write a business letter to the famous person you admire most," I announced. "You will be asking for advice and mentorship for your student business."

My students went nuts. They were enormously excited to learn that contacting a famous person is not that hard, once you've learned how. Excited shouts of "Where's Eddie Murphy?" "Where's Diana Ross?" "Where's Rocky?" filled our classroom.

I helped them find addresses for their favorite celebrities and provided envelopes and stamps. None of my students knew how to address an envelope, so I showed them how to do that, as well. I was always glad when an assignment illuminated more life skills they lacked, so we could remedy the situation.

My reward was that I got to read their letters. It is a common complaint that high school students cannot write, yet the letters I read were beautiful.

Celia, who couldn't remember how to assemble a hamburger, produced a two-page letter to Diana Ross asking for advice on how to master the craft of singing. Celia wanted to start a business giving vocal lessons. Ross wrote her a detailed, absolutely lovely letter back. Celia was on cloud nine.

About a tenth of the letters we sent out received personal responses. The people—Ross, Jimmy Carter, Sylvester Stallone, Judy Blume, and Dionne Warwick, to name a few—who had the kindness to answer a letter from a South Bronx teenager will be remembered with gratitude for a very long time. I had those letters framed for the students.

One Monday, Celia asked me who my hero was and if I had written my hero a letter.

That was when it hit me. I needed to find a hero for NFTE.

After school that day, I rode the 4 express train from the Bronx to Grand Central Station at 42nd and Park Avenue. Then I walked west to the New York Public Library on 42nd and Fifth Avenue. I was on the hunt for the *Forbes* 400 list.

The *Forbes* 400, or more accurately, "400 Richest Americans," is a feature published every September in *Forbes* magazine that lists the four hundred wealthiest US residents, ranked by net worth. Malcolm Forbes began publishing the list annually in 1982.

The library didn't have the latest *Forbes*, so I went to a newsstand on a nearby corner. It was early October and, sure enough, the newsstand had the "400 Richest Americans" issue. I bought the expensive, glossy magazine and scurried down to West 4th Street Saloon with my prize.

I spent the next four afternoons poring over the *Forbes* 400 while stuffing my face with popcorn, searching for my hero. I was looking for someone who had experienced what it was like to grow up poor, had made money through entrepreneurship, and was now philanthropic. I wanted someone, ideally, who had been raised in a tough urban environment and knew what it was like to grow up fearing for your life on a daily basis.

I started reading every bio of the four hundred millionaires and billionaires on the list, but nobody jumped out at me as the hero who might be willing to fund my mission to bring entrepreneurship education to low-income youth. Nonetheless, I highlighted seventeen people whom I thought might possibly take interest in NFTE.

On Friday, I was reading the last few bios on the last page of the *Forbes* 400 list when I needed a bathroom break. I pushed back from my table with a sigh, groaning a bit as I pried myself out of my chair. I was feeling very discouraged. I had read almost four hundred bios of wealthy people yet had not found anyone who fit my criteria.

When I returned to my table, I noticed, to my surprise, that someone or something had turned the magazine's page. I looked around, but I did not see Janet, Edie, or any other friends nearby who might have been curious about what I was doing. Had a gust of wind come through the door and ruffled the pages? I didn't think so because I always sat away from the door to avoid drafts, as my asthma made me prone to bronchitis.

Regardless, I was looking down at a new page, and on that page was an article titled "Those Who Dropped Off the *Forbes* 400." It was a list of multimillionaires who had dropped off the *Forbes* 400 list only due to their philanthropy.

The bio for one of them, Ray Chambers, said he had grown up in Newark, New Jersey, and was focused on helping low-income children. My skin prickled. I knew immediately that he was my hero.

I remember reading Ray's bio like it was yesterday. The more I read about Ray, the more certain I became that he would understand NFTE's mission and want to fund it.

From Ray's photo, I could see that he was handsome in a patrician way. He looked like a movie star typecast to play millionaires.

According to Ray's bio, though, he had been born and raised in Newark's West Ward. This was a more prosperous area than some neighborhoods in Newark, but it was still a crime-ridden, rough place. I knew Ray would understand the challenges of growing up in a violent urban environment.

It also caught my attention that Ray had been an entrepreneur in high school and college. He started his band, the Accidentals, in high school with four Italian American buddies. They worked their way through college by playing gigs together. Ray was the singer.

After graduating from West Side High School, Ray earned a degree in accounting from Rutgers. He worked as an accountant after college for about a year before becoming president of a small company in Florida. Ray did well in Florida, earning enough money to move to Morristown, New Jersey, and join the exclusive Morristown Club, a stately brick townhouse where the elite met to dine and schedule their golf dates. There, Ray met William E. Simon, the former treasury secretary under President Gerald Ford.

Bill Simon was a tall, ruddy Irishman who wore huge Buddy Holly glasses and was widely regarded as a tough SOB. The *Wall Street Journal* once ran a hit piece on him that outlined how mean he was to his Secret Service detail—making them wait outside in the heat for hours without offering them any water, for example. He had been Nixon's energy czar back in the 1970s. After Nixon resigned, Ford appointed Simon to head the Department of the Treasury.

Bill and Ray formed Wesray Capital Corporation—"Wes" stood for Bill's initials—in 1981. In 1982, Wesray became one of the first companies to use a leveraged buyout model when it acquired Gibson Greetings Cards for $80 million. Bill and Ray put up around $330,000 each and paid the rest of the $80 million purchase price with bank loans, using Gibson Greetings Cards itself as collateral.

This was a hugely risky move, but it paid off fantastically well. When Wesray took Gibson Greetings Cards public two years later, the company was valued at $290 million. Bill and Ray personally netted approximately $70 million each.

Suddenly, Ray from Newark was a multimillionaire.

Wesray moved into a small abandoned synagogue on South Street in Morristown. The company made forty-five similar deals in the 1980s, earning an estimated four billion dollars with only eight employees. Ray spearheaded the 1985 purchase and resale of Avis Rent a Car, for example, which netted a profit of $740 million on Wesray's $10 million capital outlay.

By the time I was reading about Ray Chambers in *Forbes*, he was worth around $200 million. And he was deeply devoted to philanthropy.

It took me two weeks to draft and type my fundraising letter to Ray Chambers because I felt very nervous about it. I wanted it to be perfect.

Sitting at my favorite table in West 4th Street Saloon, I read the letter yet again. I couldn't find any errors so I signed it. At the bottom of the letter, I added a handwritten note, doing my best to keep my writing legible:

> *PS: Eager to hear your stories about your entrepreneurial adventure with the Accidentals, hope to see you soon.*

I folded my letter to Ray, put it in a stamped envelope, licked the strips, and sealed it shut.

When I closed my eyes for a moment to say a prayer, I slipped into an extraordinarily calm state that I had never experienced before. I can only describe it as a moment of zen. In this deeply relaxed state, I witnessed my future unfurling before my mind's eye. Each year, each decade, like a movie trailer.

I was flooded with magical visions: Taking planes all over the world with Janet, C.J., Juan, and many NFTE executives and teachers to come; opening NFTE programs from Chicago to China; meeting celebrities and incredibly wealthy donors at black-tie galas; and even taking NFTE students to the White House to meet the president. I saw beautiful offices in a skyscraper on Wall Street with magnificent views of New York Harbor. I saw NFTE graduates going to college, becoming millionaires, appearing on television programs, in newspapers, and in magazines. I even saw myself writing books and speaking at conferences and universities.

I also saw that NFTE was going to be the most intense, exhausting, time-consuming, overwhelming, challenging thing that I could possibly do with my life.

When I opened my eyes, I was so freaked out that I almost didn't send the letter.

I felt scared, because I enjoyed my simple life as a teacher very much. I was my own boss at the DOB program. My workdays were short and filled with children I had come to love. I had a beautiful girlfriend whom I adored, and plenty of time to see her on evenings and weekends. I had saved my job and was finally on friendly terms with most of my colleagues in the typing department at Jane Addams.

Heck, even Mrs. Spratt was on my side.

If you send this letter, I told myself, Ray Chambers is going to call you and finance you. Then what?

I sat there with the letter in my hand and asked myself: Do you *really* want to change your life like this?

Then I heard a voice in my head say, "It's not about you."

I stood up, walked out of West 4th Street Saloon, and dropped the letter in a mailbox.

Three days later, Ray Chambers called me.

It was Tuesday before Thanksgiving. I went to Jane Addams that morning instead of the DOB, because I was due for a review from Marilyn Sanders. She was still not wild about me and highly suspicious about the amount of time I spent teaching off campus.

"What are you doing all day in that offsite program?" Marilyn demanded the moment I walked into her office.

I had brought all my students' business plans to show her. I was digging a couple of them out of my briefcase when she snapped, "But are you using the computers? I talked to Pat! She tells me you are not even teaching them the stenography!" Marilyn shook her stenography book at me, shouting, "ARE YOU USING THIS BOOK?!"

"Oh yes!" I replied, with as much enthusiasm as I could possibly muster. "We have computers in the room and each student types for thirty minutes a day. I do what you taught me, because you are an *incredible* teacher! You're a . . . a . . . goddess!"

I was sucking up to her like crazy. I just wanted to get the review over with and get the hell out of there.

"Thirty minutes!" Marilyn shrieked. "That is inadequate! Does the union know? How did you even get this job?"

Pat must have heard Marilyn yelling at me because she charged into the room like a linebacker, panting heavily.

"Steve!" Pat gasped. "I've been trying to find you. You have an important phone call!"

Just then, Victor came strutting down the hallway. He was

looking for me because I was taking him to my annual lunch with Dan Simmons in Brooklyn. Dan had agreed to listen to Victor's demo tape. Victor was hoping Dan would pass it on to his brother Russell, whose Def Jam record label was putting hip-hop on the mainstream map with hit albums from L.L. Cool J, the Beastie Boys, and Public Enemy.

Of course, the moment Victor saw Pat Black he started rapping "MissBlackStopFuckinWitMe" as fast as he possibly could.

All this chaos stopped Marilyn's harangue for a moment. As she glared at me, I took advantage of the opportunity to gather up my briefcase and papers and hightail it out of her office.

"I'm so sorry, Marilyn," I yelled over Victor's speed-rapping on my way out the door. "I'll be back later and I *so* look forward to more of your valuable critique!"

Pat's broad back was moving rapidly down the hall. I shuffled behind her as fast as I could, holding my briefcase in both arms and trying not to drop any papers.

I rushed into her office, dropped my stuff on a desk, and grabbed a phone, but it was the wrong one.

"No, Steve, here!" Pat cried, handing me a receiver.

I couldn't figure out why Pat was grinning from ear to ear until I said, "Hello?" and heard an exquisitely cultured female voice respond, "Hold for Mr. Chambers, please."

"I, um, sure!" I stammered.

There was a long pause, and then I heard Ray Chambers's voice for the first time.

"Hello? Is this . . . Steve Mariotti?"

Ray spoke very slowly. His voice was deep and sonorous, and he pronounced every word distinctly and carefully. He sounded like Errol Flynn or something.

"Yes, Mr. Chambers, this is Steve Mariotti."

"Mr. Mariotti. I got your letter."

Pause.

"I really want to work. With you."

Pause.

"Are you available . . . tomorrow? I know it's the day before Thanksgiving."

Pause.

"Could you come . . . to Morristown? Can you be here by ten thirty . . . AM?"

"Of course!" I practically shouted into the phone.

"I will see you then," Ray responded quietly, "and I will look forward to it."

———

There was just one problem. I was flat broke. I didn't have any money to get to Morristown. I wasn't even sure where Morristown was. I had already borrowed money from Janet for my trek to DC. I couldn't hit her up again.

Pat Black was beaming. She gave me a big hug. She was so delighted for me that I didn't have the nerve to confess my financial problem to her.

Meanwhile, Victor had followed us down the hall. He was bouncing up and down in her office doorway, rapping "MissBlack-StopFuckinWitMe" and "MissBlackSheGotThatSupaFineWeed."

Pat was nodding to Victor's beat and giving him her usual "Aren't you talented and adorable?" smile.

My head was spinning, but I still had to get Victor to his big meeting with Dan Simmons.

"Have you got your tape? Are you ready to go?" I asked Victor.

"I got it! And I'm ready," he grinned, opening his coat to flash me a big bottle of Budweiser sticking out of his pocket.

"Jeepers, let's go," I said, rolling my eyes. "Close your coat!"

We headed out of Jane Addams and down the sidewalk toward the subway. I was power walking as quickly as I could, which I always did in the South Bronx in the vain hope that the muggers would see how fast I was moving and leave me alone.

"Slow down, Mr. Mariotti!" Victor yelled after me. "You white boys always so scared of shit."

I slowed down long enough for him to catch up with me. Together, we walked past a street corner guarded by two large gang-bangers with twitchy eyes. I could practically see their prison muscles bulging under their puffy down coats. No doubt they had guns tucked into their waistbands.

Of course, right as we walked past these two scary dudes, just to bust my balls, Victor hollered at them, "Suck my cock!"

All I could think was, Oh no, oh Jesus Christ, oh fuck.

I started power walking even faster, like a duck on methamphetamine. Victor was chortling away at the sight of me. To tell you the truth, I am pretty sure he knew them, because they ignored his taunt entirely.

We finally reached the subway and took the long ride to Bed-Stuy. Victor practiced his rapping on me the entire way, which kept us both amused.

We met up with Dan at a local diner. He was wearing his usual fall uniform: a leather jacket over an argyle sweater and baggy jeans. Dan was a tall, powerfully built guy, but he squeezed into a booth with us. As we sat together munching on some burgers and fries, Dan listened to Victor's tape on headphones.

"Your material is really good!" Dan told Victor, who beamed. "You got great flow and clear delivery, good rhymes. You know how to tell a story," Dan added, "so here's what you need to do. You need to get to a real recording studio and make a better-sounding demo."

And Victor, ever the hustler, said, "Cool, cool, thank you! Could we use your brother's studio?" Victor was referring to Russell Simmons, of course.

"I don't like to ask my brother for that until you have an agent or manager," Dan replied.

"Would *you* pay for it?" Victor asked with a grin and a wink.

That was pretty darn nervy, but as I always said when we played the negotiation game in class, "If you don't ask, you don't get."

Dan threw back his head and laughed.

"You a hustler, son! I like that! Tell you what. You go figure out how to get the funding for three or four hours of studio time. Come back with one tune that sounds really dope. I'll listen to it, and if I like it, I'll take you to meet my brother and his partner."

On the ride back to the South Bronx, Victor groused nonstop about Dan's refusal to finance his recording. By the time we reached our stop, I was sick of hearing it.

"Victor," I said, "my understanding is that you've got a lot of money. Why don't you finance your demo yourself?"

He winked and said, "Yeah, but he don't know that."

After we emerged from the subway and were walking up the sidewalk to Jane Addams, I cleared my throat awkwardly.

"Um, speaking of money, Victor," I ventured, "I'm in a bit of a bind with Thanksgiving coming up. I need to take a trip out of town."

I felt like the biggest loser on the planet. I was about to hit up my drug-dealing student for a loan. But if I didn't make it to Morristown tomorrow for that meeting with Ray Chambers, all would be lost.

"Do you think you could possibly lend me, like, eighty dollars?" I continued. "I'll pay you back a week from Friday."

"Well," Victor said, "with the vig it'll be one twenty."

That little fucker.

"After all I've done for you, you're going to charge me fifty percent interest over nine days?" I exclaimed.

"Let's make it one sixty, that's a hundred vig, and I get an A in the class," Victor countered.

At the shocked look on my face, Victor burst out laughing.

"Naw, Mr. Mariotti, come on now!" He pulled out a wad of cash, handed me $200, and said, "I'm kidding. It's yours. It's a gift."

"I can't take a gift from you, Victor," I said.

"I won't take repayment from you, Mr. Mariotti," Victor replied, and he pressed the money into my hand.

CHAPTER 15

THE HAVE FUN GAME

"It takes a lot of courage to show your dreams to someone else."
—ERMA BOMBECK, *If Life Is a Bowl of Cherries, What Am I Doing in the Pits?* (1978)

Victor's $200 saved me. That evening, I laid my suit and tie out on the couch in the ramshackle loft Janet and I shared at 6 Jones Street, next to West 4th Street Saloon. I triple-checked the schedule for the morning train to Morristown, New Jersey.

I went to bed early, wanting to be bright-eyed and bushy-tailed for the most important meeting of my life. Janet was working late that night. She was always good about tiptoeing in without waking me if she knew I had an early morning. I was so worried about sleeping through my alarm, though, that I could not fall asleep. I remember praying at 4 AM: "Dear God, please let me go to sleep. Just for a few hours."

No dice. I lay awake all night.

At seven, I took a shower and then headed to Penn Station. I had my briefcase with me, stuffed with student business plans and my spiral-bound curriculum. I was also carrying a videotape of my students that I hoped to show Ray.

I was really nervous about making sure I got on the right train at Penn Station, then I was really nervous about getting off at the right stop. When I finally arrived in Morristown, I was so relieved!

I disembarked from the train and headed to the street to hail a cab, since Ray's office was three miles from the station. But in all my careful planning, I had forgotten one thing.

Unlike Manhattan, most small towns do not have fleets of yellow cabs cruising the streets.

I was panic-stricken. It was almost ten, and the meeting was at ten thirty. There wasn't time to walk three miles. I didn't see a cab anywhere.

I stood on the curb blinking back tears in the bright sunshine.

Right then, a green-and-white taxi pulled up in front of me. The driver rolled down his window and shouted, "Hey! Do you need a ride?"

"Oh my God, yes!" I cried.

Once I got inside and had given the driver the address for Wesray Capital, he said, "You know, I never come this way but I saw you over there and you looked lost or something."

He got me to 330 South Street by five minutes after ten. The office was in a former synagogue, so I started reciting to myself all the books of the Old Testament that I could remember: "Genesis,

Exodus, Leviticus, Numbers, Deuteronomy; dear God, please, please make this work."

I loved teaching, but after seven years I was feeling burned out. I also strongly believed that I could do more good outside the school system, where I could provide the entrepreneurship education to teenagers living in poverty that I believed would transform their lives. If Ray wasn't going to fund NFTE, then I didn't know who was going to fund it. Because he was perfect.

I stood outside the synagogue doors and took a deep breath, then I pushed open the door.

As I went to sit down in the reception area, a beautiful African American lady who was also sitting there gave me a warm smile. I recognized her as Barbara Bell Coleman, the president of the Boys & Girls Club of Newark. Barbara was very polished, dressed in a nice suit with three strands of pearls around her neck. She knew who I was, it turned out, and we chatted a bit.

After a few minutes, Ray's secretary emerged and said, "He can see you now." Barbara and I both rose and followed the secretary into Ray's office, which was simple and spare. The only thing on the wall was a framed article about the Accidentals.

Barbara and I sat down together at a table and waited for Ray.

When he walked in a few moments later, I was smart enough to say, "Thank you for seeing me. How much time do you have, so that I know how quickly I should make my presentation?"

Ray replied, "I'm afraid I only have fifteen minutes, because I have a busy schedule today."

"In that case," I said, "I'd like to show you this five-minute video, rather than talk, because it presents my mission to bring entrepreneurship education to low-income youth very clearly."

I could tell Ray was a bit reluctant to watch a video, but he agreed.

The video showed my students working at the school store and talking about how much they had learned from selling, and from starting their own little businesses.

Then Ray talked, and, for once, I was smart enough not to interrupt.

"I've adopted eight hundred children in the second and eighth grades from Newark schools," Ray said. "I've agreed to pay for their education, including college, if they graduate from high school.

"When Barbara and I were out walking with some of the students," he continued, "we asked them what they want to be when they grow up. Most of them said they wanted to be business owners. Barbara and I were shocked."

Barbara chimed in, "Yes, it's true. So many of them are interested in business that we would love to bring an entrepreneurship-education program to them."

"Your letter arrived at just the right time," Ray said. "I would really like to fund this. Would you be willing to do the program you proposed in your letter at the Boys & Girls Club of Newark?"

I was beyond thrilled to hear this. But I couldn't abandon my South Bronx students. And I didn't want any funding Ray might offer me to be funneled through, and potentially controlled by, the Boys & Girls Club.

"Thank you so much, Ray," I began. "I would love to work with Barbara to bring NFTE's entrepreneurship-education program to Newark. I could get started right away!" As diplomatically as possible, I added, "However, I am currently committed to Jane Addams High School and an off-campus program in the South Bronx through June. I could come out to Newark on Tuesdays, Thursdays, and Saturdays, but I would want to spend half my time and half your funding in the South Bronx."

Barbara, I sensed from her reaction, was none too pleased.

"This program should be part of the Boys & Girls Club," she asserted, "and based in Newark."

I knew it was important for me to stay independent and not let my new foundation become entirely folded into the Boys & Girls Club. Don't get me wrong—having the Boys & Girls Club as a partner was very exciting, and Barbara was clearly a strong, charismatic leader. I was going to have to be strong, as well, and stand my ground.

I felt extremely nervous. Was I about to blow my very first funding offer?

"I understand, Barbara," I said, "and I will give the Newark program tremendous effort and commitment. But I can't abandon the South Bronx Entrepreneurship Education Program and the children who are working so hard up there."

Ray gave me a long appraising look.

Then, he said quietly, "No, of course you can't." He paused, and then added, "That is very commendable, Steve."

In the end, we all agreed that NFTE would remain independent. I would divide my time evenly between my commitments in the South Bronx and partnering with the Boys & Girls Club to deliver an after-school entrepreneurship program in Newark.

"My goal is to build a global movement in entrepreneurship education," I told Ray and Barbara, "and to forever change how low-income children are viewed by themselves and by others—as assets, not liabilities."

Ray nodded.

"Well," he said, "how much money do you need for the first year?"

"I will need two hundred thousand," I replied. Just hearing that big ask come out of my mouth made me start to sweat.

"I'll go two hundred fifty thousand," Ray said, "and I'll match whatever you can raise above that."

In that moment, I learned the power and grace of giving more than you have been asked to give. I have never forgotten that lesson. Whenever I have been able, I have tried to follow Ray's example and do the same.

———————————————

Leaving the meeting, I felt absolutely euphoric. I was worried, though, about how I was going to get back to the train station. It turned out Ray's secretary had called a car service for me. The driver was waiting outside.

Clearly, I was moving up in the world.

On the train, I was blissed out but exhausted. I couldn't believe I had just raised a quarter of a million dollars. I knew I was taking on an enormous responsibility, as well. I hadn't slept, and the stress of it all knocked me out. My brain shut down and I passed out in my seat.

After exiting Penn Station, I charged down to West 4th Street Saloon to tell Janet the amazing news.

Janet had sometimes acted a little embarrassed to be seen there with me—not because she wasn't proud of me, but because some of the employees and customers hinted that she was dating beneath herself. The other waitresses were dating famous actors or wealthy businessmen. Janet was beautiful, kind, and intelligent. Frankly, she *was* out of my league. I couldn't wait to give her something to brag about and make her feel proud to be seen with me.

That night, we had a celebratory dinner together as a couple at West 4th Street Saloon, and Edie waited on us. I was so happy and tired that I could barely talk. It was an evening of pure joy.

I could hardly wait for Thanksgiving break to be over. On Monday morning, I popped out of bed extra early. I was eager to get to Jane Addams before classes started so that I could share my news with C.J., Juan, and Pat prior to heading to the DOB to teach my offsite class.

I caught up with C.J. in the teacher's lounge. He was overjoyed to hear that Ray Chambers had agreed to fund NFTE.

"Would you work for NFTE full-time?" I asked C.J., adding, "I'll get you a car and pay you well."

C.J. promised to think seriously about my offer.

That December, I went straight to West 4th Street Saloon every day after school, motivated more than ever by the check for $20,000 Ray Chambers had mailed to me with his pledge to donate an additional $230,000 to my fledgling nonprofit.

Instead of being discouraged from teaching small business to low-income youth, I was finally being invited to create an entrepreneurship-education program for them. The pressure was on to finish the curriculum I had been developing and to write a student workbook and lesson plans.

I hired Janet to help me. She proved to have a genius not only for lesson plans but also for writing grant proposals and letters to more prospective donors.

In January, C.J. resigned from Jane Addams to become my first full-time employee. I got him a Mitsubishi Galant, and he moved to a nice apartment right outside of Newark. Soon, I also hired Juan Casimiro, the other teacher who had been running the South Bronx Entrepreneurship Club with me and C.J.

C.J. oversaw NFTE's after-school program at the Newark Boys & Girls Club. I took the PATH train to Newark on Tuesday and Thursday evenings and Saturday mornings to help him teach.

Luckily, the PATH station on 9th Street and Sixth Avenue was a short walk from where Janet and I lived.

This was a ton of work for all of us. I was still teaching the offsite program at the Department of Buildings and supervising the school store at Jane Addams. C.J., Juan, and I were also running the South Bronx Entrepreneurship Club after school at Jane Addams on Mondays, Wednesdays, and Fridays. The schedule was punishing, but I felt ecstatic. I was running on adrenaline and the excitement of seeing my vision for NFTE actually come true.

Wonderful people were coming on board to support that vision. Barbara Bell Coleman became one of NFTE's strongest supporters and spent hundreds of hours mentoring me, particularly in fundraising. I learned immensely valuable lessons about leadership and running a nonprofit from her. Ray Chambers was also incredibly helpful, not only as a donor but also as a mentor and advisory board member.

Ray's gruff business partner Bill Simon was very supportive, too, in his unique fashion. Bill returned every phone call I ever made to him. He even let me shadow him at his office for a day under the condition that I not interrupt him.

"Watch, listen, learn, but do not speak," Bill warned me.

Bill's mantra was, "Make friends with the secretary." I watched him make around forty phone calls that day, and he was incredibly charming to the secretaries. Butter wouldn't melt in his mouth!

"Suzanne! It's Bill Simon! How *are* you? How are the kids? Oh, that's wonderful! How adorable! Hey, do you think I could get the boss on the phone?"

I learned insights that day about how to network and make things happen that I have used ever since.

At the Newark Boys & Girls Club, we were teaching second and eighth graders fundamental business concepts like buy low/

sell high, selling, marketing, and simple record keeping. We also helped them brainstorm fun business ideas and fill out the simple business-plan workbooks Janet and I had developed.

The eighth graders were at that perfect age when children are mature enough to behave but their hormones have not gone wild yet. They were challenging at times but not too difficult.

The second graders were bonkers.

I had never taught second grade before. I have never had more joy teaching a class, but it was also the hardest thing I have ever done.

There is something about my face that makes second graders crack up. I could not get them to obey me. Desperate to figure it out, I went to observe some classes at their schools to learn how their teachers handled them.

When the female teachers barked, "Sit down now!" those little kids would sit right down. When I barked "Sit down now!" they laughed hysterically and continued to race around the room.

My second graders were my greatest teachers, though.

I always thought teaching was about me, my lesson plans, and my presentations to the class. The second graders turned that plan upside down. They gave me a whole new view of education. Before dealing with them, I did not understand that it is okay sometimes for a classroom to be noisy. So what? The second graders were talking to each other and, I noticed, they were usually talking about what I was trying to teach them.

Since they seemed to like to talk to each other, I thought maybe they would work together. One day, I tried something that had been effective with my rowdy DOB class. I divided the second graders into small groups and assigned each group a simple project to tackle together. After a certain amount of time, one child from each group would report on the group's progress to the class.

The small-group method worked great. I have used this ever since. I lecture for no more than five minutes. Then I break the class into groups to work on their assignments. You get a lot more done, the students learn teamwork, and you don't bore them to death with long presentations.

Nonetheless, one Saturday class with the second graders was total chaos. The class was too long, for starters. It dragged on for six hours. My little entrepreneurs were tired, cranky, and completely ignoring me.

"Okay, everyone, attention please, we're going to play a game!" I shouted over the din.

A game! Yay! They all started screaming.

"It's called the Mr. Mariotti Have Fun Game!" I announced gleefully. "Now, we're all going to line up here." I herded them into a rough semblance of a line in front of the clanking cast-iron radiators on one side of our classroom.

"Now we rub our feet on the carpet like this!" I rubbed my shoes back and forth on the carpet as fast as I could.

"Harder! Harder!" I shouted as they imitated me. "Yeah! Great job! Yay!" I encouraged them. "Now, on the count of three, we all reach out and touch the radiators!"

The radiators were warm, not hot, so there was no risk of the children burning themselves, but they received mild shocks from the static electricity their eager little feet had generated.

I have to admit that I took a hint of sadistic pleasure from the astonished looks on their adorable faces. Before you judge me too harshly, please remember that they had been horrible all day long. If you have ever worked with seven-year-olds, you know. It can be torture.

Technically, I wasn't supposed to be shocking second graders. But they laughed their faces off and no one cried, thank God. Some kids were even rolling on the floor with delight. Then they started doing it on their own.

This gave me a chance to teach a simple lesson on electricity, and positive and negative charges. The second graders also began treating me with a little more respect, now that they knew Mr. Mariotti could bring the pain!

Those second graders, who are now adults, love to laugh with me about the Mr. Mariotti Have Fun Game. One kid, Leon, actually grew up to be an electrician. He still jokes with me that he was inspired by his first shock to develop a lifelong fascination with electricity.

*****

That spring, NFTE started getting national media coverage, which was exhilarating for me and my team. We were featured on the television show *World News Tonight with Peter Jennings*, which was a huge breakthrough. The episode included wonderful interviews with students sharing their excitement about entrepreneurship and their pride in their small businesses. It also included footage of our students buying products in the wholesale district, and of Victor recording in a studio.

We received very positive coverage that spring from the *New York Times* and the *Daily News*, as well. All that publicity led to a contract with the Wharton School of the University of Pennsylvania to run a two-week summer entrepreneurship education program that we dubbed NFTE BizCamp. I started to have meetings with millionaires and billionaires to find financing for it.

I ran into some wealthy people whose attitudes toward teaching poor children about business formation and ownership were shocking. One day, I met with the cofounder of a top private equity firm. He was very philanthropic and had sponsored scholarships for many young people—but he balked at donating to NFTE.

I didn't understand why.

"You're doing so much for education by enabling deserving low-income students to attend private schools," I said to him. "Why don't you spend some of that money to also teach them how to become business owners?"

A tall, imposing man, he let his glasses slide down the bridge of his nose and gazed warmly at me, like an uncle indulging a favorite, but slightly stupid, nephew. As if it were the most obvious, most rational statement in the world, he said, "But, Steve, then who would do the work?"

I wish I could say that was the only time I ever heard this. Sadly, I've heard variations of this argument from a wide range of rich and powerful people.

Owners have enormous power in the world, and this man knew it. Children raised in poverty typically do not think about who owns the stores in their neighborhood or the buildings in which their families live. Unlike the children of wealthy people, they may not be taught at the dinner table that business is a craft that can be learned, and that wealth comes from ownership. I wanted NFTE to change that and help level the playing field.

We obtained $70,000 in funding for the first BizCamp from junk-bond trader Michael Milken. The grant was administered by Lisa Hoffstein of the University Community Outreach Program for the Milken Young Entrepreneurs Program at Wharton. Lisa secured NFTE additional contracts to conduct two-week summer BizCamps for low-income teens at Columbia, USC, and Berkeley. We wound up running these summer BizCamps for ten years. They really helped us grow as an organization.

Unbeknownst to us at the time, Michael Milken was under investigation by the SEC for his trading activities at Drexel Burnham Lambert. He would be convicted of racketeering and securities fraud in 1989, sentenced to ten years in prison, and fined $600 million. After his release in 1993, Michael continued to donate to NFTE for several years, although ultimately he was motivated by his bout with prostate cancer to devote most of his foundation's resources to medical research.

By May, I was incredibly overwhelmed trying to juggle my teaching responsibilities at Jane Addams High and the Boys & Girls Club of Newark with my new responsibilities as the leader of a suddenly booming nonprofit.

I couldn't sleep because my mind was constantly racing. Janet was worried that I was going to collapse from exhaustion. Reluctantly, I finally agreed with her that I needed to resign from Jane Addams in June and devote myself completely to NFTE.

CHAPTER 16

TO SERVE IS
TO RULE

"A man may break a word with you, sir; and words are but wind. Ay, and break it in your face, so he break it not behind."
—WILLIAM SHAKESPEARE, *A Comedy of Errors* (1594)

Juan Casimiro had the South Bronx Entrepreneurship Club well in hand. I knew those students would be fine without me. But I dreaded telling my class at the Department of Buildings that I would not be returning in the fall.

My offsite students had been abused, raped, assaulted, and at least one of them had committed murder. But I believed in them, and I wanted them to believe in me, so one day I had promised

239

the class, "If you give me your word that you won't leave until you graduate, I won't leave."

We swore a solemn vow that day. We also shared a secret motto, which I have never before revealed, but I guess I can now: "To serve is to rule."

I had sworn to see my students through to earning their special ed diplomas. Most of them had only one more semester to go. I was not sure how they would take the news of my resignation. By leaving I would be breaking a sacred oath, but I had to do it in order to help more children just like them.

I did believe that my students would be all right without me, because they were doing so well and had come so far in the three-and-a-half years that we had been together.

Victor had opened a small recording studio where he could demo his own music and provide other aspiring rappers with an affordable place to record.

Mariana was working in a clothing store and had become an Avon representative.

Maurice was a regular in the wholesale district. He had expanded his business from selling sunglasses to other trendy accessories, as well.

In October, Shana had given birth to a baby boy she named Terrell.

"It was the happiest day of my life, Mr. Mariotti," she told me. She took the baby to the program for teenage mothers at Jane Addams several times a week.

I was so incredibly busy, meanwhile, that I kept putting off telling the class my news until the second to last day of the semester. It was pure cowardice on my part, frankly.

We were having a little party that day at the Department of Buildings to celebrate the end of the semester, since the next day we would have to be at Jane Addams to conduct the end-of-term inventory for the school store. There was a buffet in the back of the room with rice, beans, stewed chicken, and other goodies.

It was now or never.

I wanted to begin from a positive place, so I started by listing all our wonderful achievements as a class. Many of the students had part-time jobs, for starters. We had developed such a good reputation on Arthur Avenue that now a lot of businesses there wanted to hire students from our class.

Every student had a business card. Every student was either operating a small business or writing a business plan. Everyone was coming to class each day. Hygiene had improved, and the students were dressing better. They knew how to sell, negotiate, and keep good records. They were back at Jane Addams part-time, running the school store and taking classes.

Perhaps most importantly for these once-shunned special ed children, everyone had made not only some money but also some friends.

"You all know how to be 'in the money'!" I concluded.

That was our code for acting in a businesslike fashion. We called it "in the money," as opposed to acting "out of the money" by cursing or trying to threaten and intimidate people.

"They don't pay you for that!" the class shouted in unison.

Next, I went around the classroom and asked each student to share his or her biggest accomplishment from the semester. It was unbelievable. I wish I had picked up a camcorder. Listening to them share their pride in their jobs and their businesses, and describe how their lives had changed, was quite possibly the happiest hour of my life.

As always, Victor was the first to raise his hand. He was bouncing up and down in his chair with his eagerness to speak.

I stifled a grin. "Yes, Victor?" I said.

"I have a legit business!" Victor practically shouted. "Doing something I love and I'm making *bank*! Sometimes more than I did running drugs—I can't believe it! I feel like I can do anything now, and make my dreams come true, and I don't always have to watch my back. I'm still friends with my former bosses so they don't whack me down, but now they come record in my studio and pay *me* money."

I involuntarily winced at the thought of Victor staying friends with gangbangers, but he was right. He still had to live in Fort Apache and couldn't burn bridges if he wanted to survive.

"I used to be so angry, yo," Victor continued. "I used to want to hurt people and fuck 'em up. I never gave a shit about going to class or being on time for nothing. Until you started bringing in them music magazines for me to read, and I started seeing home-boys like me making records. Teachers always made me feel like I couldn't read and I was stupid. I ain't stupid! I can fucking read as good as anybody! If I was some rich boy, I'd have me a scholarship and awards.

"And then we met Scott La Rock," Victor added, "and . . ." Victor's voice trailed off for a moment. We were all still pretty broken up about Scott's murder.

Victor pulled himself back together, though, and continued, "We met La Rock and he gave us *vision*, man!"

At this, Mariana jumped up and cried, "God bless Scott La Rock!" and the entire class shouted, "God bless Scott La Rock!" and "South Bronx, South Bronx!"

"Mariana, what have you learned?" I asked her.

"I learned to make money, Mr. Mariotti!" she said. She started walking around the room, imitating my mannerisms and voice perfectly. "Buy low, sell high, keep good records. Buy low, sell high, keep good records." The class cracked up.

"Ah, bullshit!" Lamont said. "The most important thing I learned was to be tena . . . shit, what was the word you was always teaching us, Mr. M? To never give up?"

"Tenacious, tenacious, always tenacious!" Anton boomed before I could answer Lamont.

"What else did you learn, Anton?" I asked.

"That we are all on the same team. If we help each other with our businesses, we meet more new customers and make more money."

After every student shared something he or she had learned, we all cheered and applauded. I couldn't stall anymore. I had to share my news.

"Um, I have an announcement to make," I began. "That letter you encouraged me to write to my hero Ray Chambers using this magazine . . ." I held up my dog-eared *Forbes*. "Well, it worked! He wrote back to me, and I went to meet with him. He has agreed to fund NFTE with two hundred and fifty thousand dollars. We are going to teach entrepreneurship to students just like you all over the world."

Their eyes grew huge, and a few kids started to applaud.

I held up my hand. I had to get through what I needed to tell them before I lost my nerve.

"You all helped me so much with my business plan and composing this letter," I continued, "I can't thank you enough."

I started tearing up.

"I have been working extremely long hours traveling back and forth from the Bronx to Newark, where we are running our first program," I said. "And I'm also teaching here, overseeing the school store, and running the Entrepreneurship Club with Mr. Casimiro. Now NFTE has received a contract to run a summer entrepreneurship camp, as well."

I paused, because my voice was getting a little shaky.

"At this point," I continued, hoping I could get the next few sentences out without losing my composure altogether, "I've got to become the full-time president and CEO of NFTE so that we can fulfill our mission. I'm . . . very, *very* sorry to have to say this, but I'm not going to be able to return as your teacher in September."

"What the fuck?!" Shana yelled, and with that all hell broke loose.

"You lied to us!" Mariana screamed. "You broke your contract! Whenever we break our contracts, we get in trouble!" She pointed at me and roared, with the mighty wrath of the righteous, "I'm gonna sue you!!!"

Victor stood up and slammed his chair to the floor.

"He's just another white man inheriting a plantation!" Victor shouted to the class, waving his arms in the air. "Just another lyin' white mothafucka!"

"You played us!" Shana screeched at the top of her lungs. "You used us!"

She grabbed Victor's chair and threw it into one of our class-room's glass walls. The glass cracked from the impact. Typists came running. They stood outside our classroom looking in with shock on their faces.

I was horrified. Imagine the worst breakup you've ever had, multiplied by twenty-two upset teenagers with emotional issues. The entire class was pandemonium. Miguel was sobbing uncontrollably in his chair. Estelle was screaming, "Fuck you, you fucking liar!" jabbing the air in my direction with her long red nails.

"I'm sorry!" I yelled over the din. "I know I'm breaking my promise to you! But I have a chance here to help so many more young people! I've shared my dream with you. You know this is what I want to do. And you should dream big for *your* life! I have never lied to you!"

Anton stood up. He towered over the rest of the kids. For a moment, I thought he was going to walk over and pound my face in, but he just gave me the dirtiest of dirty looks and shook his head, saying, "Yeah, you gonna take our business plans now, and all our ideas, and use 'em with them other kids."

When he said that, I almost wished he had hit me. I *was* using their business ideas, and so much more that I had learned from them, in the NFTE curriculum. What right did I have to do that?

"We're not partners, Mr. Mariotti, you can't take my business!"

"You're dishonest! You use people! You used Miss Black!"

"You goddamn bastard!"

"You're a fucking liar! I hate you! I hate you!"

I couldn't keep track of who was saying what anymore. I felt horrible, because they were right. I was breaking my solemn vow to them by leaving. I was betraying the very trust I had fought so hard to win.

Everyone was yelling and screaming and crying. The typists looked completely freaked out. Miss Archibald was out for the day, so there was no leadership on the floor. I was terrified that one of the typists was going to call Pat Black.

"You used Mrs. Sanders!" someone shouted. At that, a few students cracked up, at least, because they all knew Marilyn Sanders scared the crap out of me.

Miguel stood up.

"I want to defend Mr. Mariotti!" he proclaimed. He raised one finger into the air and placed his fist on his hip like Clarence Darrow about to give a closing argument. To my horror, Earvin shoved Miguel and he fell down.

"Earvin, no!" I shouted, terrified that Miguel's bum leg might break. I had to get control of this mess before someone got seriously injured and we trashed the entire classroom.

"Fuck you, Mr. Mariotti, you just wanna get rich and famous!" Earvin yelled at me.

"SIT DOWN, EARVIN!" I screamed as loudly as I possibly could.

For a split second, everybody shut up.

Then someone, probably Victor, started pounding on the table, chanting, "Mouse! Mouse! Mouse! Mouse!"

The other students joined in. The room reverberated with my hated middle school nickname. "Mouse! Mouse! Mouse! Mouse!"

Those little assholes.

"Mouse! Mouse! Mouse! Mouse!"

I felt my blood boil over, and then I completely lost my shit.

"SHUT THE FUCK UP!!" I screamed, frothing at the mouth. "Have I got your attention NOW? Good! Because fuck you ALL! I have worked my ass off for you! I have taught you everything I know! You wouldn't even know what a contract *is*, or what it *means* to sue somebody, if it wasn't for ME!

"Yes, I am ambitious! Yes, I want my foundation to become a worldwide success! I want to help lots of other children! NOT JUST YOU GUYS!! Fuck you, motherfuckers, I've been here every day trying to teach you every goddamn thing I know! Don't hold me back! And don't fucking hold yourselves or each other back!!"

I mean, I really went beserko. I can't defend my behavior, other than to say that perhaps it was good for my students to see me get real. I don't know. All I know is it shut them up long enough for me to attempt to regain control of the class and try to explain to them that this was their success, too.

They had inspired and encouraged me to start NFTE. They were now part of something that was going to help many other children. They would be just fine without me. And they could always, *always* call me, anytime!

Miguel was still crying. I knew he was on my side and understood where I was coming from.

"Come on, Clarence Darrow," I implored Miguel. "Help me out here."

Miguel blew his nose loudly into a paper napkin. Then he stood up again. Everybody looked at him. Miguel had huge credibility with everyone, including me, because he was always so kind and morally upright, unlike the rest of us. We all loved him and knew he was the soul of decency and integrity.

"God has called Steve, our teacher, to a new assignment," Miguel declared.

Shana got up and left the room, slamming the door as hard as she could behind her.

With that, the noise level in the classroom began to rise again like an inevitable tide. I braced myself for more screaming accusations of betrayal to come roaring my way.

Suddenly, a thunderous fart cracked through the noise like the sonic boom of an airplane breaking the sound barrier.

"I apologize for breaking wind!" Anton announced and ripped another one.

It must have been the beans.

Anton's supersonic fart bombs kept coming, driving me and the entire class into hysterics.

This was the loudest, longest incidence of breaking wind I have ever heard. Just when you thought the bombing was over, another boom rumbled through our classroom.

Kids were falling off their chairs and rolling on the floor laughing. I was laughing so hard that I honestly feared I was going to pee my pants.

For years afterward, our favorite inside joke was to debate how loud each fart was and how many there were. Anton swore that he merely broke wind four times, and that it only seemed like more because the booms had ricocheted around our glass-walled classroom.

But as God is my witness, I am certain he passed gas eleven times.

How am I so sure?

Because even while laughing so hard that I could barely stand, I instinctively grabbed one of my green Vis-à-Vis pens and made a little mark on the transparency on my overhead machine every time he ripped one.

When the onslaught finally ceased, and we were all able to catch our breath, the vibe of the class morphed from rage into love. Kids were hugging each other and hugging me. It was a moment of sparkling happiness.

"I promise you, I will always be there for you!" I cried. "I will still come up here to visit you and check on you. I will help you with your businesses. And whenever you invite me to your house for dinner, I will be there."

Miguel, who had slid off his chair onto the floor during his laughing fit, grabbed the table and hauled himself up. He looked around at all of us with a twinkle in his eye and stage-whispered, "I have an idea."

Miguel began doing a little dance, rocking from side to side, holding his hands up like little paws. He was grinning as sweetly and innocently as Porky Pig in a Looney Tunes cartoon.

Miguel started singing, "Fannie May! You want some Fannie May! I know you want some Faaannie May!"

With that, I broke into what was left of our closet stash. We cranked up the tunes, pigged out on chocolates, and had a beautiful party. They forgave me. I forgave them, and we all cried and laughed some more.

The next day, when I arrived at Jane Addams High to oversee the school-store inventory, my students, Pat Black, and Mrs. Spratt surprised me with a lovely cake. The students unfurled a banner they had all signed that read:

Goodbye Homeboy
From the Entrepreneurs of Jane Addams High School

I couldn't believe they had remembered the story I had told them about my last day at Boys and Girls High in Bed-Stuy. I was incredibly moved and fighting back tears. I gave each student a silver dollar and a big hug. I hoped they would all stay in touch and not forget me.

I knew I would never, ever forget them.

Entrepreneurship

Guest speaker *Arthur Lipper* discussing how students can start their own business.

The South Bronx Entrepreneurship Club, Jane Addams Vocational High School, 1986

3

CHAPTER 17

EVERY CHILD NEEDS A VICTORY

"Victory is always possible for the person who refuses to stop fighting."
—NAPOLEON HILL, *Think and Grow Rich* (1937)

From that day forward, I was no longer a public school teacher. Janet and I moved into a larger, still ramshackle, loft on 23rd Street and Seventh Avenue. It served as both our home and NFTE's office. To my relief, a lot of my South Bronx students stayed in touch with me. I'm not sure I could have handled the transition if they had not.

When I left Jane Addams, I told Victor, "If you stay in school, I will hire you part-time to work for me."

True to my word, I hired Victor to work for NFTE eight hours a week. He came over after school to help Janet research potential donors and grants for which we could apply. Since I was no longer teaching, I also asked Victor to regale me with the latest street slang. I didn't want to lose my touch.

One afternoon we buzzed Victor up, and two men who had been shadowing him slipped into the stairwell behind him. Victor came tumbling into the apartment with these guys right behind him, beating the crap out of him.

Victor's attackers had the vicious demeanor and gym muscles of men who had spent a lot of time in prison. One was brandishing an ice pick. From what we could gather, Victor owed them money, and they were going to collect or kill him.

I really should not have been surprised, considering my previous experiences with Victor. I made a mental note to fire him, should we survive.

"I'm going to kill this motherfuckin' pussy!" the fellow with the ice pick shouted. He was dragging Victor by the arm. "This fucker is gonna to die today!"

Every short man's nightmare is a psychotic bigger man. I had two inside my apartment. I was sure they were going to murder me, rape and murder Janet, and kill Victor.

I whispered to Janet to make her way to the bathroom and lock herself in. As she began to edge in that direction, the other guy snarled, "Don't move, bitch."

All I could think was, "Earvin, I'm going to make you proud now. No flinching."

I puffed out my chest and stepped forward toward the murderous bastards in my apartment.

"Gentlemen," I said in the deepest voice I could muster, "there will be no violence in here. What the fuck is the problem?"

"This sonofabitch owes us three hundred dollars," guy holding Victor in a vise grip growled.

"All right," I said forcefully, pulling out my wallet, "here you go. Here's two hundred and sixty. It's all I've got. Take it and get out. Now."

I forced myself not to shrink back as his partner lumbered toward me to take the cash. He towered over me as he counted it.

"Drop that piece of shit," he muttered, "let's go."

Victor fell to the floor as his captor let go of his arm. Janet ran to the sink to get some water for him as the door closed behind the two men.

"Jeepers, we have got to get a real office!" I exclaimed. My heart was flopping in my chest like a fish on a dock.

"Ya think?" Janet said.

⁂

We moved NFTE out of our home and into a cramped office above a Chinese acupuncturist on Fulton Street in downtown Manhattan.

After I read Victor the riot act and threatened to fire him if he didn't give up drug dealing for good, he became a model employee and a true asset to NFTE.

Victor's gifts for marketing and branding proved invaluable as our team wrote and published the first-ever entrepreneurship textbook for high school students. Victor read and reviewed every word of our curriculum. He provided countless insights that helped shaped it into the award-winning curriculum that it is today.

Victor graduated and made it to adulthood without a criminal record—which was a freaking miracle. He traveled with me around the country speaking at high schools about the power of entrepreneurship education and how it had changed his life. Victor loved seeing new places and seemed genuinely happy.

Steve Mariotti in NFTE's office on Fulton Street. Photo by NFTE.

"I'm rejoicing spiritually!" he told me once.

I guess all those Sunday services at Kingdom Hall did rub off on him.

Victor also continued to hone his hip-hop skills: recording and producing other artists in his studio for $40 an hour, instead of earning $200 a day peddling drugs.

We both became friendly with notable leaders in the hip-hop community who were eager to support NFTE, including Dan and Russell Simmons, Melle Mel, Rakim, and Sean Combs.

Victor met Ray Chambers, as well, and told me it was the first time he realized that "rich people give back." Meeting a wealthy philanthropist was "a revelation," Victor said, adding, "They aren't doing it because they have to, but because they want to. I want to do that when I get the chance!"

I also stayed in close touch with Mariana, who was putting her entrepreneurship education to great use. She supported herself by selling Avon. She also started a business organizing baby showers, birthdays, and other gatherings. Mariana helped her customers decide what kind of decorations they wanted, and then made and installed the decorations herself.

"I love turning the things I already love to do into money," she told me. In the process, this once profoundly neglected child built a beautiful community around herself and made many life-long friends, including me.

When she was seventeen, Mariana started a housekeeping business. I became one of her first regular customers, and she remained my housekeeper until I moved from New York to Princeton in 2015. She was always a huge help in keeping me organized and productive. She and her husband are some of my dearest friends.

Shana's story was more painful. Overwhelmed by the combination of full-time school and parenthood, Shana dropped out before graduation. She was in and out of jail on minor drug possession charges. I lost touch with her and wondered how she was supporting herself, her son, Terrell—and her crack habit. Earvin was not in their lives at all. He had graduated and left the Bronx. I hoped he was doing all right, but we were not in touch, either.

Meanwhile, a spree of odd bodega robberies was plaguing Fort Apache. The *New York Post* nicknamed the pint-sized, ski-mask-wearing robber—who menaced victims with a sawed-off shotgun but never fired it—"Peanuts."

The police thought the robber had to be a teenage boy and asked me to come to the 41st Precinct because I had worked with at-risk teens in the neighborhood. A detective showed me a murky store surveillance photo. There was something about the petite frame with the wide shoulders . . .

"I don't think that's a boy," I muttered.

Shana was eventually caught and charged with armed robbery. She was sentenced to eleven years in Bedford Hills Correctional Facility for Women.

We stayed in touch throughout her incarceration. Shana told me that in many ways prison was good for her. She stopped using drugs, and when she was paroled she was able to rekindle a relationship with Terrell. He was raised by Shana's mother, whose hoarding problem slowly diminished with intervention after the fire department cleared her apartment.

Terrell turned out wonderfully. He graduated from high school in the Bronx at the top of his class, went to college, and built a solid management career for himself at American Airlines. He and his family live in Atlanta.

Sadly, though, the best day of Shana's life had a dark cloud over it. Terrell was born via C-section, during which Shana required a blood transfusion. In 1987, blood donation screening for HIV was not yet universal. Shana had no idea she was infected until she began getting sick frequently after she was paroled. The virus was detected during some routine blood work.

After her release from prison, I began visiting Shana the third Sunday of every month near her group home in the Bronx, so that we could go to church together. She was still such a spunky, funny person, and I truly enjoyed her company. Every time we went to church, I silently prayed that the progression of her disease would be slow.

In 1993, NFTE moved to our beautiful offices at 120 Wall Street, with the magnificent views of New York Harbor that I had envisioned long ago. We began collecting some very exciting NFTE success stories.

Malik Armstead was from a low-income neighborhood in West Philly. He attended our summer BizCamp at Wharton when he was seventeen. I noticed Malik right away because he sat in the front row and asked more insightful questions about the differences between fixed and variable costs than I had even heard from MBAs.

After the program, Malik started a little business selling candy and soda at his high school. He went to Morehouse College, where he sold hand-painted jeans and T-shirts while earning a finance degree. After graduation, he became a bond analyst at Morgan Stanley.

Malik and I stayed in touch. I did my best to help him with advice and contacts.

His was already a success story, but Malik was determined to be an entrepreneur. At twenty-five, Malik quit his $60,000 a year job and began searching for a restaurant location.

Malik told me, "Here I was, a young black man making more money than my mother had ever even seen, and I was giving it all up for a risky dream." But ever since his first NFTE class, he had wanted to own his own restaurant.

Malik walked into a restaurant equipment shop on Myrtle Avenue near Bed-Stuy one day and hit it off with the owner, Robert Morelli, who also owned a vacant building next door. Morelli rented Malik the building's storefront. In 1996, Malik opened the Five Spot, a little soul-food take-out café with three tables.

Back then Myrtle Avenue was known as "Murder Avenue." Malik did something important that a lot of NFTE graduates have done. He opened a simple business in a poor, underserved neighborhood, and in the process, helped transform and revitalize it.

A year later, Morelli, who had become Malik's mentor, retired and offered to sell his three Myrtle Avenue buildings to Malik and his fiancée, Kim France, for $500,000. The couple had trouble finding financing, so Morelli offered them a $413,000 line of credit. They would make their mortgage payments to Morelli instead of to a bank.

Next door to their take-out cafe, Malik and Kim built a gorgeous supper club called Five Spot Soul Food, with a sixty-foot mahogany bar, chandeliers, and walls of velvet curtains. The Five Spot became a profitable restaurant and jazz club employing around twenty people, and a vital contributor to the urban renewal sweeping the neighborhood now known as Clinton Hill.

Jimmy "Mac" McNeal, a high school senior, also attended the NFTE BizCamp at Wharton. Jimmy was a BMX bike racer looking to create the first black-owned bike company in the BMX market. Jimmy took NFTE's teacher training and became one of our finest teachers. I introduced him to the investment banker Peter Janssen, who helped Jimmy negotiate a lucrative deal to develop his company Bulldog Bikes.

Jimmy launched Bulldog Bikes in 1998. It was the first urban-oriented BMX bike company, blending the energy of hip-hop with the edginess of extreme sports. Jimmy pioneered a movement that connected urban brands and consumers with the world of action sports. Bulldog Bikes opened the doors of extreme sports to multicultural athletes, sponsoring some of the biggest champions in BMX.

Fortune 500 corporations were eager to hire Jimmy. He created engagement marketing campaigns for Jeep and ESPN, and brand development projects for Toyota, Dr Pepper, and more. Jimmy was featured in *Forbes* and on the cover of *Black Enterprise*.

Another NFTE student who has done extraordinarily well is Robert Reffkin, whose tech-driven real estate company, Compass, was valued at $2.2 billion in 2018.

Robert grew up in the East Bay area of San Francisco. When

he was eleven, he realized that his mother, an Israeli immigrant, was struggling financially as a single parent. Reffkin's father was an African American jazz musician with a heroin addiction who, sadly, died homeless.

When Robert saw a DJ at a party, he thought being a DJ might be a good way for him to earn money to help his mother. For the next three years, Robert saved up every dollar he could. When he had enough money, he bought the minimal amount of equipment needed to be a DJ and started his business, Rude Boy Productions.

In high school, Robert took a NFTE course and wrote a business plan that won him a $500 grant for his DJ business. Robert deejayed at school dances, homecomings, Bar Mitzvahs, weddings, NAACP parties, and Black Student Union dances. He made more than $100,000 as a teenage DJ.

Robert's success in business gave him the confidence to pursue bigger dreams. When his high school counselor said he would never be admitted to Columbia University, Robert decided to apply anyway. During the application process, Robert used everything he had learned from NFTE and running his business. He interacted with the university's admissions officers with the same level of professionalism he employed with his customers. He gave the officers his business card, sent them his résumé, and wrote them thank-you letters.

Robert was accepted at Columbia. He received a partial scholarship and paid for the rest of his college education with money from his DJ business. He earned his bachelor's degree from Columbia in just two and a half years and then earned his MBA.

Robert became an investment banker, spending five years at Goldman Sachs. In 2008, he raised $1.3 million to help open Bronx Success Academy 1, the Bronx franchise of the popular Success Academy network of charter schools that got its start in Harlem. In

2009, Robert founded New York Needs You, an intensive mentoring program for at-risk youth known today as America Needs You.

In 2012, Robert launched Urban Compass, a tech-driven real estate firm, with $73 million in funding from investors. In just four years, Compass became the first residential brokerage to leap past a $1 billion valuation.

At NFTE, we were fast accumulating stories like these—anecdotal evidence that entrepreneurship education could help low-income youth create their own pathways out of poverty and empower their communities.

Perhaps it was the financial analyst in me, but I felt that our wonderful anecdotal evidence was not enough to prove that we were fulfilling our mission. My team and I did not want to fool ourselves into believing that NFTE was making a difference if it really wasn't. That would be a waste of our donors' money. We needed to prove, with hard data, that entrepreneurship education was truly a worthwhile intervention for low-income youth.

We decided to search for a more concrete way to measure the results NFTE was achieving. In 1993, we began an intensive collaboration with Andrew Hahn of Brandeis University to create a long-term study of the impact of entrepreneurship education on low-income youth.

Today, NFTE can point to studies from not only Brandeis but also RAND, Harvard, and NYU that confirm what I observed as a special ed teacher in the 1980s. NFTE students demonstrate higher rates of high school graduation, college attendance, business formation, and employment than their peers who are not exposed to entrepreneurship education.

Steve Mariotti teaching "economics of one unit" and other business topics at NFTE summer BizCamps. Photos by NFTE.

Currently, more than 1.2 million American teenagers drop out of high school annually. A teenager drops out every twenty-six seconds. Imagine the positive impact on our economy if we could provide him or her with a reason to stay in school. *New York Times* op-ed columnist Tom Friedman offers one solution: "The president should vow to bring the Network for Teaching Entrepreneurship (NFTE) to every low-income neighborhood in America" (January 23, 2010, "More (Steve) Jobs, Jobs, Jobs, Jobs"). I, too, would like to see entrepreneurship education provided to every low-income neighborhood in the world.

Pablo Guzman, executive director of Foundacion, NFTE's

partner in Mexico City, told me there is no shortage of entrepreneurial energy among Mexico's young people. He sees NFTE as a way to break the next generation of young Mexicans away from the lure of quick profits and fabulous fortunes offered by the drug cartels, an attraction that is not dimmed by the rampant violence and high mortality rate of the drug trade.

"They prefer five years of being rich to thirty to forty years of being poor," Guzman said. "That's the mentality we're trying to break."

It's a mentality I have spent a lifetime fighting, whether I have been teaching entrepreneurship classes to low-income youth in America's inner cities, Palestinian ghettos, Muslim neighborhoods in France and Belgium, or new free-enterprise zones in China. I have personally witnessed that entrepreneurship education is our greatest weapon against the relentless efforts of both drug cartels and terrorist organizations to recruit from low-income communities.

Sadly missing from United States foreign policy is an awareness of the power of entrepreneurship education to reach frustrated low-income youth in unstable nations, help them develop small businesses, and encourage democracy. Where we ignore this opportunity, terrorist organizations and drug cartels move in, taking advantage of the dangerous combination of extreme poverty and sky-high youth unemployment that creates fertile ground for recruitment.

Imagine if all young people, instead, were business literate enough to create their own pathways out of poverty. To sell a product or service to another human being is an act that has the power to revolutionize lives, rebuild families, and forever change communities. Why aren't we teaching all the world's children how to do it?

As NFTE's president, I worked eighty hours a week for thirty-plus years, including Sundays.

This was not great for my relationships. Janet and I eventually broke up, and I moved from our 23rd Street loft to a two-bedroom apartment in the West Village. I am happy to report that Janet is a married pastor living in the Berkshires, as well as an accomplished artist and musician. I have been engaged twice but never married.

I am not saying my workaholic lifestyle was healthy or right. But I found a mission that I fell in love with, and I always felt strongly motivated to put in the extra time.

If you are doing what you love, and you see that your efforts are making a real difference, you can have a wonderful career. I am not sure that you can make a major impact globally and still have a normal life, though. I don't know if you can be happily married or have children. Maybe some of us are meant to take the energy we would have spent on family life and share it with the world instead.

I was on a flight to visit NFTE's program in Israel a few years ago, and the young man sitting next to me turned out to be a NFTE grad. He told me that NFTE had changed his life. He had been a troubled African American kid from a low-income neighborhood in San Francisco when a NFTE after-school program helped him discover that he was talented at selling. He became a successful salesman, traveling the world for an industrial manufacturer.

Devon told me that he used to feel so bad about himself in school because other kids were earning good grades and praise from the teachers. After NFTE, he was no longer the worst student in class; he was the student who was doing the best with his business. Once he found something he was good at, he felt like he could be successful, too.

Every child needs a victory. I learned that from my mother.

When I was growing up in Flint, my hero was Mark Whittaker, the state wrestling champion. Mark was a small, feisty young man from a solid, well-off family. His home was a few blocks from mine, so I knew Mark personally. He was a wonderful guy who always looked out for us younger kids. I still look up to him to this day.

In 1969, Mark was wrestling Tobias Young for the city championship. Tobias was a special ed kid who went to Flint Northern and lived in a foster care home.

I remember saying to my mother, "I'm really worried that Mark is going to lose to Tobias Young."

My mother looked at me and said, "Oh yeah? And what does Tobias have?"

She made me realize that Mark had everything and Tobias had nothing. And it is the child who has nothing who needs a victory most.

EPILOGUE: ONE MORE DAY

"It's the emptiest and yet the fullest of all human messages," I said.
"Which is?" she asked.
"'Goodbye,'" I said.
—KURT VONNEGUT, *Bluebeard* (1987)

My mother never regained consciousness in that Grand Blanc nursing home.

Nancy Mason Mariotti passed away on October 3, 1994, after spending nearly ten years in a coma, kept alive by a feeding tube.

My father visited her almost every day. He sat in her room, reading her favorite books aloud.

When I went to visit my mother, I could not bring myself to enter her room. I sat outside, gritting my teeth until my gums were bloody, trying not to cry.

My father, brother, and I became painfully familiar with the strange and unanticipated challenges of tending a loved one in a long-term coma, from prevention of tooth decay to preservation of bone mass. Although we knew she was unconscious, it was hard not to imagine her experiencing this limited existence in a state of constant torture.

In late September 1994, I was at my parents' home in Flint for the weekend when an author named Dennis Dunn called. His excellent book *Every Child Is Our Child: A Plan for Education That Leaves No Child Behind* had recently been published.

Dennis was calling to tell us that his book included a chapter on his seventh-grade teacher in Indiana back in 1946. She was a young unmarried teacher named Miss Mason.

"Your mother saved my life," Dennis told me. "When I went astray, she was kind enough to help me find myself."

I was supposed to fly back to New York that day, but I told Dennis that if he could possibly mail me a copy of his book, I would postpone my flight.

Two days later, the book arrived. Carrying it with me, I finally entered my mother's room at the nursing home. As I grasped her hand for the first time in nearly ten years, I read aloud the moving words Dennis had written about her.

In the seventh grade, I moved very close to the top of my class, in spite of my poor academic record. That achievement was due to Miss Mason, one of the teachers who came to teach in our new school. She was the person who taught me the importance of self-worth.

Miss Mason had noticed that he could draw, Dennis explained in his book. She had steadily encouraged him to nurture his drawing talent as something unique and special that he had to offer.

"Miss Mason had shown me that I had worth as a person—a person who could draw," Dennis wrote. By helping him feel better about himself, he added, Miss Mason also helped him become a better student.

It meant so much to me to read that chapter to my mother. I hoped she somehow sensed how deeply loved she was, not only by her family but also by the many students she had cared for throughout her career.

After visiting her, I left immediately for our local airport and caught a flight to Detroit, and from there to Madrid, where I was scheduled to speak at an international conference on at-risk youth. I was preparing to step onstage to address the conference when my Spanish guide handed me a phone.

"*Emergencia*," he whispered.

My father was on the phone. Mom had died. She had finally let go.

To my surprise, instead of grief, I felt tremendous relief.

After receiving the news, I gave my talk. Then, I ran out of the building and down the street in a state of exhilaration.

She was free. She would no longer suffer.

I went right into a bar and ordered a bottle of champagne. The bartender asked me why I was so happy.

"My mother just died!" I exclaimed.

That didn't go over too well.

I explained that she had been in a coma for nearly ten awful years. The bartender nodded knowingly. He joined me in toasting her memory, and her freedom.

At her funeral three days later, my father and I hugged. We cried together, lamenting the loss of a wonderful human being and teacher—his wife, my mother.

"Perhaps we should have let her die ten years ago," I said.

In an honest moment of deep grief, my father responded, "I wish you had told me that ten years ago."

<hr />

As I was going through her belongings, I found a letter taped to the top of a cardboard box. Dated July 19, 1968, the letter read:

> *Dearest Steve,*
> *As you know, I have decided to take a break from teaching for a year or so.*
>
> *I wanted to share my handouts, assignments, activities, lessons, quizzes, group activities, and outlines that I used at Northern with you. They have worked so well as teaching tools for me.*
>
> *I know right now the last thing you are wanting to do with your life is to become an educator. I know you know that your father and I will support you and love you whatever you decide to do with your life.*
>
> *Deep down, though, I sense that someday you may teach, and perhaps these materials will help you to help a child. That is a beautiful thing to be a part of, if even for just a moment in time.*
>
> *Never forget: "A great teacher affects eternity."*
>
> *Love,*
> *Your Mother*

Inside the box was a treasure trove that any teacher would be overjoyed to find. The box was packed with papers from my mom's years as a special ed teacher and contained the daily teaching diary she had kept.

I pored over her detailed diary. It astonished me most to discover that she had developed and taught a class called "Learning About Money" during the mid-1960s at Flint Northern High School.

I think my mom would be proud to know that, because of that box, many of her ideas and strategies for teaching low-income youth were incorporated into NFTE's award-winning curriculum. I wish she had lived to attend NFTE galas and BizCamps, as my father, John Mariotti, did often before he passed away in 2009.

She would have also loved seeing Jack become NFTE's chief financial officer in 1995. My brother is every bit as practical and organized as I am not. He served as CFO until 2001 and was invaluable. Jack has since cofounded Molecular NeuroImaging, which develops brain-imaging technology to help find cures for neurological disorders.

I was also fortunate to have my fellow teachers and good buddies C.J. Meenan and Juan Casimiro on the NFTE team. Thank goodness they stuck around, because otherwise I would have really missed them!

C.J. brought his irrepressible energy to NFTE for twenty years. He served as regional director of NFTE Pennsylvania and NFTE California. He was also director of NFTE New Jersey and NFTE University, our teacher-training program. For his groundbreaking work, C.J. received the Price-Babson Fellowship for Entrepreneurship Educators.

Juan, one of the most committed and effective teachers I have ever known, co-ran NFTE BizCamps at Wharton, Columbia, Berkeley, and USC with me. After ten years at NFTE, Juan continued to deliver entrepreneurship education to underserved youth as founder of BIZNOVATOR and the Casimiro Global Foundation.

Back in 1988, though, we were three schoolteachers with zero experience running a nonprofit. We ran into financial trouble pretty quickly. On December 3, 1988, I placed a desperate call from our tiny office to a friend who was successfully running two foundations.

"You need a fundraiser," she said.

She gave me some names. I began feverishly calling all of them.

Most didn't want to meet until January, after the holidays. NFTE would be sunk by then. Only Mike Caslin said, "I can come down right now."

Mike got on a plane in Boston and arrived four hours later. He was so cheerful and positive that the moment he walked through our door, I felt all my anxieties drain away. I looked at the stack of checks on my desk that we had been afraid to mail out, and I knew that we were saved. Within a week, Mike raised $40,000.

Mike served as NFTE's CEO for the next fourteen years. He helped transform a barely solvent nonprofit into a prominent foundation with a multimillion-dollar annual budget. His leadership was instrumental in enabling NFTE to provide entrepreneurship-education programs to low-income youth throughout the US and around the world. As our company went international, we changed its name from the National Foundation for Teaching Entrepreneurship to the Network for Teaching Entrepreneurship.

My mentor Bella Frankel, who helped me raise the reading levels of my offsite students, became one of NFTE's first advisory board members. I still regret not doing the only thing Bella ever asked of me: attend her daughter's wedding. I was too worried about meeting some grant proposal deadline. I was so focused on getting NFTE off the ground that I often failed to be there for the people in my life who meant the most.

Ten years later, I apologized to Bella, who reassured me, "No worries, Steve. NFTE was worth it." I also stayed in touch with Pat

Black, my principal at Jane Addams High. I still receive a lovely email from her every year, recalling our fun times together.

Miss Archibald, our Department of Buildings champion, retired in the 1990s. When I visited the typing pool years later, people still spoke of her as they would a legend. What natural leaders she and Pat Black were! I learned so much from their fine examples.

As I had once dreamed, former guest speakers to the South Bronx Entrepreneurship Club like David Dinkins and Percy Sutton became committed NFTE supporters. Ray Chambers, NFTE's first donor, became a long-term supporter, as well, and a valuable mentor and friend to me. Today, Ray is widely recognized as a legendary philanthropist and humanitarian. I also developed a great friendship with Barbara Bell Coleman while she was president of the Boys & Girls Club of Newark that has continued throughout her illustrious and socially conscious career.

Even though I couldn't open my rusty office door when he visited me in the South Bronx, Mike Hennessy became a close friend and advisor, and an important NFTE donor as president and CEO of The Coleman Foundation. Mike still jokes that he, not Ray, was NFTE's first donor, because he contributed those irresistible boxes of Fannie May chocolates to the South Bronx Entrepreneurship Education Program.

Philanthropist Diana Davis Spencer and her daughter Abby Spencer Moffat, John C. Whitehead of Goldman Sachs, and many more of our extraordinary donors became not only committed NFTE supporters but also some of my dearest friends.

And, yes, NFTE students have visited the White House! I escorted NFTE National Youth Entrepreneurship Challenge finalists to the Oval Office to meet President Barack Obama in 2012, and our finalists have been invited back again several times. I met many additional world leaders while serving as a member of the Council on Foreign Relations and regularly attending, and speaking at, the World Economic Forum in Davos, Switzerland.

All these friends and every one of my students enriched my life profoundly, making it even more meaningful, fun, and challenging than I foresaw that long-ago afternoon at West 4th Street Saloon, when I sat nervously clutching my letter to Ray Chambers.

Above all, founding NFTE gave my life purpose and joy, because we have helped nearly one million young people and counting discover the entrepreneurial mindset and use it to transform their lives and communities.

In 2014, NFTE put terrific leadership in place that enabled me to transition into a consulting role, with every confidence that NFTE will continue to provide entrepreneurship education to low-income youth globally for decades to come.

Steve Mariotti and Sean "Diddy" Combs shake hands at the 2013 NFTE National Youth Entrepreneurship Challenge, where Combs donated $250,000 to NFTE's mission.

I am currently the Senior Fellow in Entrepreneurship at Rising Tide Capital in Jersey City. My work involves interviewing entrepreneurs who have survived genocide, war, and natural disasters in order to share their stories of entrepreneurial grit in books, films, and television programs. In 2018, I cofounded ExperienceCounts, a nonprofit foundation that helps Americans over fifty recharge their careers, start small businesses and nonprofits, and achieve financial security.

My students are still my biggest inspiration, and I have been fortunate to stay in touch with many of them. Watching them grow into successful adults has been extremely gratifying.

Steve Mariotti at the 2016 NFTE Global Showcase at Cipriani Downtown in New York City with Nakeia Chantal Jones and Johnetta Hardy. Photo by NFTE.

To my complete astonishment, I ran into one of my East River muggers years later in an entrepreneurship class I taught at Seward Park High School on the Lower East Side. We immediately recognized each other when he walked into my class but did not at first realize why. When we did, we both burst out laughing. We shook hands and agreed to let bygones be bygones. He turned out to be a wonderful young man who was working hard to change his life and improve his prospects.

Within a year, I had dinner with him and several of the other young men who had assaulted me by the river that day. That, more than anything, ended my flashbacks and nightmares for good.

My former student Mariana still runs her successful housekeeping business and we remain great friends. She lives in the Bronx with her husband and has raised two children. She and her husband also open their home to foster children.

I stayed in touch with Miguel throughout the surgeries he needed after he slipped and fell on a wet floor at his maintenance job and broke his leg again. He was such a trouper through it all, even when he had to be put into a dreaded cast.

I was heartbroken when Miguel's sister called to tell me that he had passed away from complications of diabetes at thirty-four. I grieved the loss of one of the finest human beings I have ever known.

When I attempted to track down Anton, I learned that he was sentenced to Mid-State Correctional Facility in 1989 for attempted robbery. He was released on parole in 1991, but in 1998, he went to Sing Sing Correctional Facility for sale of a controlled substance. He was released in January of 2002, yet I have been unable to find him.

As I had often feared, Earvin was arrested for assaulting someone. He was sentenced to Queensboro Correctional Facility in 1996 and released on parole in 1999. Shana got in touch with him and told me that, against all odds, Earvin turned his life around. He is a hardworking husband and father living in Virginia.

I continued to travel to the South Bronx to attend church with Shana until she became too weak to make the trip, even in her wheelchair. Instead, we spent our visits in the group home for AIDS patients where she lives with her wife of eight years, who is also sick with AIDS.

Shana and I speak on the phone nearly every day. She calls me "Dad," and I call her my daughter.

Shana had to have brain surgery a few months ago. Terrell came up from Atlanta and stayed in her room for two days. I know it meant everything to Shana to have her beloved son there.

The brutal physical suffering that AIDS is putting Shana through is almost unbearable for me to witness, yet she remains one of the most interesting, funny, and upbeat people I know. She is still that feisty girl who will never give up, no matter what is happening in her world.

Every day now, when Shana calls, I ask, "Do you want God to take you today, sweetheart?"

And every day she declares, "Absolutely not! I want one more day!"

"When you do meet Saint Peter," I always add, "put in a good word for the short, bald-headed guy."

That makes her laugh.

"Oh, I will, Dad!" she giggles.

I really don't know how I am going to say goodbye to her.

Victor worked for NFTE part-time for twenty-six years, so I'm not sure how we fell out of touch. All I know is that he slipped away.

The phone number I had used for two decades was disconnected. I flashed back to the brash boy who had slapped $18,000 on the table of my classroom and bragged, "I'm the richest fifteen-year-old motherfucker in the world!"

I hoped Victor had not fallen back into old ways.

Luckily, I managed to track him down. Victor explained that he had fallen off the radar because his three sisters were paying him to take care of his mother full-time. She was very sick with complications from diabetes.

I headed to the Bronx to visit him. Instead of the subway, I took a car service so I could see how the old neighborhood was doing. To my surprise, formerly dilapidated Fort Apache—once plagued with arson and overrun by crackheads and murderous gangbangers—was booming. There were busy construction sites everywhere, beautiful new buildings, people walking around shopping, and an energetic, positive vibe in the air.

As I got out of the car and walked toward 149th Street, I sensed Victor's rambunctious presence. Sure enough, I turned the corner, and there he was, standing in front of the projects as if time had stood still.

"Look, Mariotti's back, and he got that vanilla white-boy gut!" Victor shouted, pointing out to the entire neighborhood that I had put on fifteen pounds.

Old acquaintances waved from their windows. Some ran up to say hello to me. They made me feel like a returning war hero.

Victor and I entered the same project building where so much had happened more than thirty years ago. Same smells, same sounds. I was flooded with memories.

"Aw, you gonna cry, Mariotti?" Victor joshed.

I just smiled. We walked off the creaky elevator and down the narrow hall into the apartment Victor shares with his mom and one of his sisters. Angela, whom I last saw when she was a little girl, was a social worker now.

It was lovely to see Victor's mother again, although she was clearly in ill health. Victor handled her with tremendous gentleness. It touched my heart to see him taking such care with her.

After he took her back to her room, Victor and I sat side by side on the couch in the living room, watching the news and drinking Kool-Aid.

Thanks to an intense exercise regimen, at forty-eight Victor barely looked a day over thirty. As we chatted, he told me that he kept busy not only taking care of his mother but also teaching young men in the neighborhood how to start small businesses, and running Bible study groups.

"You need to be working out, Mariotti!" he declared.

I nodded ruefully.

When he started proselytizing about religion, though, I raised my hand an inch or two. We both laughed as he got the message.

President Trump came on the television.

"We got a special ed kid as president now," Victor joked, adding, "He gets shit down though!"

"Done," I said, ever the teacher, instinctively correcting him.

"Down!" Victor insisted, laughing, "Shut the fuck up, vanilla gut!"

Same old Victor, and yet so much more. Today, he is a survivor of an upbringing in a violent war zone that would have given anyone PTSD. He walked away from a thriving criminal career that provided the kind of easy money and respect from his peers that would seriously tempt any human being. He is kind, loving, responsible, good to his family, and an asset to his community.

He is the real war hero.

We sat watching TV for about three hours. Finally, I had to go.

"Yo, white boy, you saved my life," Victor began. "You saved a lot of people's lives and now you're old and . . ."

"I'm just getting started, Rap Mouth!" I exclaimed, shoving his shoulder hard enough to almost knock him off the couch.

We both started giggling hysterically, as it had been forever since I had called him by that goofy nickname.

Thirty-three years ago, when I was trying to wrest Victor and Mateo apart in our DOB classroom, I had screamed, "Stop fighting, Rap Mouths!" It sounded so ridiculous that they had both burst out laughing and stopped swinging at each other long enough for me to separate them.

Victor walked me out of his apartment. We took the elevator down to the street, where I flagged a cab.

As I was climbing into the back seat, Victor said, in a serious tone of voice, "Hey, Mariotti."

I turned to look at him, realizing a millisecond too late that it was the old standby tease he had used on me so many times before.

"Gotcha, homeboy!" he shouted, laughing and jogging backward up the street, waving goodbye.

ADDITIONAL CREDITS

The Message
Words and Music by Edward G. Fletcher, Clifton Nathaniel Chase, Melvin Glover, Sylvia Robinson
Copyright © 1982 by Universal Music Publishing Group
International Copyright Secured   All Rights Reserved
Reprinted by Permission of Hal Leonard LLC

Heroes
Words by David Bowie
Music by David Bowie and Brian Eno
Copyright © 1977 EMI Music Publishing Ltd., Tintoretto Music and Universal Music Publishing MGB Ltd. Copyright Renewed
All Rights on behalf of EMI Music Publishing Ltd. Administered by Sony/ATV Music Publishing LLC, 424 Church Street, Suite 1200, Nashville, TN 37219
All Rights on behalf of Tintoretto Music Administered by RZO Music
All Rights on behalf of Universal Music Publishing MGB Ltd. in the US Administered by Universal Music – Careers
International Copyright Secured   All Rights Reserved
Reprinted by Permission of Hal Leonard LLC

South Bronx
Words and Music by Lawrence Parker and Scott Sterling
Copyright © 1986 by Universal Music – Z Tunes LLC
International Copyright Secured   All Rights Reserved
Reprinted by Permission of Hal Leonard LLC

ACKNOWLEDGMENTS

Goodbye Homeboy: How My Students Drove Me Crazy and Inspired a Movement is loosely based on journals I kept as a New York City public high school teacher from 1982 to 1988. I am thrilled to finally share the story of the brave and resilient students who inspired me to found the Network for Teaching Entrepreneurship (NFTE) in 1987, thanks to my literary agent, Jeff Herman, and BenBella Books publisher Glenn Yeffeth, who decided *Goodbye Homeboy* would not only be an entertaining read but would also add value to the international discussion of this pressing issue: How can we improve the education of low-income youth in order to help them create pathways out of poverty?

I want to thank all the wonderful students, colleagues, donors, friends, and family I have been lucky to know throughout this journey. I salute nearly one million NFTE alumni around the world, and thousands of NFTE teachers and staff members who have built a worldwide movement in entrepreneurship education. I hope you, especially, will enjoy this story of how NFTE came to be.

My talented writing partner, Debra Devi, kept this memoir

alive by believing in its potential even when at times I had lost my own vision for it. Her gift for telling my stories clearly and succinctly while weaving them into a narrative by turns moving and hilarious is a blessing for which I am very grateful. I also thank our thoughtful, patient BenBella Books editor, Vy Tran, whose insights helped Debra and me streamline this book without diminishing its rawness, honesty, or humor; our perceptive, diligent copy editor, Scott Calamar; and the rest of the BenBella team, which has been terrific. In addition, I thank Lili Hopkins for reading an early draft of *Goodbye Homeboy* and providing her insights, and my friend and colleague Tony Towle for proofreading the galleys.

I have been blessed with wonderful mentors. First, I'd like to thank Landon Hilliard of Brown Brothers Harriman, a key mentor to me when I was a financial analyst at Ford Motor Company, who has served as chairman of NFTE's board of directors, and chairman of the NFTE Endowment Fund. When I struggled as a teacher, two people, in particular, saved my career. Pat Black, the principal at Jane Addams Vocational High School in the South Bronx, saw something in me even when I was failing as a teacher. Her unflinching support gave me one last chance to find my strengths and fulfill my dream of making a difference in the challenging lives of my students. In the process, Pat taught me how a true leader operates—with humility, kindness, and grace—and became a lifelong friend. Bella Frankel, the great special education reading expert, was also my friend and mentor, sharing invaluable insights into helping children with learning disabilities read.

At Jane Addams High, I taught with two of the finest teachers I have ever known: C.J. Meenan and Juan Casimiro. I am deeply honored that they became not only my best friends but also some of NFTE's most valuable executives. I learned a great deal, too, from the mentorship of teaching legend Jaime Escalante, with whom I studied in Los Angeles; and teacher and novelist Frank McCourt, who encouraged me to write in my own voice. I am very grateful to Janet McKinstry for her encouragement, hard work, and insightful suggestions into how to teach entrepreneurship to low-income youth.

There is no way I can describe the joy of having been part of our NFTE community for more than three decades. NFTE would not have survived its first year, however, without our first CEO, Mike Caslin, who guided a fledgling nonprofit expertly and with immense energy and positivity through fourteen years of growth beyond my wildest dreams. His ability to think outside the box and inspire people was just what was needed to build NFTE into the worldwide leader in entrepreneurship education that it is today. My brother, Jack Mariotti, played a pivotal role, as well, as NFTE's head of curriculum from 1991 to 1995 and our CFO from 1995 to 2001.

So many remarkable executives have worked at NFTE that it is impossible to list them all, but in addition to Mike Caslin, I would also like to thank David Nelson, COO during a high-growth period between 2000 and 2010, and Jane Walsh and Leslie Koch, who also played key roles during crucial years. These talented leaders were ably assisted by many great NFTE executives and teachers, including Deidre Lee, Rupa Mohan, Neelam Patel, Daniel Rabuzzi, Suzanne Taylor, Victor Salama, and Kevin Wortham, just to name a few.

NFTE would never have gotten off the ground during the early years chronicled in *Goodbye Homeboy* without the support and mentorship provided by Ray Chambers, Charles and Liz Koch, Michael Hennessy of the Coleman Foundation, and Barbara Bell Coleman. Kim LaManna, Abby Moffat, Karen Pritzker, and Diana Davis Spencer have been key long-term supporters of NFTE, and wonderful, supportive friends. I would also like to thank Matthew Gilmore of Strategic Asset Services for many years of mentorship. Marty Zupan, former president and CEO of the Institute for Humane Studies, was the first to read an early draft of *Goodbye Homeboy* and encourage me to stick with it. I am proud that these donors have seen fit to support NFTE for decades, and have become some of my closest friends.

Philanthropist and former Goldman Sachs chairman John Whitehead tutored me regularly and introduced me to many top philanthropists who became key NFTE supporters, including Tucker York, Wendy Kopp, and Bill Drayton. I received crucial mentoring from Babson College president Steve Spinelli and Babson College's pioneering entrepreneurship professor Jeffry Timmons, as well as CEO Clubs founder Joe Mancuso and Entrepreneurs' Organization founder Verne Harnish. I am grateful for the important role played in NFTE's success by McKinsey & Company, and its senior partner Peter Walker; and by NFTE's publishers at Random House, Pearson, and Prentice Hall.

Today, NFTE is thriving under the skilled leadership of president and CEO Shawn Osborne and a wonderful, committed board of directors. My confidence in their leadership has enabled me to take on new projects, such as writing *Goodbye Homeboy* and serving as a Senior Fellow in Entrepreneurship at Philadelphia University and at Rising Tide Capital in Jersey City. I have also cofounded ExperienceCounts—a nonprofit focused on empowering Americans over fifty to retire with confidence—with my former NFTE colleagues Kevin Greaney, David Nelson, and Peter Patch.

I greatly enjoy my friendship with Rising Tide Capital founders Alfa Demmellash and Alex Forrester; with Empact cofounders Michael Simmons and Sheena Lindahl; and with Robin Hood Foundation CEO Wes Moore and his wife, Dawn, who has served as NFTE's Director of Business Development Corporate, and Foundation Philanthropy. It's been a gift in my life to support these young leaders and, in turn, be inspired by them to continue my work, which is currently focused on researching and writing about the entrepreneurial mindset. I am also profoundly grateful for my inspiring, lasting friendships with Serena Felder, Marisol Burgos-Ortiz, and Vincent Wilkins.

I would also like to thank the many friends I have made since moving to Princeton, New Jersey, who offered steady words of encouragement as I wrote *Goodbye Homeboy*, including Jonathan Hanke, Doug Hopkins, Aniceto Cadenas, US 1 editorial director Richard Rein, Nell Whiting, the Unitarian Universalist Congregation of Princeton, and the wonderful staff of the Princeton Public Library.

My hometown, Flint, Michigan, is in every one of my genes. I thank my three best hometown friends for their love, support, and inspiration: Joseph Farah, currently a 7th Circuit Court judge in Genesee County; Gary Voight, who got me started in entrepreneurship with a paper route when I was ten and was my partner in numerous childhood enterprises; and Paul Christopher, who inspired me to love literature as he did and grew up to become the award-winning author Christopher Paul Curtis.

Lastly, I thank my father, John J. Mariotti, and my mother, Nancy Mason Mariotti, a legendary special education teacher in Flint, for relentless unconditional love and never-failing belief in me. To my mother and father, I sense both your wonderful loving presences in my life every day and know that we will see each other again someday. Thank you for encouraging me to be the hero of my life, so that I, in turn, could encourage my students to become the heroes of their lives, too.

ABOUT THE AUTHORS

Photo by Samuel Lahoz

Steve Mariotti is the founder and former president of the Network for Teaching Entrepreneurship (NFTE), a global leader in providing entrepreneurship education to low-income youth from Chicago to China. Nearly one million young people have graduated from its programs since Mariotti founded NFTE in 1987 while working as a high school teacher in the New York City public school system.

Mariotti currently serves as Senior Fellow for Entrepreneurship at Rising Tide Capital and the chairman and cofounder of

ExperienceCounts, a nonprofit that empowers Americans over fifty to achieve financial independence.

Mariotti wrote groundbreaking textbooks for NFTE, including the high school textbook *Entrepreneurship: Starting and Operating a Small Business* (Pearson) and the junior college textbook *Entrepreneurship and Small Business Management* (Pearson). Mariotti also authored the popular *Young Entrepreneur's Guide to Starting and Running a Business* (Random House) and *An Entrepreneur's Manifesto* (Templeton Press), in which he made a convincing case for the power of entrepreneurship education to raise millions out of poverty and combat terrorism and totalitarianism.

Mariotti is the recipient of numerous awards including the Bernard A. Goldhirsh Social Entrepreneur of the Year Award, the National Director's Entrepreneurship Award from the Minority Business Development Agency of the US Department of Commerce, Ernst & Young Entrepreneur of the Year Award, the Association of Education Publishers' Golden Lamp Award and Best in Category Award, the ACE/Currie Foundation Humanitarian Venture Award, and America's Top High School Business Teacher. Mariotti served on the Council on Foreign Relations for eleven years and attended and spoke at the World Economic Forum for thirteen years. He is a featured speaker at conferences, seminars, and universities.

Raised in Flint, Michigan, Mariotti received his BBA in economics and his MBA from the University of Michigan, Ann Arbor. He began his career as a financial analyst for Ford Motor Company before moving to New York City to start an import/export business. He has also studied at Harvard University, Stanford University, Brooklyn College, Babson College, the Institute for Advanced Studies in Princeton, and Princeton University.

Photo by Samuel Lahoz

Debra Devi is an award-winning author, journalist, and rock musician. Her book *The Language of the Blues: From Alcorub to Zuzu* (Crown) received the ASCAP Deems Taylor Award for Outstanding Book on Music. She has also been honored for her articles in the *Village Voice* and other publications.

Devi has coauthored numerous books with Steve Mariotti, including *An Entrepreneur's Manifesto* (Templeton Press), NFTE textbooks and workbooks, and *The Young Entrepreneur's Guide to Starting and Running a Business* (Random House). She also coauthored the top-selling *The Idiot's Guide to Investing Like A Pro* (Penguin) and *Jivamukti Yoga: Practices for Liberating Body and Soul* (Ballantine).

In addition, Devi has written about music and pop culture for *American Blues Scene, RollingStone.com, Yoga Journal, Guitar World, Guitar,* and the *Huffington Post.* She appears as an expert on the blues in the films *America's Blues* and *Mr. Handy's Blues.*

Devi has a master's degree in journalism from Columbia University and a BA in economics from the University of Wisconsin–Madison.

31192021804115